Epics of the Sea

Epics of the Sea

A. A. Hoehling

cbi Contemporary Books, Inc.
Chicago

Library of Congress Cataloging in Publication Data

Hoehling, Adolph A.
  Epics of the sea.

  Bibliography: p.
  1. Seafaring life.   I. Title.
G540.H59   910'.45   77-75723
ISBN 0-8092-8129-5

Published by Contemporary Books, Inc.
180 North Michigan Avenue, Chicago, Illinois 60601
Manufactured in the United States of America
Library of Congress Catalog Card Number: 77-75723
International Standard Book Number: 0-8092-8129-5

Published simultaneously in Canada by
Beaverbooks
953 Dillingham Road
Pickering, Ontario L1W 1Z7
Canada

Contents

Foreword

ON AN EARLY SPRING DAY, 1944, the author stared out from a beach in front of the Galle Face Hotel, just south of Colombo, Ceylon, at the beguilingly calm Indian Ocean. It was blue, beautiful; the air itself had just been washed by one of the afternoon's clockwork thunderstorms. The war seemed very far away.

Yet it was not.

A top secret briefing at the Royal Navy Operations Office had just elicited disquieting information. Little red flags pinned onto the map of the ocean, between Colombo and Laurenco Marques, Mozambique—the destination of the Liberty ship on which the author was gunnery officer—were as plentiful and bright as lanterns strung for a garden party. Each flag denoted a reported enemy submarine, Japanese or German.

That he could safely transit some 3,000 miles of such imperiled waters, even though his ship was armed with two three-inch guns and several rapid-firing twenty mm, seemed wholly improbable. The sea, "the broad sea," even as the German sailors of the raider *Emden* had penned in World War I, surely would be "thine to keep."

As it turned out, *Joseph Le Conte* did play cat-and-mouse with the enemy all the way to Laurenco Marques and won. The author would lose a ship, but not this time. Yet the sea had spoken, perhaps merely whispered off these calm shores not only of the majesty and wonder but latent threat and overriding uncertainty.

Earlier in that same war, in late May 1940, Harold Denny, correspondent for the *New York Times,* stood at a southeast England port and took notes for a story he would be cabling:

"It was an odd sight to see the fleet of transports which, with destroyers and other naval craft, came steaming into these waters today crowded to the gunwales with cheering and smiling lads who a few days ago never had hoped to see the shores of England again. There were steamboats of all sizes, many of them had been pleasure boats in happier days, coastal tramp ships, dingy fishing boats and motor boats. A tug chugged in towing a string of five barges loaded with soldiers. One party of soldiers was brought by an officer—a yachtsman in civil life—in a sailboat he had 'pinched' near Dunkirk when he could not find a transport . . . the soldiers' torn and stained clothing gave a hint of what they had been through. Most of them had lost all their kit except rifles and had only the clothes they stood in . . . most of them were too tired to talk."

Denny, of course, was writing on the backwash of Dunkirk, and again the sea had supplied the all but infinite canvas for drama.

When, 151 years before Denny was sculpturing his next morning's "lead," another sea epic was brought to a close, no reporter was present to provide future generations with a firsthand account of what he saw. Thus in the summer of 1789 did Captain William Bligh, late of H.M.S. *Bounty,* touch shore in the Dutch East Indies with fellow crewmen set adrift by his mutinous crew. He had navigated his open boat across thousands of miles of uncharted or imperfectly charted ocean in an amazing feat that would challenge future generations of mariners.

If Bligh's long sail has been approximated, surely it has never been exceeded. The feat was memorial to a stubborn, complex seaman of unusual skill as a navigator, a man whose many facets of character did *not* include likableness.

The story began in the South Pacific. . . .

1

The Ordeal of William Bligh

CAPTAIN WILLIAM BLIGH was sleeping heavily in his cabin aboard H.M.S. *Bounty* that Tuesday, April 28, 1789.

The hour was a few minutes before a sultry sunrise. The position of the three-masted former merchantman *Bethia* was about 30 miles south of Tofoa in the Tonga Islands group, green dots in the wilderness of the South Pacific. But 91 feet long, 230 tons, *Bounty* herself was an even smaller dot in the vast ocean.

Bligh, 34, already a skilled circumnavigator of the globe, had reason to be tired. He had put Cowes, England, astern more than two years earlier, on Christmas Eve, 1787, for a seemingly endless, at times meandering voyage to the South Pacific. The square-rigged ship had initially encountered such ferocious headwinds rounding Cape Horn, at the tip of South America, that Bligh had hauled her about and recrossed the South Atlantic only to smash into equally foul weather off the Cape of Good Hope, at Africa's southern extremity.

Superior seamanship had brought ship and complement of 45 finally into calm, tropical waters. Now, with nearly 1,000 potted breadfruit plants snug in *Bounty's* especially fitted 'tween-decks "greenhouse," complete even to irrigation, Bligh felt the satisfaction

1

of one who had almost if not quite accomplished his mission: to introduce the highly utilitarian, versatile breadfruit tree to the West Indies. The "fruit," which grew up to eight inches in diameter, could be ground into flour and baked. The wood of the tree was fashioned into furniture, the inner bark or fiber was woven into cloth, and even the thick white sap was suitable as glue.

Since October 1788, the *Bounty* had been anchored off Tahiti in Matavai Bay while the precious plants were carried on board. The crew all the while had languished in pleasure and indolence, enjoying the caresses of the Polynesian girls, whose sexual favors were historically as free and uninhibited as the island breezes.

Laxity, inspiring minor misconduct as well as bloody violence and desertions, had alternated with stern discipline. Bligh himself was not averse to enjoying the abundant fruits and exotic foods of Tahiti. Yet in countering the crew's demands for more and better rations, he had shouted, "You damned, infernal scoundrels, I'll make you eat grass or anything else you can catch before I've done with you!"

Measured against the tough, unruly, often criminal element that made up the seagoing fraternity of the eighteenth century, Bligh was no more arrogant a martinet than his fellow commanders. Among that company, one who had contributed to Bligh's training and experience, was Captain James Cook, with whom he had sailed on an early voyage of discovery in the South Pacific as master of the ship *Resolution.* In fact, Bligh had been present on the ill-fated day in 1779 when that eminent navigator-explorer had been set upon and brutally stabbed and beaten to death by natives of the Hawaiian—or Sandwich—Islands.

In quitting the long, hedonistic weeks at Tahiti (known to the *Bounty* sailors as *Otaheite*) on April 5, Bligh was filled with inward satisfaction, as he would write his wife Betsy, " . . . I had sailed with my expectations to the highest pitch . . . with a ship in most perfect order and all my plants in a most flourishing condition, all my men and officers in good health, and, in short, everything to flatter and insure my most sanguine expectations and success."

The muse of history, however, was active that last week of April 1789—even as it was on the other side of the world, where on Thursday, April 30, George Washington would take the oath in Federal Hall, New York, as the first President of the United States.

As Bligh attested in his journal, he was taken completely by surprise by the crisis developing in the vulnerable hour before sunrise when he was roughly awakened by four of the crew. In the gloom, he recognized the leader as Master's Mate Fletcher Christian, 24, who had sailed with him on two previous voyages. The men quickly tied the captain's hands with a cord and threatened him with "instant death" if he spoke or made "the least noise."

Events progressed swiftly. It became obvious that the captain was not to be murdered but set adrift with those of the *Bounty* considered loyal to him. Each time he inquired the reason "of such violence," or attempted to persuade the mutineers to abandon this mutiny, one of the group would shout, "Hold your tongue, sir, or you are dead this instant!"

Although he would write that he was kept "securely bound," Bligh managed to dress himself in clothing better suited for the open sea than his night attire. Eighteen of the crew were assembled to accompany him in a 23-foot boat, with but a six-foot, nine-inch beam. Among them, almost all men in the twenties, were John Fryer, master; Thomas Ledward, acting surgeon (Dr. Thomas Huggan, the ship's original surgeon, having died in December of alcoholism); David Nelson, botanist, good friend of Bligh as well of Sir Joseph Banks, the noted naturalist who had conceived the expedition in the first place; William Peckover, gunner; William Cole, boatswain; William Purcell, carpenter; William Elphinston, master's mate; Thomas Hayward and John Hallet, midshipmen; and John Norton and Peter Linkletter, quartermasters. Others would have loyally gone along but there was no room.

With them went 150 pounds of bread, sixteen pieces of pork (two pounds per man), six quarts of rum, six bottles of wine, twenty-six gallons of water, oars, sails, hammocks, twine, the captain's precious journals and other papers and—essentials of essentials—Bligh's sextant and a compass. As the launch was about to be shoved from the side of the *Bounty,* Bligh, thinking that he had detected "some signs" of remorse in Christian, again asked him why he was acting thus. The latter replied, "That—Captain Bligh—that is the thing. I am in hell! I am in hell!"

To the now ex-commanding officer of the *Bounty,* however, the impetus for the mutiny was already obvious: "The mutineers had flattered themselves with the hopes of a more happy life among the Otaheiteans than they could possible enjoy in England."

Whatever the reason for his present situation, Bligh now faced the supreme challenge of a seagoing career which had commenced when he entered the navy at the age of eight. He needed a plan if he were to sail his eighteen charges back to civilization—and, to the best of the knowledge of this experienced cartographer and voyager of the Seven Seas, the Dutch East Indies constituted the closest "civilization."

They were more than 3,000 miles to the west.

First, he must make the nearest landfall for further provisioning and generally inspecting the seaworthiness of his small craft. Under favorable breezes, the boat actually made the shadowy coast of Tofoa by dark—a five-mile long volcanic island in the southern Togatabu group of the Tonga or "Friendly Islands." But since Bligh could not be certain that either the rocky, steep coast or the inhabitants were truly hospitable, he held off the shore by rowing.

To salve a situation which was unhappy at the very best, the captain "served to every person half a pint of grog," while a heavy surf beat ominous lullabies the night through.

In the morning, the castaways sighted a cove with a stony beach which offered a landing. Several men, put ashore, were able to find only "a few quarts of water," retrieved not from springs but from depressions in the rocks. In the afternoon, farther along the same coast, the more nimble of the group scaled "high precipices" to pick some twenty coconuts.

The next day, deserted huts and plantain trees, with their banana-like fruit, were discovered, along with vines arranged by the natives for ascending the cliffs. When it came time to descend by these crude ropes, Bligh, frightened by the height, was "seized with such a dizziness" that he had to be assisted by the others.

On Friday, the fourth day following the mutiny, Bligh met inhabitants of the island for the first time. From them he obtained modest quantities of breadfruit, plantains, and water. Although initially uncertain as to how he might explain his presence, with no ship in sight, Bligh had agreed among his men on the myth that their vessel had "overset"—capsized and sunk—and only *they* had survived.

While the Polynesians appeared "satisfied" with the explanation, the observant Bligh noted that "there did not appear the least symptom of joy or sorrow in their faces." Indeed, even they must have known that there had been no severe storms in many weeks.

Bligh, having previously been among the Polynesians, was able to "talk" in mongrel English laced with the natives' own limited vocabulary and punctuated by long-familiar gesticulations. But he really couldn't communicate. He could not know what was going on behind the islanders' bland expressions. Time was running out faster than he could have possibly imagined.

By evening, whatever their earlier mood, it became apparent the Tofoans were assembling to attack the party of the *Bounty's* launch —perhaps for cannibalism. Bligh, "in a silent kind of horror," led his men down the beach for the boat. The islanders, now 200 strong, held onto the mooring rope while hurling stones "like a shower of shot."

John Norton, a big, corpulent quartermaster, then counter-attacked single-handedly, charging up the beach while Bligh hacked at the boat line with his knife. Norton diverted the mob's attention momentarily, allowing the launch to shove off. But his actions were sacrificial—he died almost instantly under a brutal hail of rocks. The others, unable to assist, watched the insanely infuriated natives continue to beat and mutilate his obviously lifeless form, aiming especially at his head. And still there was no apparent motive for the savagery.

The survivors, "everyone . . . more or less hurt," had to fight their way to sea. Filling their canoes with the murderous rocks, the islanders pursued the heavily laden launch. Soon Bligh was surrounded and once more dodging missiles reminiscent of the cave age. While the Englishmen attempted to field the rocks and toss some back, they found their pitching ability "very inferior" to that of their adversaries.

The captain, however, proved himself equal to this crisis even as he had the many gales through which he had sailed the *Bounty* and other commands. He "adopted the expedient" of throwing clothes overboard. The ruse worked. In the time it required the Tofoans to stop and retrieve the articles, the launch had lengthened its distance from the war canoes and dark was falling. As a providential bonus, a breeze "fresh from the eastward," had sprung up, filling a reefed lug foresail.

They had escaped the "Friendly Islands." Even so, there was scant basis for rejoicing. Bligh would write that such was the trend of his thinking when his men "solicited" him "to take them towards home." He reminded them that with the possible exception of the doubtful coasts of New Holland (Australia) the nearest white settlement was Dutch-owned Timor "a distance of full 1200 leagues," every bit of 3,000 miles, probably closer to 4,000.

It was obvious to Bligh that his seventeen shipmates preferred any extreme to hazarding another uncivilized island. He obtained their solemn promise to subsist on one ounce of bread and a quarter of a pint of water per day, then was wryly amused to observe that "everyone seemed better satisfied with our situation than myself."

The next day the castaways were buffeted and drenched by a "severe gale," with "the sea curling over the stern." This necessitated constant bailing and underscored the necessity of wrapping the bread against the seawater and also lightening the boat to avoid its being swamped. Determining that only two suits per man were necessary, Bligh then ordered extra clothing jettisoned together with some rope and spare sails. This radical measure produced the desired effect, leaving the boat with more freeboard.

The gale continued for several days, until May 4. Then, land again—an island, another, another. The survivors sailed so close to some two dozen that Bligh believed them to be inhabited "as they appeared very fertile." But none aboard wanted to touch shore, even though food was needed. For much of the bread had rotted because of the impossibility of keeping it wholly protected from seawater.

A hooked fish momentarily raised spirits, but they plummeted again as the men failed to land it.

Bligh, no mean cartographer, sketched the islands, concluding that they were the little known "Feejee" group. He would one day be credited as their true discoverer. Carefully, on May 6, he sailed the launch over a coral bank, with but four feet depth "and without the least break on it."

On the seventh two large sailing canoes put out from one of the islands, impelling the Englishmen to add oar power to that of their sails. All day long the two strange boats kept after the launch, one of them gaining until a late afternoon thunderstorm whipped up the seas and provided a fortuitous mantle under which Bligh made good his escape, not knowing in his "defenceless situation" the intent of the "Feejees."

He remained apologetic that he could not provide a better record of these interesting islands, some of which were distinguished by "extraordinary high rocks."

"Being constantly wet," Bligh explained, "it was with the utmost difficulty I could open a book to write, and I am sensible that what I have done can only serve to point out where these lands are to be found again, and give an idea of their extent."

"We experienced cold and shivering scarce to be conceived," Bligh added. The teaspoonfuls of rum or ounce and a half of port he was compelled to dole out were not sufficient to allay the shivering. A fishing line dragged constantly astern hooked nothing "though we saw great numbers of fish."

On the eighth, the sun came out, enabling the men to remove and dry their clothes as well as clean out the boat. Bligh then demonstrated that he was not only ingenious but also a good psychologist, given the extremity of the moment. He devised a scale out of coconut shells with pistol balls as weights, to be used in daily rationings. And he "amused all hands with describing the situation of New Guinea, and New Holland (Australia), and gave them every information in my power, that in case any accident happened to me, the survivors might be able to have some idea of the way to Timor, which at present they knew nothing more of than the name and some not even that."

The next few days were stormy. Athough Bligh had built up the stern with some of the boat's seats, much water was shipped. This demanded renewed bailing. However, canvas stretched as a kind of awning caught some twenty gallons of much-needed water. The tendency to "poop" or founder because of too much sea pouring in over the stern inspired the captain to label the situation "extremely dangerous."

He did glimpse enough stars on the evening of the eleventh to calculate position with his precious sextant and determine that they had progressed 102 miles since the previous day. On the twelfth, Bligh saw "a kind of fruit on the water" and the next morning "men-of-war," probably broad-winged frigate birds wheeling overhead. Now he was certain that land was not far distant.

He was right. For several days they sailed between islands which he judged to be the New Hebrides. Although he was certain they were "fertile and inhabited" since he saw smoke rising in various locations, he dared not land. It was a hard decision since the condition of all was "very little better than starving" and "the sight of them [the islands] only served to increase the misery of our situation." Yet, philosophically, Bligh was thankful for the cloudy, wet weather that had been their almost constant fare, since "hot weather would have destroyed us with thirst."

On Monday, May 18, three weeks after Bligh was cast adrift, the sun appeared to warm the little group after a drenching rain. Every one "complained of violent pains in his bones." Their condition, in spite of much better weather—somewhere in the Coral Sea—continued to deteriorate.

"At dawn of Wednesday, the 20th," Bligh wrote, "several of my people seemed half dead. Our appearance was shocking and I could look no way without catching the eye of some one in distress. Extreme hunger was now too evident, but no one suffered from thirst, nor had we much inclination to drink, that desire, perhaps, being satisfied through the skin.

"The little sleep we got was in the midst of water, and we always awoke with severe cramps and pains in our bones. All the afternoon we were covered with rain and salt water, so that we could scarcely see."

Gale winds returned and by Friday Bligh considered "our condition as extremely calamitous," running with a monstrous sea, with waves frequently foaming over the stern and quarters. Bligh rationalized with reason that the least mistake at the helm would have caused the overloaded boat to founder at once. Yet the heavy winds resulted in a record day's run of 130 miles.

On Sunday, May 24, with the return of sunshine and relatively flat seas, Bligh could log the sight of "some cheerful countenances and, for the first time for fifteen days past . . . comfort from the warmth of the sun." Seabirds, including boobies (or goose-like gannets) and noddies (terns or more typical seagulls) began to appear in significant numbers—so much so that one of the castaways, on Monday, reached up and caught a noddy.

"About the size of a small pigeon," it was nonetheless divided into 15 small portions, entrails included, excluding only beak, bones, feet and, of course, feathers. The distribution, commencing with the more desirable portions, was effected in a curious but time-honored seafarers' version of drawing lots. One person turns his back and designates another who then asks "who shall have this?" while pointing to a portion. Then the man with his back turned names the recipient.

That evening one of the larger boobies was caught and three more on Tuesday. Two held fish in their stomachs which also were devoured by the ravenous sailors. Now beaks and feet were also stripped of any flesh. Bread, dipped in salt water, completed the "feast."

Starvation appeared less imminent.

Two days of "serene" weather and hot sun followed, causing some "languor and faintness." There was more booby sustenance and then, on Wednesday, May 27, so much driftwood appeared that Bligh reckoned they were nearing "the reefs of New Holland." At 1:00 A.M. Thursday, this proved to be the case, as the helmsman reported the sound of breakers.

Bligh ordered the boat around and on a northeast course until the sound disappeared. At 9:00 A.M. the reef came into full view: "The sea broke furiously over every part, but we saw smooth water within." This was the Great Barrier Reef of Australia's northeast coast, already charted by Captain Cook, who also discovered what he named "Providential Channel."

With difficulty, since the men were too weak to row effectively, Bligh found a channel "about a quarter of a mile broad" and "happily" transited the reef. It proved to be another entrance, several miles north of Cook's discovery.

The survivors were now about three-fifths of the way to Timor and about 120 miles south of the northeast tip of Australia: Cape York. Wherever they were, Bligh "returned God thanks for his gracious protection," then "with much content took our miserable allowance of a 25th of a pound of bread, and a quarter of a pint of water, for dinner."

On Thursday, May 28, after nearly four weeks continuously at sea, the launch touched shore. It was near what Bligh called Direction Island, which actually was an Australian headland, now named Cape Direction. Some slept ashore, others in their more familiar "home."

The next day, Friday, a delicacy—oyster stew. After starting a fire with "a small magnifying glass," Bligh discovered a piece of brimstone and a tinder box on board. A copper pot which someone with much forethought had carried from the *Bounty,* some pork and bread completed the essentials for the stew. The oysters themselves grew to the rocks so firmly that "it was with difficulty they could be broken off." It did not take the men long to learn that it was more expeditious to open them where they were and perhaps devour them at once since they were "of a good size and well tasted."

Springs were discovered, two "ill-constructed" native huts, a pointed stick, possibly used in warfare, and tracks of an animal which Nelson, the botanist, thought was a kangaroo. This piqued Bligh's curiosity since he wondered "whether the animal swims over from the main land, or is brought here to breed by the natives."

That day was spent in further exploring their surroundings. Some two to four miles in circumference, the island was covered with rocks and low, scrubby trees, including some palms. Wild pigeons, parrots, and other birds flew over the higher ground. There was a bountiful supply of berries which proved to be edible, Bligh having first noted that they were eaten by the birds. Lizards were seen, "and the blackberry bushes were full of ants' nests, webbed like a spider's but so close and compact as not to admit the rain."

On Saturday, May 30, "being the restoration of King Charles the Second," Bligh named the area "Restoration Island." In the afternoon, readying for sea, and after finishing a prayer service, the former commanding officer of the *Bounty* noticed some "20 natives" on the opposite shore, armed with spears or lances and "halloaing to us." They appeared to be "black with short bushy hair or wool."

The men did not tarry. They pushed off the beach and continued their journey up the coast, well inside the Great Barrier Reef. On Sunday, off a sandy, more barren coast, they saw natives of similar appearance, but "waving green branches of the bushes near them as a token of friendship." Others appeared to be making motions which were "less amicable." Nonetheless, about four miles farther along, Bligh determined it was safe to land again—on a small island. Now, this Sunday evening, there arose the first serious grumbling since the Englishmen had been put over the side of the *Bounty.*

"Fatigue and weakness," Bligh would chronicle, "got so far the better of their sense of duty, that some of the people expressed their discontent at having worked harder than their companions, and declared that they would rather be without their dinner than go in search of it. One person in particular (Purcell, the carpenter) went so far as to tell me, with a mutinous look, that he was as good a man as myself. It was impossible for me to judge where this might end; therefore to prevent such disputes in future, I determined either to preserve my command, or die in the attempt.

"Seizing a cutlass, I ordered him to take hold of another and defend himself; on which he cried out, that I was going to kill him and immediately made concessions."

John Fryer, the master, who had always felt a sense of rivalry with Bligh, then grasped the moment to interfere, suggesting that Cole, the bosun, put the captain under arrest. Bligh wheeled on him and told Fryer he'd put him "to death, the first person," if he did not mind his own business.

Fryer, who seemed to have no particular strength of his convictions or stomach for real conflict, now assumed a semiapologetic attitude. Bligh would write his own amen. "I did not allow this to interfere further with the harmony of the boat's crew, and everything soon became quiet."

The confrontation produced the salutary effect Bligh had desired. The men dispersed to collect a generous amount of oysters, clams, and dogfish for their dinner. Before they ate, walking about the island, which Bligh named "Sunday," an old canoe, about 30 feet long, was discovered. Fearing that warriors might not be far away, he led his group to "a more retired place for lodging," where they enjoyed their relatively sumptuous repast.

Monday, June 1, was a day of mingled discovery and continuing vexation for the leader of the castaways. Turtle tracks and cracked-open turtle shells were observed, leading to the supposition that natives were about. No living turtles were to be found.

Many of the group took sick with "a violent heat in the bowels, loss of sight, and great thirst." Bligh correctly enough diagnosed the cause as excessive eating of raw or half-cooked food and also the heat of the sun. Robert Lamb, who had been the *Bounty's* butcher, was caught devouring, raw, nine birds. For his gluttony and, as his shipmates charged, for frightening off other noddies and boobies, Bligh administered to the offender "a good beating."

In the evening, while he "strolled about the beach," Bligh noticed with shock that the islands "appeared all in a blaze." A campfire had spread to the surrounding grass. Certain that their presence was betrayed, the captain took his launch to sea early the next morning.

Now the men no longer could know the time. William Peckover, the gunner, had the only watch. While it had prevailed faithfully through continued drenchings, it finally had expired. Bligh logged, "noon, sunrise and sunset are the only parts of the day of which henceforward I can speak with certainty."

They sailed on up the coast . . . an island, another, the second of which Bligh, the dedicated name-fixer, called "Booby Island" since it appeared to be primarily a resting place for those tough, hardy birds. He logged, "no more land was seen on the coast of New Holland; and at 8 o'clock in the evening we were once more launched into the open ocean."

Bligh, usually a faithful recorder of details, had neglected to note that he had rounded Cape York and was proceeding west through what was to be known as Torres Straits, towards Timor.

On the fourth of June, "we saw a number of water-snakes; they were ringed yellow and black." The weather worsened and the survivors became wet again "with much cold and shiverings."

On the sixth, Bligh took inventory and estimated another nineteen days' rations of bread. However, he saw "every prospect of a quick passage" to Timor. On Monday, June 8, a small dolphin was caught, affording the men their first substantial meat. Even so, their resistance was going down, so much so that by Wednesday Bligh was forced to log "a visible alteration for the worse in many of the people," adding:

"Extreme weakness, swelled legs, hollow and ghastly countenances, with an apparent debility of understanding, seemed to be the melancholy presages of approaching dissolution. The surgeon and Lebogue, in particular, were most miserable-looking objects. I occasionally gave them a few tea-spoonfuls of wine out of the little that remained, which was of infinite use; the hopes of being able to accomplish the voyage, were our principal support.

"The boatswain very innocently told me, that he really thought I looked worse than any one in the boat; I was amused by the simplicity with which he uttered such an opinion, and returned him a better compliment. Our course since yesterday was 111 miles."

This proved to be the darkest hour before their particular dawn. Early Friday, June 12, "with an excess of joy," Bligh picked up the east coast of Timor. He would write:

"It is not possible for one to describe the pleasure which the blessing of the sight of this land diffused among us. It appeared scarcely credible to ourselves, that in an open boat, and so poorly provided, we should have been able to reach the coast of Timor, in forty-one days after leaving Tofoa; having, in that time, run by our log the distance of 3,618 miles; and that, notwithstanding our extreme distress, no one should have perished on the voyage."

Two days later, on Sunday, when he finally came ashore at the town and fort of Coupang, he added, "A painter might have delineated the two groupes of figures, which, at the time, presented themselves to each other; an indifferent spectator would have been at a loss which most to admire, the eyes of famine sparkling at immediate relief, or the horror of our preservers at the sight of so many spectres, whose ghastly countenances, if the causes had been unknown, would not so much have excited pity as terror. Our bodies were nothing but skin and bone, our limbs full of sores, and we were clothed in rags. In this condition, with tears of joy and gratitude flowing down our cheeks, the people of Timor beheld us with a mixture of horror, surprise and commiseration."

The ordeal of Captain William Bligh was at an end.

2

Blue Riband

". . . an impractical, impossible dinosaur of a vessel!"

ONE ORDEAL WAS PAST, but turbulence and confrontation persisted for William Bligh as well as for those who had sailed on the *Bounty*.

In 1792, on his second try, Bligh successfully transported bread-fruit trees from Tahiti to the West Indies. However, in August 1797, he was involved in a general Royal Navy mutiny, known as the "Nore," from a tributary at the mouth of the Thames. With customary resilience, or great luck, he commanded the same mutinous ship, H.M.S. *Director,* victoriously a few weeks later against the Dutch at Camperdown.

Bligh, in 1801, was on the quarterdeck of the *Glatton* during Lord Nelson's bombardment of Copenhagen, afterwards being commended by that naval immortal. Almost immediately, the erstwhile captain of the *Bounty* faced a new challenge when he was court-martialed for abusive treatment of a lieutenant. Reprimanded only, Bligh was appointed in 1806 as governor of a penal colony in New South Wales. There seemed some doubt whether the post was punishment or reward.

Two years afterwards, in 1808, he was swept up by mutiny for yet a third time. It arose from his over-zealousness in attempting to stamp out corruption, including contraband liquor traffic. He was

15

arrested and returned to England, where once more he was able to parlay adversity into something closer to success. He was promoted to rear, then vice admiral, although he would never be entrusted with another command. Home from the sea, the lonely widower with six daughters sat in his house in the Lambeth section of London, thinking long thoughts of a chaotic and not readily duplicated career. He died in 1817 of cancer.

Of the *Bounty* mutineers, some remained on Tahiti, only to be taken prisoners in 1791 by a special search party dispatched on H.M.S. *Pandora*. When the *Pandora* was wrecked en route to England, four of the prisoners drowned in their manacles. The survivors sailed in small boats to Timor as if to retrace Bligh's own voyage. Three were hanged at Spithead after a court-martial, in testament to the implacable Royal justice of the eighteenth century. The trio's previous testing by man and the elements had been ruled insufficient penance.

Christian, with eight from the *Bounty* and eighteen Polynesian men and women, settled on tiny Pitcairn Island after burning His Majesty's breadfruit ship. Disputes over the women resulted in several murders and at least one suicide, and fever wiped out all but one of the mutineers, Alexander Smith, also known as John Adams. The cause of Christian's own demise would remain obscure. It was variously reported as murder or suicide (by leaping off a cliff).

Not until the American merchantman *Topaz* happened by Pitcairn in search of fresh water in 1808 was this postscript to an almost forgotten mutiny finally written. Even as Bligh was continuing to cope with mutiny and other adversity, old Alexander Smith was fathering a colony—over which, a few decades hence, the Union Jack would proudly fly, unattainable as this new possession—Pitcairn—was.

Of those non-mutineers who accompanied Bligh to Timor two succumbed in the East Indies from their exhaustion, one (Lamb, the butcher of the immense appetite) died on the voyage home, and a fourth was lost with all others aboard an England-bound ship.

In the nineteenth century much of the course of United States history would be shaped at sea. In 1803, a stripling but aggressive America was showing the Barbary Pirates that Old Glory was not, with impunity, to be trampled upon. In that year Stephen Decatur led a boarding party onto the U.S.S. *Philadelphia* (which had fallen into pirate hands when it became stranded on a sandbar off the north coast of Africa) and burned the big, handsome frigate. He could not rescue the American crew, which had been imprisoned.

The daring naval officer went on in the War of 1812 to capture the British frigate *Macedonian.* In the same conflict the 1,576-ton *Old Ironsides,* under Isaac Hull, which had herself pummeled the Barbary brigands, won the surrender of H.M.S. *Guerriere* off the Maine coast.

Nonetheless, the British Empire was not without her victories at sea, some of them spectacular. In October 1805, after a long pursuit across the Atlantic to the West Indies and back again, Lord Nelson finally caught up with the French Admiral Villeneuve and destroyed his combined French/Spanish fleet off Cape Trafalgar, Spain. Fifteen of the enemy were sunk in imperishable testimony to euphemism—"the Nelson touch."

France was no longer a sea power, nor would be again, ever. Napoleon fought land actions alone, culminating in Waterloo.

All this while, preeminently peaceful forces were in motion. They would, through commerce and colonization, have a far more profound effect on world destiny than that wrought merely by armies and armadas. Just before the American Revolution, James Watt had perfected his steam engine, inspiring Robert Fulton, just two years after Trafalgar, to create and launch his *Clermont.* If not, perhaps, the first, it was indisputably a very early steamboat.

Then, in brave challenge to the sailing packets which pitched and rolled a wearisome 40 days on the Liverpool-New York run, the 320-ton *Savannah* set out in 1819 to introduce steam to the North Atlantic. She was pathetically under-powered. Her single cylinder was rated at only 72 horsepower, roughly equivalent to that of a small automobile of today. She required nearly a month to reach England, but used her engines to paddle only three days of that protracted time. She was under sail the remainder. For that matter, *Savannah* did not possess bunker capacity for more than a few days' coal fire.

The pioneering vessel never repeated her dubious feat. In fact, her engines were removed as if to underscore the truth that the era of the seagoing steamer may have glimmered, but surely had not yet dawned.

For nearly two decades travelers continued to patronize the big, relatively comfortable packets, especially those of the Black Ball Line. It did not seem to bother them that at best the eastbound passage required three weeks or more sailing, plunging through the wild, virtually year-'round gales. Too, there was something disquieting about those craft, appearing year-by-year on inland waterways, belching sparks and smoke like railroad locomotives, setting fire to the fields ashore, and, with their grotesque paddle wheels, churning up the mud and frightening away the fish, perhaps forever.

However, the pioneers and the daring had not lost sight of the "Atlantic steam bridge" during this score of years. At least five others beside the *Savannah* had made the voyage, partly under steam, during this time. One was the little known Canadian ship *Royal William,* hardly more than an island ferry, which paddled partly across in 1833. By the mid-1830s two ships were being groomed which possessed the capability of reversing the failures of the past.

In 1836, the keel was laid for the first true ocean steamship, even though she was fitted with four schooner-rig masts, just in case. The *Great Western,* owned by the British railway of the same name, was the brainchild of the civil engineer Isambard Kingdom Brunel. She was an impressive 236 feet overall, 1,340 tons, with engines which developed 750 indicated horsepower to turn paddles via a six and one-half-ton shaft about 29 feet in diameter. Her top speed was some eight knots.

By March, 1838, the first newspaper advertisements were singing the attributes of the great coal-burning vessel: 128 staterooms, "divided between the upper saloon, under saloon, fore cabin, poop and cuddy [small cabin, often near galley]," with the fare only 35 guineas, or $150. Also offered were "20 good bed places" for servants who, along with children, were transported at half fare.

The grand saloon boasted painted panels ranging from landscapes, the arts, and sciences to Cupid and Psyche—thus setting a precedent for yet more lavish maritime decor.

Far less pretentious was little *Sirius,* a coastal vessel some 60 feet shorter and about half the displacement of the *Great Western.* She had been chartered by a Connecticut-born, Yale-educated London merchant, 58-year-old Junius Smith, who with his nephew, Henry Smith of New York, had already founded the British and American

Steam Navigation Co., generally acknowledged to be the first trans-Atlantic steamship line.

The Smith enterprise was already building a vessel some 40 feet longer than the *Great Western* and more elaborately fitted: the *British Queen*. But she wasn't ready for sea. So the competitive Junius leased the *Sirius* in the hopes of beating his lumbering rival which, by her owners' advertisements, was coaling up to sail that very spring.

The *Sirius* put out from Cork on April 4, 1838, carrying 40 passengers, including eleven women. The *Great Western* was delayed four more days at Bristol. The weather was unfavorable; there were cargo problems; and as further bedevilment, a small fire erupted in the boiler room.

During the fire Brunel lost his footing on a charred ladder, and all but seven passengers were scared off. In this group of stouter nerve was one lady.

Both steamships, however, arrived in New York harbor on April 24. The *Sirius,* which had averaged slightly under seven knots, had been compelled to burn cabin furniture and other woodwork the last days at sea, and took on 50 tons of coal at the pilot station to complete the passage in twenty days.

The *Great Western*, able to clock nearly nine knots, made New York only three and a half hours behind the *Sirius.* She accomplished her historic, all-steaming voyage in 16 days with more than 100 tons of coal to spare, having consumed some 456 tons. However, a minor mutiny among the stokers had temporarily marred an otherwise smooth crossing.

The two ships were greeted by the firing of shore guns along Brooklyn and Staten Island. Church bells rang and small boats clustered about the steamships. Toasts were drunk to President Van Buren and to Queen Victoria.

"Nothing," exclaimed a correspondent of the *London Times* concerning the *Great Western,* "could exceed the beauty of her appearance as she gallantly breasted the waves."

The *New York Enquirer*'s reporter concluded that the two vessels had presented "the most irrefragable testimony of the practicability of steam navigation between the Old and New Worlds." Had he been clairvoyant, he might also have added that the two had paddled in their own fashion a channel for the fickle Blue Riband: a theoretical award for the fastest vessel on the North Atlantic. Competition was destined to become continually keener.

The *Sirius* would brave the Atlantic but once more; the *Great Western* 64 more times, reducing her own mark, eastbound, to thirteen days. She carried to England varied cargoes, including cotton for the Great Western Cotton Mills in Bristol and a commodity never before seen in Europe: two weeks' old American newspapers, thousands of copies in one voyage. In thumping out a sturdy reputation for dependability, the *Great Western* inevitably attracted many notables or future notables including, in November 1839, John Ericsson the inventor.

As a matter of fact, the brilliant if irascible Swede had already introduced the screw propeller to two ships, the *Francis B. Ogden* and the *Robert F. Stockton,* both named after Americans with whom Ericsson held business associations. As with others of his visionary creations, this type of stern propeller, replacing the familiar side or beam paddle wheels, met with many rebuffs. For example, Sir William Symonds, Surveyor of the Royal Navy, who had attended a successful demonstration on the Thames nonetheless sneered, ". . . even if the screw has the power to propel a vessel it would be found altogether useless in practice because, the power being applied to the stern, it would be absolutely impossible to make the vessel steer."

The next year, however, 1839, the tiny *Stockton,* a mere 35 tons, 71 feet long, proved she could and did steer, as she crossed to New York. But she had her problems, losing a man overboard and relying on her schooner rig almost the entire passage, which required a month and a half.

Now, too, Junius Smith's *British Queen,* complete with a bright blue funnel and a full-length figurehead-sceptre of her regal namesake, was finally in service. When she dropped anchor in Gravesend Bay on July 28, 1839, the *New York Sun* put out an extra, with a rendering of the handsome steamer across the top of page one. The same paper had been meeting the *Great Western* with its own sailing ships to take ashore such timely items as London newspapers.

These two steamships, which were already instilling a measure of confidence in a packet-oriented traveling public, would not have the ocean to themselves for long. A new name was about to appear over the long, green combers, from Nantucket shoals to the Kerries: that of Samuel A. Cunard. He was born in Halifax of loyalist parents who had fled the American Revolutionists. No newcomer to the merchant marine, Sam Cunard, with his brother Joseph, had operated sailing ships since early in the century between Nova Scotia, Newfoundland, Boston, and as far south as Bermuda under the name Abraham Cunard & Son. His father, Abraham, had originally been a carpenter.

Following Abraham's death, the Cunards, their ranks swelled by sons of Sam and Joseph, migrated to England the year of the *Great Western's* maiden voyage. They lost no time. By 1840 the Cunards, with one ship—the *Britannia*—had established the British and North American Royal Steam Packet Co., controlled by several parties in addition to the Cunard family. At that time it was known only informally as the Cunard Line.

Its success was underwritten by the Crown, which subsidized the company to carry mails across the Atlantic. *Britannia* put Liverpool astern on July 4 to launch a shipping empire. The choice of that public relations-inspired date seemed to indicate that the passions of the War for Independence as well as the hateful little War of 1812 were cold.

Somewhat shorter than the *Great Western* but of similar tonnage, *Britannia* embodied Cunard's desires for a plain sort of ship. She could accommodate 115 passengers and 225 tons of cargo at a top speed of nine knots, only a fraction faster than the *Great Western.* On *Britannia's* maiden voyage she raised Halifax in twelve and a half days, then proceeded to Boston which, to New York's profound annoyance, would be Cunard's western terminus. The "Hub" would also port her sisters, now building: *Caledonia, Acadia,* and *Columbia.* Daniel Webster was among those who welcomed the "immense" ship, *Britannia,* at banquets and receptions.

Most passengers spoke favorably of the food, which included steak for breakfast, fresh milk provided by a stable of cows, or chicken stew and eggs courtesy of a large, cackling hen coop astern. However, sailing masters long ago had brought their livestock and poultry along. Some more critical alluded to the "stale eggs" and "cold tea," while Charles Dickens, on a subsequent crossing, would fill his pen with acid for numerous observations.

He described his cabin as "an utterly impractical, thoroughly hopeless and preposterous box." Among the potpourri of passengers and their peculiarities was a man who "carried more guns with him than Robinson Crusoe, wore a shooting coat, and had two great dogs on board. On further consideration, I remember that he tried hot roast pig and bottled ale as a cure for seasickness; and that he took these remedies (usually in bed) day after day, with astonishing perseverance. I may add, for the information of the curious, that they decidedly failed."

Of the weather and the ship's "outrageous antics," he wrote:

". . . . anything like the utter dreariness and desolation that met my eyes when I, literally, 'tumbled up' on deck at noon, I never saw. Ocean and sky were all of one dull, heavy, uniform, lead colour. There was no extent of prospect even over the dreary waste that lay around us, for the sea ran high, and the horizon encompassed us like a large black hoop. Viewed from the air, or some tall bluff on shore, it would have been imposing and stupendous no doubt, but seen from the wet and rolling decks, it only impressed one giddily and painfully.

". . . In the gale of last night the life-boat had been crushed by one blow of the sea like a walnut shell; and there it hung dangling in the air; a mere faggot of crazy boards. The planking of the paddle-boxes had been torn sheer away. The wheels were exposed and bare; and they whirled and dashed their spray about the decks at random. Chimney, white with crusted salt; topmasts struck; storm-sails set; rigging all knotted, tangled, wet, and drooping; a gloomier picture it would be hard to look upon."

Foul weather and the inability of ship or crew to cope with it dominated all seaboard existence and thought.

"The head engineer has distinctly said that there never was such times—meaning weather—and four good hands are ill, and have given in, dead beat. Several berths are full of water, and all the cabins are leaky. The ship's cook, secretly swigging damaged whiskey, has been found drunk; and has been played upon by the fire-engine until quite sober. All the stewards have fallen down stairs at various dinnertimes, and go about with plasters in various places. The baker is ill, and so is the pastry-cook.

"A new man, horribly indisposed, has been required to fill the place of the latter officer; and has been propped and jammed up with empty casks in a little house upon deck, and commanded to roll out pie-crust, which he protests (being highly bilious) it is death to him to look at. News! A dozen murders on shore would lack the interest of these slight incidents at sea."

All in all, Dickens provided unintentional endorsement of his contemporary, Junius Smith, who had complained in a letter, "passengers in general know nothing about a ship and yet are the most arrogant and opinionated of all Adam's descendants . . . they do not care one button for the owners or for their welfare."

"Speed, Comfort, Safety" had become Cunard's slogan. This proved largely fact in the line's early decades. And Sam Cunard was especially sensitive to public fears in stressing "safety." While Dickens was out of sorts over matters of physical comfort, the majority who allowed themselves to be transported across the North Atlantic did so in persistent fear of their very lives. Solemn bon voyage groups at dockside holding back their tears with varying success were more the rule than the exception. Conscientious family attorneys urged their clients to take another look at their wills and possibly increase life insurance.

The concern was by no means wholly unfounded. Bad years lay just over the horizon.

There was, for example, the *President,* as ill-fated as she was beautiful and ornate. She became, in 1840, Junius Smith's latest contribution to the British and American Navigation Co. Somewhat larger than the *British Queen,* she was complete with a "remarkably well executed bust figurehead" of George Washington at her bowsprit and other nautical frosting, including an American eagle and British lion, on her stern.

Plowing into service, she proved at once disappointingly slow. Laid up for the winter, the *President* reappeared in the spring of 1841 in New York. On March 4, she sailed, carrying 30 passengers and a crew of about 90. The passengers included Lord Fitzroy Lynnox and an Irish actor, Tyrone Power, plus his servant. Her paddle wheels splashed down the bay through a crisp, bright late winter afternoon as she sailed eastward—into oblivion.

She ran into a nor'easter the very next morning off Nantucket shoals, by the loggings of other vessels. Then: nothing. Friends and relatives waited in Liverpool as did representatives of the steamship company and merchants expecting cargo. Weeks passed. Bits of wreckage picked up at sea, at first associated with the *President,* proved inconclusive. For example, there was a figurehead that on closer scrutiny turned out not to bear the least resemblance to the Father of His Country, since it was of a sailor with a black kerchief. The disappearance not only wrecked her owners but cast a long shadow over the seaworthiness of ships of steam. The *Great Western* sailed with most of her cabins empty. Even Cunard, with its excellent record, suffered although that very year, 1841, its newest ship, the *Acadia,* accomplished the first ten-day crossing of the Atlantic.

Undaunted in the face of grave public apprehension, the builders kept working. Brunel was producing a gargantua, the *Great Britain,* 3,270 tons, 274 feet long. Multi-decked, six masts, she proved to be the largest steamship yet to be groomed for the Atlantic and the first of her size with a propeller and an iron hull.

She arrived in New York in July 1845, after an unspectacular crossing of fifteen days. She did not long remain, however, in transatlantic service. A subsequent grounding off the Irish coast hastened her sale to another company and ultimately her employment in the Australian gold rush trade. (Remarkably, she is in existence today, having been towed back to Bristol from the Falkland Islands where she was found rotting and rusting away inside a cerement of barnacles.)

As the 1840s ended, passages were shortened. Cunard, with six ships on regular schedules, could point to records being broken successively. In 1847, her *Hibernia* crossed in nine days; the *Asia,* in 1850, crossed in eight days.

By that same year, three new lines—one British, the second American, the third German-American—offered their own innovations in speed and choice of accommodations, and attracted a varied clientele. William Inman, an Englishman, pioneering a company bearing his name, started out with the 1,600-ton iron, screw-driven ship, *City of Glasgow,* boasting, of all banal luxuries, flush toilets and an apothecary's shop. She could transport 400 immigrants from Liverpool to Philadelphia for a fare of $45 each. Inman thus anticipated by at least a century mass transatlantic excursion rates.

The Ocean Steam Navigation Co. of New York, which would become a forerunner of North German Lloyd, was founded primarily to compete with Cunard. Its *Washington,* sailing first in 1847, was larger than Cunard's *Britannia* and offered fares of $120 England to New York ($150 from Bremen) compared with Cunard's fare of $190. She required some fifteen days for the passage.

Excepting Cunard, the Collins Line would exert the most far-reaching influence upon type, quality and speed of ocean travel. It was founded by Edward Knight Collins, of Cape Cod, whose father and uncle both were sailing masters. He dreamed of a vastly gaudier fleet than Cunard's. He wanted big steamers—upwards of 3,000 tons, nearly 300 feet long—complete with bathrooms, smokerooms, barber shops, upholstered drawing saloons, carpeting, rosewood paneling, table tops of brocatelli marble, mirrored walls, scrollwork, stained glass, drapes, a royal cuisine, steam heat, ice lockers—in short and in Collins's own words, each "a floating palace."

A subsidy of half a million dollars from Congress, almost immediately doubled, enabled Collins to turn dream into reality. He built four such ships, wooden-hulled and paddle wheel-driven, the *Atlantic, Arctic, Pacific,* and *Baltic.* They contained all the accoutrements desired plus such innovations as the first engine room telegraphs and clockwork to force-feed oil lamps.

More than all these Lucullan and technological *ne plus ultras,* Congress also desired that the Blue Riband be snatched away from Cunard. Implicitly, if not in fact, the Collins Line captains were ordered to maintain "full speed ahead!" and damn the weather, fog, sleet, ice, or the dark of night.

The *Atlantic* in 1850 proved that she could cross her namesake ocean on a regular schedule a bit in excess of ten days. The *Pacific,* two years later, clocked a day's run of 330 miles, which would stand for a dozen years. In the same year the *Arctic* crossed eastbound in nine days, seventeen hours.

Congress applauded these ornate greyhounds which made Cunard's ships appear, if not quite barges by comparison, at least very drab. Also, passengers were eating food they had never tasted at home. Delmonico-like menus offered green turtle soup or potage au choux, turkey with oyster sauce, croquette de poisson à la Richelieu, epigram d'agneau, sauce truppe. The cuisine was a leap forward from the "stale eggs" and "cold tea" of a scant decade ago.

Collins's principal *bête noire,* however, soon became obvious. He spent too much money, even with the crutch of governmental subsidy. The first class fare of $125 (certainly not the second class of $70) just did not and could not bring in sufficient revenue to offset the Park Avenue fashions of his steamships.

He overpaid his crew. His captains, for example, earned $6,000 annually, almost triple the Cunard scale. And his liners were driven so hard that annual maintenance began to approximate the original cost. At twelve knots, any one of them consumed 85 tons of coal a day—astronomical compared to the intake of a railroad locomotive. Critics obtained fierce satisfaction, asserting that this merely proved an earlier hypothesis that any steamship over 1,200 tons could not be run economically because of the great and unavoidable ravenings of coal.

Then came a sobering year for transatlantic travel: 1854. In the spring, the *City of Glasgow* vanished as mysteriously and as completely as the *President* had. The 399 passengers and 74 crew members made the loss the greatest yet of any single disaster at sea. Some speculated, without any substantial foundation, that she might have burned or even been pirated.

In September 1854, the *Arctic* was en route from Liverpool with 233 passengers. These included Collins's wife, Mary Ann, his youngest son and only daughter, his brother-in-law and family, as well as seven members of the family of James Brown, one of the bankers supporting the Collins Line.

Off Newfoundland, as often happened, the *Arctic* plunged into fog. But Captain James C. Luce, whose crippled eight-year-old son was along, kept the ship paddling ahead at full speed, while the bow lookout pumped the foghorn bellows to warn fishing boats and other traffic to get out of the way—if possible. There was that "fastest" record to maintain. Also in current vogue was the theory that the faster one went the sooner out of a fog. That theory presupposed an illusion of indestructibility.

It did not work out quite that way this time.

About 60 miles from Cape Race, the 250-ton, iron-hulled French coaster *Vesta* smashed into the *Arctic's* starboard side below the water line. Sails were draped over the gouges in the *Arctic's* hull as Luce ordered full speed ahead for Cape Race, in the hopes of beaching her.

Soon the inrushing waters extinguished the fires. *Arctic* was dead in the water. A huge raft was knocked together. But most of the crew did not wait. They lowered and rowed off in all but one of the lifeboats.

About four hours after the collision the *Arctic* sank. Of the 368, including crew, only 45 reached shore, and most of those were crewmen. Captain Luce was among them. Not one woman or child survived in this display of brutal cowardice.

When the news belatedly reached New York, the *Times* would note, "the city was filled with mourning for the loss of so many valuable lives and all classes of the community felt for the calamities of others as though they had been their own."

Collins himself had lost much of his family and inlaws. His line, nonetheless, appeared to have ridden out of the tragedy and might have continued to do so had not the *Pacific,* less than eighteen months later, sailed from Liverpool with nearly 200 aboard—and into the same oblivion as the *President* and the *City of Glasgow.*

Based on the experience of several other ships at that time, plus a bit of floating wreckage, it was theorized that the beautiful *Pacific* had smashed into an iceberg.

Curiously, Cunard's first iron ship, the 3,300-ton *Persia,* rival of the Collins steamers, had struck a berg at about the same time but made it to New York in spite of heavy damage. Captain Asa Eldredge of the *Pacific,* had previously boasted, "If I can't beat the *Persia* I'll send the *Pacific* to the bottom."

In 1858, Collins's subsidy was canceled. This proved the requiem for what was left of his line of fast, nine- to eleven-day, sumptuous ships which had ushered in a new era of transatlantic travel. It meant, also, that, aside from Inman, which had lost its *City of Glasgow,* Cunard was the only company which could steam a fleet of robust consequence into the North Altantic.

During the preceding ten or fifteen years Americans had been witness to a seaborne phenomenon not wholly unrelated to the race to conquer the Atlantic—the gold rush to California and the coming of the clipper ships. Some 500 of the tall-masted, graceful clippers were constructed between the early '40s and late '50s, almost as if blatantly defying the trend to steam.

The New England merchants knew what they were doing, however, since the big sailing vessels were cheaper and faster to build than steamships (in fact could pay for themselves and even make a profit on the first voyage), were endowed with capacious cargo holds, and often could log a day's run equal to or exceeding that of the steamers. The record was 374 miles in a day, set by the *Flying Cloud.*

Probably no steamship, with her need for coal and the tendency of her engines to break down if operated for extended periods, could have equaled the record run of the *Sea Witch,* which, in 1849, sailed from China to New York in 74 days. Nor would the average steamship of that year been likely to have survived the pounding of "the Horn." Josiah Cressy, on the *Flying Cloud,* logged the results of a not wholly unusual spell of dirty weather:

"June 6 (three days out of New York). Lost main and mizzen topgallant masts and main topsail yard. June 7—sent up main and mizzen topgallant masts and yard. June 8—sent up main topsail yard. June 14—discovered mainmast badly sprung about a foot from the hounds [part of the framing of the masthead] and fished it. July 11—very severe thunder and lightning, double-reefed topsails, split fore and maintopmast stay sails. At 1 P.M. discovered mainmast had sprung. Sent down the royal and topgallant yards and studding sail booms off lower and topsail yards to relieve strain. July 13—let men out of irons in consequence of wanting their services with the understanding that they would be taken care of on arriving at San Francisco."

Cressy, along with Nat Palmer and Charles Low, one of the great clipper captains, had also alluded to crews not much improved in their character, conduct, or social amenities since Bligh's mutinous ruffians. In this case, Josiah Cressy had caught the culprits drilling and smashing holes in the side of the clipper with marlin spikes. No explanation was provided.

The high water mark of clipper building came in 1853 with the launching of the 4,555-ton *Great Republic* in the Boston yard of the famous Donald McKay. Larger than any steamship then in service, the *Great Republic* sported four decks and the same number of masts. With a 53-foot beam, she drew the immense draft of 38 feet, and required the innovation of a steam winch to hoist her blossoming acres of canvas.

Then—disaster. The day after Christmas, in the same year she'd been launched, she took fire in New York while awaiting her first voyage. Although rebuilt, she emerged a cutdown and depressing impersonator of the immense, beautiful ship conceived by her designers.

Probably the clippers would have come along anyhow in the evolution of the U.S. merchant marine even if there had not been a gold rush, sparked by the strike of gold at Sutter's Mill (the future site of Sacramento) in January 1848. Ships were already picking up hides and seal skins in California in addition to cargo waiting on the opposite shores of the Pacific: tea in China, wheat in Australia, and even opium in Turkey to be transported to China and possibly elsewhere.

The clippers, in particular, introduced a volume of varied and sometimes exotic cargoes: satin, taffeta, cocoa, sugar, coffee, lace from Belgium, cotton from Nanking, Italian silk, brandies, porcelain, china baked from exceptionally pure clay, cigars, rum, whiskey, and immigrants, notably from Germany and Ireland.

And they introduced or furthered at the same time far less welcome stowaways: measles, smallpox, Norway (or Asian) rats, German cockroaches, Japanese (or Siberian) beetles, sparrows, starlings, pigeons, Hessian flies that decimated grain crops, river-clogging water chestnuts, and a devil's brew of fungi, including the Dutch elm disease, which could rot and level whole forests.

While British companies were concentrating on the North Atlantic steam "ferry," enterprising Americans were cashing in on the sea route to the gold fields, well aware that many could not and would not face hostile Indians and other perils of the overland route. In fact, it was estimated that more than 90,000 persons arrived via sea in sailing ships of every description, sidewheelers, large and small, even Hudson River ferry boats. Many, if they got there at all, were abandoned along the flats of San Francisco Bay or the Sacramento River to rot and expose their ribs as a lure for maritime archaeologists of generations hence.

The rush also sparked the growth of serious-minded, dollar-hungry corporations like the Pacific Mail Steamship Co. and the Vanderbilt Line. The latter, created by the crusty but successful Commodore Cornelius Vanderbilt, erstwhile operator of Long Island Sound ferries, carried passengers to the Atlantic side of the Isthmus of Panama, leaving them to struggle through fever and bandit-ridden Chagres swamps the twelve miles to Panama City, "the unhealthiest spot in the world."

"Ho, for California!" read a typical ad in the *New York Herald:* "to sail on the 25th Instant, the splendid ocean steamer *Senator* of 754 tons burthen, 240 feet long by 30 feet beam. . . ."

Vanderbilt's Line for San Francisco itself advertised "the only line giving tickets for crossing the Isthmus! The shortest and cheapest route. The Favorite Double-engine Steamship *Prometheus,* 1800 tons, will leave from Pier No. 2 N. River at 3 o'clock P.M. precisely on Friday, for San Juan del Norte connecting with the Pacific Steamer over the Nicaragua Transit Route leaving but 12 miles of land transportation.

"These steamers are unrivalled in their accommodation and ventilation. For information or passage apply to . . . D. B. Allen, Agent, No. 9 Battery Place, New York."

The appetite for journeying to the gold fields would be further whetted by dispatches such as this one, in the *New York Times,* of September 19, 1851, under a Baltimore dateline:

"The steamship *Illinois* from Chagres for New York put into Norfolk today, short of coal. She brings the California mails, 400 passengers and $1,800,000 in gold and freight besides a large amount in the hands of passengers."

Aside from inherent dangers, monotony became its own corrosive *enfant terrible* during these voyages which could and often did consume four months. Nerves of passengers and crew alike were frayed until they could stretch no further. Aboard the sailing packet *Washington Irving* Captain Samuel Plumer, according to a traveler, "ranges the ship like an enraged lion." On another vessel, one passenger offered $10 reward for an untold joke or some personal recollection not already recounted time and again. Weeks later, the same man, almost driven mad, repeated his bonus for anyone who consistently did not talk to him *at all.*

Men and women, wishing desperately that they had *never* thought of the gold rush, read books, periodicals, and old newspapers until these literally crumbled in their hands. There was card playing, fishing when becalmed, even palmistry. Some took to drink, brawled with the crew, and found themselves in irons.

Food invariably ran low, even with such major ports of call as Charleston and Rio, and others in between. The gold hunters toted along their own chocolate cubes, pickles, cheese, bread, sardines, and salted meats. Canned meat was a menace since the poorly sealed containers generally exploded after a few days at sea. The master himself ordered "tinned meat" hunts. It was a race to see if the cans burst before they hit the sea.

Sometimes sharks jumped for them, leaving the bemused passengers to speculate if these rapacious fish would regret their hunger.

And yet, with provision problems and boredom added to the unseaworthiness of the "gold" ships, these hardy American argonauts were persistent. Mrs. D. B. Bates, of Kingston, Massachusetts, for example, survived the loss through fire of four sailing ships. She arrived in California ten months after she left home.

By 1857, with the fever for the precious yellow metal largely abated, steamship operators such as Commodore Vanderbilt again focused their primary energies upon the North Atlantic. That year there was added to a considerable fleet of lesser craft the magnificent 5,000-ton *Vanderbilt,* 355 feet long. The largest steamship on the run to Europe, she cost her owner at least a million dollars.

The *Vanderbilt* offered, as a sort of one-steamship super line, service to Europe every forty days, making the run—at her best time—in about nine and a half days. First class cabins sold for rates commencing at $100, with a maximum of $130. Second cabin was $75.

Size was burgeoning, even as the *Vanderbilt* furrowed the gray waters of the North Atlantic with her impressive avoirdupois. Being groomed for her maiden voyage was the ailing Brunel's tour de force, the *Great Eastern,* originally named *Leviathan,* which might have been more apt. She was gaped at and extolled by poets of the time, including Longfellow, who would lyricize:

> Sublime in its enormous bulk
> Loomed aloft the shadowy hulk.

Also pronounced "the wonder of the seas," *Great Eastern* merited all hyperboles: 27,000 tons displacement, 24,360 tons gross (or about five times that of the mighty *Vanderbilt,* by either measure); an unbelievable 700-foot long, metal double hull, towering 60 feet from keel; 30,000 iron plates fastened by three million rivets; eight engines and 112 furnaces to power a 24-foot diameter propeller as well as mammoth paddle wheels; five funnels; six auxiliary masts which could carry 7,000 yards of sail. . . .

She had the capacity to haul 4,000 passengers plus 6,000 tons of cargo (greater than the *Vanderbilt* in toto), staterooms at least twice the size of comparable accommodations on any previous Atlantic steamship. Her grand saloon seemed no less than a Buckingham or

Versailles palace, with decor of gold cloth and flowered glass walls, mirrors, claret plush chair or sofa upholstery, teakwood paneling, deep carpets. The stretching amplitude of the main or promenade deck appeared to some a veritable parade ground.

When the *Great Eastern's* voracious coal potential was branded an economic hurdle, Brunel scoffed, "our good Isle has abundant coal."

A London reporter, seeing her for the first time, exclaimed, "an impractical, impossible dinosaur of a vessel!"

Perched high on her blocks at Millward, the Isle of Dogs in the Thames, she dominated the countryside, vying in her own grotesque nautical majesty with St. Paul's Cathedral a few miles to the west in London or Canterbury, to the east.

She was so big, mountain-like, bulky, utterly unwieldly and intractible that it required three months merely to launch her, sideways. An extra $300,000 (equivalency) was expended for this purpose alone, culminating in the wrecking of jacks, steam rams, tackles and other precious special equipment.

Indeed, her successive owners had already lavished nearly four million dollars upon her. It was a sum more identifiable with the Royal Exchequer. The cost in lives, too, had been far greater than normally associated with the construction of a ship. At least half a dozen workmen had already perished, most in a single explosion. Brunel himself, in ailing health, succumbed before the *Great Eastern's* maiden voyage.

She arrived in New York the last of June, 1860, after an unspectacular fifteen-day crossing, carrying about one-tenth of her rated passenger capacity. The *New York Times,* on June 30, devoted its entire front page to the iron dinosaur from the Old World, upending a cutaway diagram to bisect page one vertically.

For a solid month she was a P.T. Barnum curiosity, even though the flamboyant showman somehow never kindled an interest in her. The curious came from Chicago, St. Louis, Savannah, and other distant cities, old and young, firm and infirm, 144,000 visitors "lost in the ship," according to the late James Dugan, as "they wandered through her like children discovering marvels." They brought picnic lunches, cards, books, knitting, the young ones dolls and toys—and why not? For one dollar the visitor could inhabit the vast premises the day long.

The pattern of accidents set at the Isle of Dogs continued. At least two crewmen toppled off her superstructure to the dockside, paying the supreme price for their carelessness. Visitors stumbled over rigging and davits and broke or sprained arms and legs, while children became lost in the below-decks labyrinth for hours—but there was no record of a fatality that month among their curious numbers.

At the end of July the *Great Eastern* carried cruise passengers to Cape May and Old Point Comfort, Hampton Roads, Virginia. Again, at the end of summer, she returned to Old Point, then up Chesapeake Bay to Annapolis before sailing home. She had, in spite of her qualities as a crowd magnet, been a mixed success. Attending her cruises there had been at least confusion and misunderstanding if not, perhaps, actual misrepresentation. Excursionists found that their passage had not necessarily secured them a cabin. That had to be bought, extra. Nor was dining assured. And if through surcharge or bribery they did buy their way into the dining saloon, they found the food skimpy and the heat so overpowering (the area being between funnels) that they had to flee with their plates onto deck or somewhere else.

At summer's end, *Great Eastern* steamed for home.

She returned in 1861, on one voyage impaling herself upon rocks in Long Island Sound, which would thereafter carry the name, "Great Eastern Ledge." Her double bottom precluded any serious consequences. However, the accident lent further embellishment to a standing rumor: that two workmen had been sealed in the double hull. What else would explain curious poundings and wailings in the dead of night? Or so the superstitious among the crew reported.

Now the same shaky witnesses would attest they heard the weird sounds no longer. Obviously, the imprisoned men had been freed into the waters of Long Island Sound.

On September 7, 1861, the *Great Eastern* again sailed from Liverpool, carrying, among her other voyagers, a wealthy Liverpool merchant, Thomas B. Forwood, and his 21-year-old son, William B. Forwood. As the youthful Bill would observe, "it was a memorable voyage." This proved understatement, as Bill's account reveals.

"Three days out we encountered a heavy gale, which carried away our boats, then our paddle wheels. Finally our rudder broke, and the huge ship fell helplessly into the trough of the sea. Here we remained for three days, rolling so heavily that everything moveable broke adrift, the saloon was wrecked, and all the deck fittings broke loose. Two swans and a cow were precipitated into the saloon through the broken skylights."

These had come down from the cow shed and the poultry coop, located topsides for milk, eggs, and other food.

"The cables broke adrift, and swaying to and fro burst through the plating on one side of the ship. The captain lost all control of his crew, and the condition of things was rendered still more alarming by the men breaking into the storerooms and becoming intoxicated. Some of the passengers were enrolled as guards; we wore a white handkerchief tied round our arms, and patrolled the ship in watches for so many hours each day."

At one juncture, a small sailing ship appeared, dwarfed by the piteously thrashing *Great Eastern.* The senior Forwood communicated through the master of the liner that he would pay the little brig $500 a day if she would just stand by. When there was no reply, the Liverpool merchant offered to purchase her outright. Again, no answer although the craft remained by the *Great Eastern*'s side a little longer. Bill Forwood continued:

"My father was badly cut in the face and head by being thrown into a mirror in the saloon during a heavy lurch. I never knew a ship to roll so heavily, and her rolls to windward were not only remarkable but very dangerous, as the seas broke over her, shaking her from stem to stern, the noise reverberating through the vessel like thunder. We remained in this alarming condition three days, when chains were fixed to our rudder head and we were able with our screw-engines to get back to Queenstown. My father returned home, not caring to venture to sea again, but I embarked on board the *City of Washington* of the Inman Line, and after a 16-day passage arrived in New York."

As a matter of fact, he was arrested upon disembarking and detained for several days by the Metropolitan police. Was he not really an English agent in the pay of the Confederacy?

The mood and preoccupations of America were far altered since the *Great Eastern*'s maiden voyage. The citizens of the North cared not a whit whether the big liner had nearly sunk that fall, or about who might hold the Blue Riband, if indeed they had ever thought about the Blue Riband at all.

After all, there was a war on.

3

Cruise of the *Alabama*

". . . the lightness and grace of a swan."

THE NORTH marched uncertainly off to war in the spring of 1861 against the secession and "intolerable impudence" of the South. Both sides were almost equally unprepared for battle, on land or upon the sea. The Federal navy of 90 ships was less than fifty percent steam propelled, and of the latter proportion only some 18 vessels could be termed relatively "modern." None was an ironclad.

The South flexed even less muscle afloat, in fact none at all except what she had "appropriated" from the Union: revenue cutters, governmental survey steamers, tugs, and river craft which happened to be in ports claimed by the seceding states. Her asset, in addition to unmitigated brass, lay in the surprise historically associated with the acts of an aggressor—catching an adversary off balance.

When President Lincoln proclaimed boldly, on April 19, 1861, a blockade of the Confederate sea coast, Secretary of the Navy Gideon Welles reached for his ledger books and came up with a sobering statistic: only eleven vessels available for blockade duty. Yet the North pointed to one plus, a huge merchant marine.

With an enviable facility for innovation, the navy purchased ships outright, received some ships as gifts (the *Vanderbilt,* for example), or simply commandeered segments of the merchant fleet. These included relatively large coastal sidewheelers, New York ferry boats (adaptable by their design to harbor patrol), schooners, and other sailing ships. All were lightly armed and sent to such southern ports as Norfolk (for most of 1861 in Confederate control), Wilmington, Charleston, Savannah, Mobile, and New Orleans.

If in its varied and sometimes barnacled character it bore similarities to Pinafore's navy, the blockading fleet—perhaps 150 vessels all told—at least spread out its tentacles octopus-like to throttle slowly Richmond's lifeblood, trade. For example, in the first two years of the Civil War exports of cotton to England had shrunk from 816 to merely 6 million pounds. Such strangulation could spell, even by the calculation of the dullest, nothing less than defeat.

Denial of the grain ships' cargoes from Australia sparked the so-called "bread riots" in Richmond at Easter time, 1863. But the riots transcended bread, as angry mobs raided all kinds of stores, demanding a variety of merchandise denied them, from shoes to Spanish brandy and wines.

What, then, could be a counter-measure on the part of the weaker power? To Stephen Mallory, Jefferson Davis's able secretary of the navy, a major answer lay in attempted destruction of the enemy's considerable merchant marine. And to effect this there must be commerce raiders, an asset in zero supply at the outset of the war. The South's only real warship prize, the steam frigate U.S.S. *Merrimack,* converted into the ironclad C.S.S. *Virginia,* had been scuttled in May 1862, just two months after her battle with the little *Monitor* in Hampton Roads had ended, more or less, in a draw. She was top-heavy, underpowered, and not fit for the open sea anyhow.

Thus, Richmond had to look to foreign nations to create her navy. While both England and France had issued neutrality proclamations, there was considerable sympathy for the South. Napoleon III, cotton-hungry, did not disguise his feelings. However, although the belligerents were free to purchase all needed food, cannon, ammunition, and uniforms provided they could transport them safely to their destinations, buying or building men o' war was another matter. This was not allowed under international law.

Nonetheless, as early as the summer of 1861, Secretary Mallory resolved to take a chance. He dispatched a former U.S. Navy captain, James D. Bulloch, to England to see if the law—like most—could not be circumvented.

It could, indeed, and soon the *"Oreto,"* patterned after a Royal Navy steam sloop, was being built in Liverpool. Officially she was under order from a firm in Palermo but this fooled few persons, certainly not the American minister, Charles Francis Adams. He protested vigorously, but futilely.

The raider sailed in March 1862, and was fitted out in Nassau as the *Florida.* A varied career, including the seizing of fourteen prizes in spite of several near apprehensions by the Union navy, culminated in October 1864 in her own capture in the neutral harbor of Bahia Brazil by the U.S. sloop-of-war *Wachusett.* Strong diplomatic notes to Washington inevitably resulted, but it was a *fait accompli.*

The *Florida* was still on the ways when the keel was laid at Laird's of Birkenhead for another and quite superior raider, the 220-foot, 1040-ton "No. 290," or *"Enrica,"* which the world would subsequently know as the C.S.S. *Alabama.* Barkrigged, she was powered by double engines of 300 horsepower each, which could propel her at upwards of fifteen knots. Her armament was quite formidable: a Blakely 100-pounder rifled gun, pivoted forward, one eight-inch solid shot gun and six 32-pounders mounted in broadside. She was built and armed to hold her own with any warship except an ironclad, and there were not as yet very many ironclads, or "impregnable" floating batteries, as naval designers such as John Ericsson thought of them. Her speed, anyhow, was probably antidote against an ironclad.

With bunkerage for 300 tons of coal, plus her basic capability as a sailing ship, *Alabama* could stay at sea for half a year. It was assumed she could be provisioned from the larders of her prizes.

"Hull No. 290," the cost of which had now totaled a quarter of a million dollars, slipped out of Liverpool on July 29, 1862. Yet that very day legal advisers to the Crown had concluded that she had indeed been constructed for warlike purposes against the United States, with which Great Britain maintained friendly relations. However, such an eventuality had been anticipated. A shipyard crew had invited wives, sisters, mothers, and sweethearts along, as though this were merely a trial excursion down the Mersey.

At the Bar, a shallows well known to generations of mariners inbound from the Irish Sea, a tug took off the female guests and "No. 290," like a tadpole metamorphosing into a frog, soon became the C.S.S. *Alabama.* She steered full steam ahead for the picturesque hills of Porto Praya, the Azores. She arrived there August 20, to be met by her crew and commanding officer, Raphael Semmes.

No "face in a crowd," the tall, slender Semmes was a most distinctive personality and an experienced naval officer. "Old Beeswax," the sobriquet by which he was generally known, only partially described him. It referred to his sharply pointed red moustache, which blended with a markedly florid complexion to present an imposing if not especially handsome appearance.

More noteworthy was the person behind the sad, smoldering eyes—dour at best, generally vain, opinionated, often hot-tempered and arrogant, thus sharing some traits with Captain Bligh. On the other hand, at 53, Semmes was correct, chivalrous, and capable both as a commander and as a navigator. He was highly intelligent with an ever inquisitive mind.

A Marylander who later adopted Alabama as "his" state, Semmes went to sea as a midshipman at the age of 17, before the U.S. Naval Academy came into existence. Mingling nautical experience with the study of the law, especially international, he had served on the *Constellation* and also on the brig *Somers,* which claimed the dubious distinction of becoming the only U.S. Naval vessel ever to hang mutineers. Three of the alleged plotters, including the son of the secretary of war, were executed at sea in 1842. Later, Semmes was her temporary commander.

He participated in the blockading of Vera Cruz during the Mexican War. The years immediately prior to the firing upon Fort Sumter in April 1861 found this studious, aloof man alternately practicing law in Mobile and serving as secretary of the Lighthouse Board. He became, upon Alabama's secession, one of the first naval officers to volunteer to the provisional Confederacy at Montgomery.

His withdrawn, singularly humorless qualities now blossomed into a lusty fanaticism. He began hurling such epithets as "devoid of Christian charity" or, simply, "hyenas!" at his erstwhile countrymen and fellow officers.

Given command of the *Sumter,* a mail steamer which had plied between New Orleans and Havana, Semmes in a year's time racked up seventeen captures, of which six with their cargoes were burned, two ransomed, and the remainder released in Cuban ports. She was finally blockaded in Algeciras, Spain, by the chain-armored new U.S. cruisers *Kearsarge* and *Tuscarora.*

When "Old Beeswax" had first sighted his new command sweeping in over the long, blue groundswells toward the Azores it became love at first sight. "She sat upon the water," he would confide to his ever-fattening journals, "with the lightness and grace of a swan."

Alabama entered commission in the Confederate Navy with a crew of 80. The second in command, executive officer, or first lieutenant was a Georgian, John McIntosh Kell. Heavily whiskered, portly, he was characterized by a friendly manner, quite the opposite of his captain, who was about ten years his senior. Kell's own naval career had been interrupted by a court-martial (for refusing to obey an order), dismissal, then reinstatement. Kell would describe the motley crew:

"It was made up from all the seafaring nations of the globe, with a large sprinkling of Yankee tars (among whom are to be found the best sailors) and with a nucleus of southern pilots and seamen from the ports of Savannah, Charleston, and New Orleans."

A number, too, had signed on from the Liverpool ferrying crew in response to an impassioned speech, sometimes more of a diatribe, by Semmes, explaining the threat to the South by the North of "subjugation," and emphasizing that the fight would be of the "oppressed against the oppressor"—this alone "enough to nerve the arm of every generous sailor."

Captain Bulloch, who had accompanied the *Alabama,* now left on the *Bahama,* which had transported Semmes to the Azores. The raider was off.

Eleven days after her formal commission, on September 5, the *Alabama* captured the Edgartown, Massachusetts, whaler, *Ocmulgee,* off Fayal, the Azores. Using a former subterfuge, Semmes had hoisted Old Glory, thus coming upon the whaler unprepared. He removed the 37 crewmen and burned the ship.

Next the *Alabama* stopped a French ship but waved her on her way, after offloading the prisoners. The raider within a few days overhauled the schooner *Starlight,* of Boston, which had angered Semmes by attempting to outrace him. Semmes soon stopped her by a shot whistling through her rigging. This crew he put in irons as retaliation for the imprisonment of the paymaster of his erstwhile command *Sumter* after the U.S. consul at Tangier had secured his arrest.

Next, the *Ocean Rover,* out of New Bedford. As Semmes found himself tempted to pity he would rationalize " . . . when I come to reflect for a moment upon the diabolical acts of his (the master's) countrymen of New England who were outheroding Herod in carrying on against us a vindictive war filled with hate and vengeance, the milk of human kindness which had begun to well up in my heart disappeared . . . ."

In his first month, Semmes destroyed twenty merchant ships. He would note with wry amusement that he had been "peopling" the little island of Flores with crews of the destroyed vessels until there were "nearly as many Yankee sailors as there were original inhabitants." He had taken especial satisfaction in burning the whaler *Elisha Dunbar,* 24 days out of New Bedford, on a stormy night:

" . . . the scene . . . wild and picturesque beyond description. The black clouds were mustering their forces in fearful array . . . the sea was in a tumult of rage; the winds howled, and floods of rain descended. Amid this turmoil of the elements, the *Dunbar,* all in flames and with disordered gear and unfurled canvas, lay rolling and tossing upon the sea."

Changing her theater of operations, *Alabama* set course for Newfoundland, lost her main yard in a hurricane, then headed south again for the more halcyon Caribbean. She captured en route the schooner *T.B. Wales,* some 200 miles east of New York, from which Semmes took aboard his first women prisoners. In addition to the captain's wife, a second was the wife of an American consul, with her three daughters. They remained for a week in cabins from which the *Alabama's* officers had been turned out, until they were landed in Martinique in mid-November.

Leaving Martinique, and quelling an incipient mutiny of drunken sailors by simply dousing them with buckets of cold sea water, Semmes lingered in the Caribbean. By early December, having captured at least 21 additional vessels, he overhauled Vanderbilt's California-bound *Ariel,* of 1,295 tons. The boarding officer reported 500 women and children on the steamer "in a great state of alarm."

This piqued the Confederate captain's innate chivalry. He dispatched his "handsomest young lieutenant," a clean-shaven, sunken-eyed Georgian, Richard F. Armstrong, together with a prepared speech for the ladies.

"The captain of the *Alabama,*" said Armstrong, "has heard of your distress and sent me on board to calm your fears by assuring you that you have fallen into the hands of Southern gentlemen under whose protection you are entirely safe. We are by no means ruffians and outlaws."

Harboring no affection for Commodore Vanderbilt, Semmes was eager to burn the small liner. However, in addition to the many women and children, there were 150 U.S. Marines and U.S. Navy personnel aboard. Together with a crew of some 100 more, the count of souls compressed within the *Ariel* posed an impossible accommodation challenge for the *Alabama.*

Semmes waited two days for another "less valuable ship" to blunder along, one large enough for the mob on the *Ariel.* This did not happen. It was too dangerous to linger in these patrolled sea lanes; besides he was wasting time. From the *Ariel's* captain he secured the promise of a "ransom bond," about $261,000, although with no fixed time or place for collection—leaving hundreds of grateful women as well as "paroled" marines and sailors to continue an interrupted passage to California.

By now the year 1862, which had flamed with disasters on land and sea to both North and South, was ending. Casualties had soared already past the quarter million mark and it was only the second year of the war. The Federal navy, however, after a tardy start, was now building up with ever increasing rapidity a whole class of scrappy little *Monitors,* big ocean-going steam propeller sloops, fleets of ironclad river gun boats, mortar barges. Preeminent certainly was the 4,120-ton *New Ironsides,* 232 feet long, mounting a crushing battery of sixteen powerful eleven-inch Dahlgrens, backed up by yet more cannon of only slightly less destructive potential. Of all the diverse ships built or being built by North or South, she became the best harbinger of battleships of the twentieth century. She was, beyond refutation, ahead of her time.

North and South Atlantic and Gulf blockading squadrons were on an urgent alert to seek out and destroy the *Alabama,* which was devastating shipping and depriving the Union of a spectrum of needed raw materials, from cotton, wool, and food stuffs to coal and metal ores. Semmes learned this from newspapers found aboard his prizes and obtained fierce satisfaction from the knowledge.

He railed only at the repeated references to his *Alabama* as a "private." The *New York Times,* in fact, maintained its ever-accumulating file on the raider under the heading, "Piracy." And the

Evening Star, of Washington, as but one of many other examples, headlined an article on December 6, 1862, "More Captures of the Pirate Steamer *Alabama!*"

Diverted from coastal blockade was the big, hefty sister of the *Ariel,* the *Vanderbilt.* She had earlier waited at Hampton Roads for a crack at the *Merrimack,* and subsequently had intercepted a Confederate runner. She could pack on sufficient speed to catch the *Alabama* even though her firepower was debatable. As a plus, with shored-up bow, stowed tight with cotton bales, she was a formidable ram. On December 11, the *Vanderbilt* boiled out of New York harbor, hell-bent for the "pirate steamer *Alabama,*" even though her officers had no certain idea of the latter's location.

The *Alabama* was, as a matter of fact, cruising in the Gulf of Honduras, where Semmes was evolving a plan to destroy the "Banks Expedition." General Nathaniel P. Banks, in a much publicized operation, was to lead an army through Galveston up north to the Red River on the Arkansas border, hopefully to knock Texas back into the Union. Events would alter such a master plan, but Semmes could not know this, nor apparently did he attempt to obtain later or corroborating information from his prisoners. Instead, he resolved to cruise the Gulf of Mexico toward Galveston and sink the transports of what to him was a wholly problematical fleet.

The weather turned foul, inspiring Semmes, ever fascinated with meteorology, to write, "The clouds look hard and wintry . . . the gale has continued all day, with a rough sea in which the ship is rolling and tumbling about . . . weather cloudy and gloomy-looking, and the wind moaning and whistling through the rigging—enough to give one the blues."

On Christmas, anchored off the Arcas Keys, west of the Yucatan Peninsula in the Gulf of Mexico, Semmes allowed a run on shore for the men who, he penned in a moment of consuming pity, were "terribly pressed in this wicked and ruthless war." A few days later, "Old Beeswax" had again lashed down his emotions, refusing permission to his chief bosun's mate to return to England aboard a barque of that flag which had come alongside to coal the *Alabama.* At the same time he threw a seaman into double irons for getting drunk, and all-in-all took satisfaction in the fact that he had "jerked them (other recalcitrant crewmen) down with a strong hand."

Meanwhile, Galveston had just fallen back into Confederate hands after a strong attack by General "Prince" John Magruder, who had earlier in 1862 done much to thwart General John McClellan's peninsular campaign for Richmond. The loss of Galveston, vital "cotton port", gateway to all of Texas and the Southwest and major funnel from the Confederacy to England, could be measured only by the yardsticks of disaster. The Banks Expedition must be diverted and postponed.

In fact the entire Federal position off Galveston Island was imperiled. Confederate officers had assembled a weird, comic-opera fleet of harbor craft and armored their sides with bales of cotton as a novel substitute for iron. They then rolled artillery pieces from shorebound breastworks onto the wooden and, in some cases, rotting decks. Tatterdemalion as they were and manned primarily by soldiers who had never before set foot on any sort of ship, the "men o' war" on New Year's Day nonetheless destroyed two of the Federal blockaders (themselves largely make-do) with heavy loss of life.

Bloodied and stunned, the surviving units drew off to a more respectable distance to await the arrival of the heavy, 2,070-ton sloop of war U.S.S. *Brooklyn,* sister of Admiral David Farragut's flagship U.S.S. *Hartford,* now blockading Mobile. Both were among the newest and most formidable Union ships of the line, mounting 25 guns apiece.

Among this little flotilla was the *Hatteras,* 1,100 tons, a "third class" sidewheeler with five guns, snatched from her prosaic if utilitarian career as a Delaware River ferry, where she was known as the *St. Mary's.* She had been a familiar sight carrying carts, cattle, assorted cargo, and people between Wilmington and Pennsville and other small ports on the New Jersey shore. Children, picnicking with their families, remembered the *Hatteras's* master, good-natured Homer C. Blake.

Now wearing the stripes of a lieutenant commander, Blake had whipped his crew of about 124 into a salty, well-disciplined naval force. He had captured about half a dozen blockade runners, mostly schooners. However, since the pummeling of the blockaders, Blake considered himself fortunate merely to be afloat. He contemplated with much relief the new presence of the big, glowering *Brooklyn.* She was commanded by Fleet Captain Henry H. Bell, also chief of staff to "Davy" Farragut and just about as senior and tough as his superior.

At 2:30 P.M., January 11, a gray, cheerless Sunday, the lookout on the *Brooklyn* spotted a sail on the horizon. The small flotilla was about 30 miles off Galveston, but even so in relatively shallow waters. Since this seemed routine to Bell, he ordered Blake to steam out and investigate.

The *Hatteras* at once signaled compliance, by flag, and soon her heavy sidewheels were churning the green sandy waters of the Gulf.

On board the "sail," which turned out to be the *Alabama*, Semmes was experiencing disappointment, since he had found no trace of the "Banks expedition." However, watching the approach of the *Hatteras*, and having recognized the unmistakable outlines of the mighty *Brooklyn* at anchorage, he resolved to lead his pursuer well away from "his consorts." He lowered the propeller, which had been designed for easy attachment so as not to slow the raider when under sail, and steamed slowly southward.

By dusk, only the *Hatteras* was in view. Semmes ordered his engines stopped and waited. Finally, Blake maneuvered his sidewheeler to within speaking distance, about 75 yards. Unfamiliar with the big Confederate raiders, he shouted, "What steamer is this?"

"His Britannic Majesty's ship *Petrel!*" came the reply. Semmes then ordered a signalman to ask, in turn, "What ship's that?"

The *Hatteras*'s response was not clearly heard on the *Alabama*. Blake, however, was lowering a boat for the purpose of coming alongside and examining papers. It was an improvident act. The former Delaware River skipper would write, "Almost simultaneously with the piping away of the boat the strange craft replied, 'We are the Confederate steamer *Alabama*,' which was accompanied by a broadside."

In marginal keeping with the rules of naval warfare, Semmes ran up the Confederate flag and prepared for another broadside. Somehow, *Hatteras* survived the first devastating blow and returned the fire. The range was so close that crewmen were firing muskets and pistols at each other.

"The firing continued with great vigour on both sides," Blake wrote. "At length a shell entered amidships in the hold, setting fire to it, and at the same instant . . . a shell passed through the sick bay, exploding in an adjoining compartment, also producing fire. Another entered the cylinder, filling the engine-room and deck with steam, and depriving me of power to maneuver the vessel, or to work the pumps upon which the reduction of the fire depended."

In thirteen minutes or less, the *Hatteras* was blazing furiously in two distinct places, her decks awash. Two of the crew were dead, five wounded. Blake hoisted a white light in token of surrender.

The transfer to the largely undamaged *Alabama* commenced. Semmes, accepting Blake's sword, welcomed him with stiff cordiality, "I am glad to see you on board the *Alabama* and we will endeavor to make your time as comfortable as possible." Proving that he meant what he said, he insisted that Blake occupy his own cabin. And the victorious commander ordered full speed ahead for Jamaica, not waiting for his victim's final, fiery plunge.

Meanwhile, taking short respite from the brutal realities of war at sea, Semmes put on his scientist's cap. His ever restless mind mused on the dynamics of the Gulf Stream as the *Alabama* steered eastward.

" . . . the old theory of Dr. [Benjamin] Franklin and others was that the Gulf Stream, which flows out of the Gulf of Mexico, between the north coast of Cuba, and the Florida Reefs and Keys, flows into the Gulf, through the channel between the west end of Cuba, and the coast of Yucatan, in which the *Alabama* now was. But the effectual disproof of this theory is, that we know positively, from the strength of the current, and its volume, or cross section, in the two passages, that more than twice the quantity of water flows out of the Gulf of Mexico, than flows into it through this passage. Upon Dr. Franklin's theory, the Gulf of Mexico in a very short time would become dry ground. Nor can the Mississippi River, which is the only stream worth noticing, in this connection, that flows into the Gulf of Mexico, come to his relief, as we have seen that that river only empties into the Gulf of Mexico, about *one three thousandth* part as much water, as the Gulf Stream takes out. We must resort, of necessity, to an under-current from the north, passing into the Gulf of Mexico, under the Gulf Stream, rising to the surface when heated, and thus swelling the volume of the outflowing water."

Ten days later, the *Alabama* dropped anchor in Kingston, Jamaica, where the prisoners were freed and the British allowed the raider to languish for five days, coaling and repairing. This along with Nassau and Bermuda was a transfer port for "depot" ships from England, which were employed in concert with swift steamers to run the blockade and return with cargoes principally of cotton.

The period in Kingston was respite for Semmes, who spent much of the time ashore, horseback riding in the hills. He also demonstrated that he was not unlike other seafarers in his affinity for members of the opposite sex. Finding that a Royal Navy friend, "Captain Kent," was away in England, he partook of the hospitality of his "English-looking cottage" at Blocksburgh, where he as well confided to his diary that he enjoyed "some lady-visitors."

The *Alabama* put to sea again on January 25, and the next day overtook and burned the sailing ship *Golden Rule.* From newspapers found aboard her he learned several bits of "good news": the "sister cruiser" *Florida* had escaped from Mobile, partly because the blockading squadron had been weakened by the detachment of the *Brooklyn;* the *Monitor* had foundered in a gale off Hatteras, New Year's eve; and General William T. Sherman was bogged down on the Yazoo attempting to slog his way to Vicksburg. There, too, on the same tributary of the Mississippi, the U.S. gunboat *Cairo* had become the first victim of a Confederate electric "torpedo," or mine.

For the next four months *Alabama* ran amuck in Caribbean and South Atlantic waters. Brigs, schooners, and other sailing vessels fell before her like fragile clay ducks in a shooting gallery: the *Chastelain, Palmetto* (which restocked the raider's own larders with biscuits and cheese), *Olive Jane, Golden Eagle, Washington* (ransomed), and *Bethia Thayer* (ransomed). The *John S. Parks* became the thirty-fifth prey of Semmes, who paused in his methodical bookkeeping like an over-conscientious mortician or executioner to pen comments.

" . . . this boisterous Sabbath is the second anniversary of my resignation from the United States Navy. I have more and more reason as time rolls on to be gratified at my prompt determination to quit the service of a corrupt and fanatical majority . . . aggressive and unscrupulous."

The roster of the victims rolled on: *Morning Star* (ransomed), *Kingfisher, Charles Hill, Nora* (all on one day, March 23) and *Louisa Hatch* (taken as a supply ship since she carried coal). Then Semmes anchored at the penal island, Fernando de Noronha, 225 miles northeast of Natal, Brazil: ". . . in the wayside of the commerce of all the world, is sighted by more ships, and visited by fewer than any other spot of earth. It is a broken, picturesque, volcanic rock, in mid-ocean, covered with a pleasing coat of verdure, including trees of some size, and the top of the main island is cultivated in small farms, etc. Awfully hot when the sun shines."

Ignoring the niceties of neutrality, Semmes knocked off two more vessels hailing from New England which had stumbled into the anchorage: *Kate Cory* and *Lafayette.*

One captured ship, the barque *Conrad,* of Philadelphia, was commissioned the C.S.S. *Tuscaloosa* and piped on her way with a small crew from the *Alabama.* She would capture and ransom a prize of her own.

Having taken upwards of a dozen victims more during the early summer of 1863, by August *Alabama* had crossed the South Atlantic and cooled her sizzling engines at the Cape of Good Hope, anchoring at Simonstown. There Semmes was informed that the *Vanderbilt* had just missed him and in likelihood was still sniffing about in these waters. In fact the hefty liner had already bunkered much of the locally available coal supply. He also learned with deep distress of the fall of Vicksburg and Lee's repulse at Gettysburg by "the Northern hordes."

According to the second in command, John Kell, "We played 'hide and seek' with the United States steamer *Vanderbilt* whose commander Charles H. Baldwin had explained to Sir Baldwin Walker, the English admiral of the station at Simonstown, that he did not intend to fire a gun at the *Alabama* but to run her down and sink her.

"We were not disposed to try issues with the *Vanderbilt* so one night about 11 o'clock while it blew a gale of wind from the southeast we hove anchor and steamed out of Simon's Bay."

Heading past lovely St. Paul's Island in the Indian Ocean for the East Indies, Semmes learned, in late October, that the 997-ton United States sloop *Wyoming* was waiting for him in the Sunda Straits, Java. Guessing that he was equal to a fight with her, the captain kept his raider on course. Hunting was slim, however; in the six weeks since leaving Simonstown he had destroyed but one ship.

On November 10, boldly flying the Stars and Bars, the *Alabama* swept through the Sundra Straits, so close to shore that "naked natives" were plainly seen gaping at the warship. Semmes had every reason to be bold. Not only was the *Wyoming* hardly in sight, she was off somewhere in the Pacific licking her wounds. The seven-gun, third class screw sloop had blundered into a gunboat and Japanese shore batteries off Honshu. There seemed no special provocation for the affair, but nonetheless, it had knocked the *Wyoming* out of action for the time being.

Semmes bagged two more prizes, including the clipper ships, *Winged Racer* and *Contest*. The latter, bound from Yokohama to New York, almost outran the *Alabama*. The two thereby met the fate of other stately California clippers lost to the war, including the famous McKay *Stag Hound*, burned by the *Florida* off Brazil along with the *Jacob Bell*.

For the month of December Semmes behaved more like a tourist than the captain of a warship, in part because of his insatiable curiosity, in part because the machinery of the raider was worn and more or less literally screeching and rasping for repair. At the picturesque, mountainous little island of Pulo Condore, a French possession, Semmes was fascinated by numbers of "sedate old babboons sitting on the sand-beach opposite, and apparently observing the ship very attentively." He concluded that the place must be "a paradise for monkeys."

Then, three days before Christmas they reached the fabled Singapore. Semmes, with a pilot on board, hauled his command alongside a coaling wharf, noting:

" . . . crowds gathered to look curiously upon her, and compare her appearance with what they had read of her. These crowds were themselves a curiosity to look upon, formed, as they were, of all the nations of the earth, from the remote East and the remote West. Singapore being a free port, and a great centre of trade, there is always a large fleet of shipping anchored in its waters, and its streets and other marts of commerce are constantly thronged with a promiscuous multitude. The canal—there being one leading to the rear of the town—is filled with country boats from the surrounding coasts, laden with the products of the different countries from which they come. There is the pepper-boat from Sumatra, and the coaster of larger size laden with tin ore; the spice-boats from the spice islands; boats with tin ore, hides, and mats from Borneo; boats from Siam, with gums, hides, and cotton; boats from different parts of the Malay peninsula, with canes, gutta-percha, and India-rubber. In the bay are ships from all parts of the East—from China, with silks and teas; from Japan, with lacker-ware, raw silk, and curious manufactures of iron, steel, and paper; from the Philippine Islands, with sugar, hides, tobacco, and spices. Intermixed with these are the European and American ships, with the products of their various countries . . . "

Then, Semmes proved once more that he could not resist political philosophizing.

"Singapore, which was a fishing village half a century ago, contains a hundred thousand inhabitants, and under the free-port system has become, as before remarked, a great centre of trade. It concentrates nearly all the trade of the southern portion of the China Sea. There are no duties on exports or imports; and the only tonnage due paid by the shipping, is three cents per ton, register, as a lighthouse tax. The currency is dollars and cents; Spanish, Mexican, Peruvian, and Bolivian dollars are current.

"Great Britain, with an infinite forecaste, not only girdles the seas with her ships, but the land with her trading stations. In her colonization and commerce consists her power. Lop off these, and she would become as insignificant as Holland. And so beneficent is her rule, that she binds her colonies to her with hooks of steel. A senseless party in that country had advocated the liberation of all her colonies. No policy could be more suicidal."

The *Alabama*'s captain, guilty of a number of contradictions, seemed to have forgotten his own opposite views on the "oppressors" in "Yankee land."

He found good hunting in the Malacca Straits, bordering Singapore on the southwest. The raiders celebrated Christmas eve by burning the bark *Texan Star,* sailing low, heavy with a cargo of rice. Two days later he destroyed the *Sonora* and *Highlander,* both in ballast, and, in fact, sitting ducks. They were languishing at anchor at the western approaches to the straits, sails furled, washing hung on the rigging.

"They were monster ships," Semmes enthused, "being eleven or twelve hundred tons burden."

The master of the *Highlander* confided to his captor, "Well, Captain Semmes, I have been expecting every day for the last three years to fall in with you. And here I am at last. The fact is, I have had constant visions of the *Alabama,* by night and by day; she has been chasing me in my sleep, and riding me like a nightmare, and now that it is all over, I feel quite relieved."

If, for the moment, the *Alabama* had "paralyzed" the China trade in these distant seas, as Kell the "exec" declared, the raider's success was no barometer of the fortunes of the Confederacy itself.

On December 26, 1863, Henry Hotze, Confederate commercial agent in London (since Great Britain had shied from accepting a minister or ambassador in formal recognition of the Secessionist government) had written to Secretary of State Judah P. Benjamin in Richmond, " . . . it is absolutely hopeless to expect to receive any really serviceable vessels of war from the ports of either England or France, and . . . our expenditures should therefore be confined to more practicable objects and our naval staff be employed in eluding, since we can not break the blockade."

Already, in September, Charles Francis Adams, the U.S. minister to Great Britain, had bluntly warned Lord Russell, the foreign secretary, against allowing two powerful "Laird [built] Rams" to leave Liverpool, to be used by the Confederacy for breaking the blockade: "It would be superfluous for me to point out to your honor lordship that this is war."

The rams did not leave the Mersey—ever. On the other hand, with a fleet of *Monitors,* some double-turreted, deployed along the U.S. East Coast like seagoing mastiffs, there was reasonable doubt as to the ability of two rams to challenge the tightening Union blockade, now some 750 ships strong.

Even so, Bulloch, by a most devious plan, did sneak one more raider out: the *Sea King* which became the *Shenandoah.* The elaborate ruse, which would have challenged the unraveling powers of the most suspicious lawyer, involved spurious ownership by an Englishman, her sailing for Bombay in ballast of coal, and her first captain's possession of power of attorney, enabling him to sell the vessel once he cleared the British Isles. Masquerades were the warp of the war, on sea and land.

Richmond could toast the New Year, 1864, with bitter gall. In Europe the tide of support was turning toward the North. No sentiment, only cold, hard pragmatism was involved. The crushing attrition at Gettysburg, Lee's broken, groaning army limping back across the Potomac, the unconditional surrender of Vicksburg to a new champion, Ulysses S. Grant, had spoken in clear, unmistakable tones—the Confederacy was being bled white. It was an apocalypse. Total defeat was to be measured in the dwindling sands of the

South's own doomsday hourglass. Even now, in these early days of the war's fourth year, William Tecumseh Sherman was marshaling the mightiest army yet assembled by the North to assault Atlanta—the Military Division of the Mississippi.

On January 8, 1864, the *Alabama,* with the momentary nom de plume, U.S.S. *Dacotah,* searching for the Confederate raider, was advised by a British barque, "It won't do! The *Alabama* is a bigger ship than you, and they say she is iron-plated besides!"

En route to England, the *Alabama,* on February 9, dropped anchor at Johanna Island, lying between Africa and Madagascar, hoping to provision. Semmes recorded the following interlude:

"I gave my sailors a run on shore, but this sort of 'liberty' was awful hard work for Jack. There was no such thing as a glass of grog to be found in the whole town, and as for a fiddle, and Sal for a partner—all of which would have been a matter of course in civilized countries—there were no such luxuries to be thought of. They found it a difficult matter to get through with the day, and were all down at the beach long before sunset—the hour appointed for their coming off—waiting for the approach of the welcome boat. I told Kell to let them go on shore as often as they pleased, but no one made a second application."

At the same time, the *Florida,* in heavy rain and mist, slipped out of Brest, France, where she had been under repairs since the preceding August. It was a wrenching frustration for 53-year-old Captain John Ancrum Winslow, who had been waiting offshore in the screw sloop *Kearsarge* for many weeks. In fact he had patrolled European waters for slightly more than a year hoping to bag at least one of the Confederacy's birds of war as they were hatched in English yards.

Blind in one eye as a result of a fever contracted while on duty in the festering bayous of the Mississippi, Winslow was heavy and rather stooped, hardly an imposing figure compared to Semmes. A humble man, North Carolina-born, he was in fact the antithesis, in both appearance and personality, of the captain of the *Alabama.*

The two officers, however, were old shipmates, having served in the Mexican War at the blockade of Vera Cruz. Both had been commended for bravery, and both, while in temporary command, had lost a ship. Semmes's ill-fated brig *Somers* foundered in a storm. Winslow ran his little gunboat, *Morris,* which had been captured from the Mexicans, onto a reef. The two officers enjoyed friendship as warm as possible considering the austerity of Semmes. They ribbed one another on the need for paying closer attention to navigation and keeping their commands afloat.

The navy did not hold a little matter like shoal water much against John Winslow. In fact, Navy Secretary Welles considered the command of the handsome, two-year-old *Kearsarge* quite an honor. Winslow had been dispatched, aboard the ever-voyaging *Vanderbilt* (now dubbed "that huge old coal box" by Semmes), to the Azores in December 1862, to meet this "third class" powerful sloop. It was also hoped that Winslow's health would improve in the balmy waters far removed from America's southern swamps.

At 1,031 tons, *Kearsarge* was comparable to the *Alabama* if not as "rakish." Her superiority lay in two eleven-inch smooth bore Dahlgren semi-pivot guns (or at least relatively maneuverable) among her total armament of seven cannon, augmented by one and one-half inch thick chain armor over her sides.

And so, as Winslow restlessly patrolled the English Channel and worried about his own future should he permit another Confederate cruiser to tiptoe past his bows, the *Alabama* continued on her roundabout course for the British Isles. This was by way, again, of the Cape of Good Hope and Brazilian waters. On March 4, Semmes admitted to his journals, "my ship is weary, too, as well as her commander and will need a general overhauling by the time I can get her into dock."

John Kell himself wrote, "Her boilers were burned out, and her machinery was sadly in want of repairs. She was loose at every joint, her seams were open, and the copper on her bottom was in rolls."

In early April, *Alabama* paused at Napoleon's remote island of final exile, St. Helena, then "jogged along leisurely under topsails" the remainder of the distance across the South Atlantic. On April 22 and 27, Semmes sank his last ships, the *Rockingham* and *Tycoon,* respectively. The *Rockingham,* after she was abandoned, was used for target practice. It might have been a portent that many of the raider's shells failed to explode, indicating that the powder had deteriorated from months at sea in hot, humid climates.

The "long chase" had ended. *Alabama* had stopped some 300 ships, burned 57 and ransomed 14 additional (for a record which stands to this day, two World Wars removed).

On June 11, the *Alabama* steamed into Cherbourg harbor, past the long rows of waterfront buildings with their red terra cotta roofs. Semmes felt "like a crippled hunter limping home. . . ." He prepared a letter for the Confederacy's naval emissary in Paris, Flag Officer Samuel Barron, asking for repairs and also his own relief, noting that his "health has suffered so much."

The French Ministry of Marine, however, did not welcome this visitor flying the flag of rebellion. For one consideration, even a few squadrons of the Union navy could now take on the French fleet with full expectation of victory.

Testily pointing out that Cherbourg maintained only naval docks and asking why the *Alabama* hadn't put into Le Havre with its ample commercial facilities, the local maritime prefect did convey the marine minister's concession—the *Alabama* could coal but not repair, then speedily be on her way again. Or Semmes might wait for permission for repairs from Emperor Napoleon III, who was away enjoying the baths at Biarritz. Apparently, Semmes never entertained the possibility of returning to Liverpool, where now his presence would be more uncomfortable.

Meanwhile, aboard the *Kearsarge,* anchored in the murky waters of the Schelde, off Flushing, the Netherlands, Winslow was electrified by an early morning visit from the U.S. consul. He rowed out to the man o'war bearing a telegram from William L. Dayton, U.S. minister to France. The *Alabama* was in Cherbourg!

Semme's old shipmate lost no time. He bowled into Cherbourg on the fourteenth, steamed past the *Alabama,* hove to long enough to put over a boat, but did not anchor. Although the aggressive Raphael Semmes interpreted the *Kearsarge*'s normal enough maneuvers as a challenge, Winslow's immediate purpose was to ask that any prisoners the *Alabama* might have put ashore be released to his custody. This was refused by the French on the grounds such an act would constitute "an augmentation of military force."

Winslow then steamed outside of the breakwater and dropped anchor about three miles distant—to wait.

Half-sick or not, Semmes was breathing fire again, "tired of running from that flaunting rag! [the U.S. flag]." He summoned Kell to assert, "I am going out to fight the *Kearsarge;* what do you think of it?" It wasn't really a question, since Semmes had made up his mind. Kell knew that the *Alabama* was in no condition to meet a well-armed sloop like the *Kearsarge.* But what could he do, or say?

Semmes went further. Like a gentleman whose challenged honor demands a duel, he hastened a note to the Confederate port representative in Cherbourg, "I desire you to say to the United States consul that my intention is to fight the *Kearsarge* as soon as I can make the necessary arrangements ... I beg you she will not depart before I am ready to go to sea."

Semmes commenced coaling ship and readying the guns, certain that his "crew seemed not only willing but anxious for the combat." And so a fateful week in June, 1864 passed.

Sunday morning, the nineteenth, Winslow ambled on deck after a leisurely breakfast to comment on the brilliance of the sun and brightness of water and sky. About 10:15 A.M. the church flag was hoisted above the ensign, and the captain, following tradition of the sea, conducted services on the quarter deck. He read from a well-worn prayer book of the Protestant Episcopal Church.

He had barely started the opening confessional when his chief quartermaster, whose attention had been caught by a lookout, stood up and sidled out of the congregation. In a moment, the quarter-master returned with the announcement; "She's coming!"

Services were dramatically interrupted as Winslow ordered anchor upped for steaming about four more miles to seaward. This would put *Kearsarge* seven miles from land, well outside of France's territorial waters. Guns were already loaded; side chains were draped. No further action stations needed to be piped.

The captain then sat down on an arms chest upon the quarterdeck beside the rail, glasses in hand, in easy speaking distance of his quartermaster, officer of the engine hatch bell and the gunnery officers. He sat on the little chest, and he did not leave it, watching, with his one good eye the ever-enlarging mass of the *Alabama* sweeping toward him over the gentle morning swells. Winslow preferred the sedentary position, given as he was to shortness of breath.

The *Alabama* was accompanied by two "neutral" consorts, the ironclad frigate *Couronne,* flying the Tricolor, and the steam yacht *Deerhound,* flying the Union Jack, owned by a wealthy Englishman, John Lancaster. Since word of an impending naval engagement had swept Cherbourg, the breakwater, rooftops, other heights, also the rigging of ships in the harbor were swarming with some 15,000 spectators, basking in the sunshine.

Many of the curious had brought their children and picnic baskets and campstools; a few who could afford them brought spy glasses. Some had journeyed all the way from Paris on a special excursion train.

The average Frenchman hadn't been afforded such an opportunity for likely bloodletting since the nostalgic days of the Place de la Concorde during the French Revolution.

After the *Alabama* had cleared the breakwater, Semmes found it impossible to resist recreating a snatch of the Nelson flamboyance. He stepped onto a gun carriage located on the aft deck and addressed the assembled crew.

"Officers and seamen of the *Alabama:* You have at length another opportunity of meeting the enemy. . . . " His oration lasted some moments, concluding, "The flag that floats over you is that of a young Republic, which bids defiance to her enemies, whenever and wherever found! Show the world that you know how to uphold it! Go to your quarters!"

As Semmes would subsequently report to Flag Officer Barron, ". . . we were distant about one mile from each other, when I opened on him with solid shot, to which he replied in a few minutes, and the engagement became active on both sides." Minor damage was inflicted to the *Kearsarge's* rigging.

The *Alabama* fired two more shots broadsides before the *Kearsarge* closed to 900 yards (about half a mile) and opened up. According to Winslow, "I ordered the *Kearsarge* sheered, and opened on the *Alabama.* The position of the vessels was now broadside and broadside, but it was soon apparent that Captain Semmes did not seek close action. I became then fearful, lest after some fighting he would again make for the shore. To defeat this, I determined to keep full speed on, and with a port helm to run under the stern of the *Alabama* and rake, if he did not prevent it by sheering and keeping his broadside to us. He adopted this mode as a preventive, and as a consequence the *Alabama* was forced with a full head of steam into a circular track during the engagement."

Semmes was dismayed at the battle fought, at close range, on Winslow's terms and the protection offered by the *Kearsarge's* chain armor. This offset the disadvantage occasioned by the Federal sloop's low bunker supply—only about 120 tons of coal, less than half of her opponent's—which caused her to ride high in the water.

The raider's captain now called to his executive officer, "Mr. Kell, use solid shot; our shell strike the enemy's side and fall into the water!"

That didn't help much. The firing continued "rapid and wild," according to Winslow. The gunners alternated shell and shot as the two combatants kept steaming in concentric circles, loading and firing. Kell admitted, "The enemy's eleven-inch shells were now doing severe execution upon our quarter-deck section. Three of them successively entered our eight-inch pivot-gun port; the first swept off the forward part of the gun's crew; the second killed one man and wounded several others; and the third struck the breast of the gun carriage and spun around on the deck ... our decks were now covered with the dead and the wounded and the ship was careening heavily to starboard from the effects of the shot-holes on her waterline."

Semmes sought vainly for an opportunity to elude the terrible fire of the *Kearsarge* and make for French territorial limits and sanctuary, steering by sail as the rudder had been damaged.

Lieutenant Arthur Sinclair, a Virginian and sailing master of the *Alabama*, chronicled the continuing unequal fight:

"Our bulwarks are soon shot away in sections; and the after pivot-gun is disabled on its port side, losing, in killed and wounded, all but the compressor-man ... the spar-deck is by this time being rapidly torn up by shell bursting on the between-decks, interfering with working our battery; and the compartments below have all been knocked into one. The *Alabama* is making water fast, showing severe punishment; but still the report comes from the engine-room that the ship is being kept free to the safety-point. She also has now become dull in response to her helm, and the sail-trimmers are ordered out to loose the headsails to pay her head off. We are making a desperate but forlorn resistance, which is soon culminated by the death-blow. An eleven-inch shell enters us at the water-line, in the wake of the writer's gun, and passing on, explodes in the engine-room, in its passage throwing a volume of water on board, hiding for a moment the guns of this division. Our ship trembles from stem to stern from the blow. Semmes at once sends for the engineer on watch who reports the fires out, and water beyond the control of the pumps."

The commanding officer then ordered Kell, "Go below, sir, and see how long the ship can float."

Kell would write, "As I entered the ward room the sight was indeed appalling. There stood Assistant-Surgeon (David Herbert) Llewellyn at his post, but the table and the patient upon it had been swept away from him by an eleven-inch shell which opened in the side of the ship an aperture that was fast filling with water."

Kell ran back to the quarterdeck to tell Semmes, "We cannot float ten minutes."

Without hesitation, Semmes said in a strong, but somber voice, "Then, sir, cease firing, shorten sail, and haul down the colors; it will never do in this 19th century for us to go down and the decks covered with our gallant wounded."

However, Winslow "was unable to ascertain whether" the colors "had been hauled down or shot away, but a white flag having been displayed over the stern, our fire was reserved. Two minutes had not more than elapsed before she again opened on us with the two guns on the port side. This drew our fire again, and the *Kearsarge* was immediately steamed ahead, and laid across her bows for raking.

"The white flag was still flying, and our fire was again reserved."

The battle was over. Good gunnery, experienced command, two big eleven-inch Dalgrens, and luck had won for the Federal navy. A 100-pound shell from the *Alabama* lodging in the stern post had not exploded, like so many Confederate shells. Had it not failed, the sloop would have been sunk or at least disabled. The *Kearsarge* had fired but 173 projectiles, some half the number of her opponent.

"Boats were now lowered from the *Alabama*," according to the *Kearsarge's* surgeon, Dr. John M. Browne. "Her master's mate, (George T.) Fullam, an Englishman, came alongside the *Kearsarge,* with a few of the wounded, reported the disabled and sinking condition of his ship and asked for assistance. Captain Winslow inquired, 'does Captain Semmes surrender his ship?' "

" 'Yes,' was the reply. Fullam then solicited permission to return with his boat and crew to assist in rescuing the drowning, pledging his word of honor that when this was done he would come on board and surrender . . . it was now seen that the *Alabama* was settling fast."

It was quite true. Kell was stumbling over the bodies and the litter on the slanting decks, urging every man to take hold of a spar and jump overboard: "all hands save yourselves!" Some, such as Arthur Sinclair, however, lingered, fascinated.

"The scene," he would report, "was one of complete wreck. The shot and shell of the enemy had knocked all the compartments into one; and a flush view could be had fore and aft, the water waist-deep, and air-bubbles rising and breaking with a mournful gurgle at the surface. It was a picture to be dwelt upon in memory, but not too long in the reality. I returned hastily to the spar-deck (upperdeck). By this time most of the officers and men had left for the water. The battery was disarranged, some guns run out and secured, some not. The spars were wounded woefully, some of them toppling, and others only held by the wire rigging. The smoke-stack was full of holes, the decks torn up by the bursting of shell, and lumbered with the wreckage of woodwork and rigging and empty shell-boxes. Some sail was set; and the vessel slowly forged ahead, leaving a line of wreckage astern, with the heads of swimmers bobbing up and down amongst it.

"Toward this the boats from the yacht (*Deerhound*) were rapidly pulling. The *Kearsarge* lay a few hundred yards on our starboard quarter, with her boats apparently free from the davits, and pivot-gun ports not yet closed, nor her guns secured."

About an hour and a half after the firing of the *Alabama*'s opening broadside, the Confederate raider made her last plunge, about four and a half miles off the Cherbourg breakwater. She settled "stern foremost," according to Kell, "launching her bows high in the air. Graceful even in her death-struggle, she in a moment disappeared from the face of the waters. The sea now presented a mass of living heads, striving for their lives."

Semmes, among them, would simply report, "She could swim no more, so we gave her to the waves."

Her passing was more violent, in the measure of Sinclair, who would record that her bow "made a wild leap into the air, and she plunged down on an inclined plane to her grave ... there was a crash, her main topmast going by the board. ..."

"Graceful" or "wild" in death—and either could have described her ephemeral existence—the dread *Alabama* was no more.

4

The *Jeannette* Expedition

". . . a great, gaunt skeleton clapping its hands above its head . . ."

THE CROWDS, strangely stunned and silent, filed off the Cherbourg breakwater, the adults' baskets and the children's dolls limp in their hands. Steam was being raised on the locomotive of the Paris excursion train, even as a second one, too late, was chugging in. It was all over. There would be no second performance.

For correspondents, however, it had been a top story. The gentleman from the *London Star* wrote that it was "by far the most interesting naval engagement that has taken place of late years near to our shores." The *London Times* pronounced it a "magnificent . . . spectacle!"

Londoners, for that matter, would have the first flash Monday morning. Americans would not know for more than two weeks, not until the Inman Liner *City of Baltimore* arrived with British papers, official dispatches, and an assortment of personal letters. On July 6 the *New York Times* headlined, "The Pirate Sunk off Cherbourg by the *Kearsarge*" and inked its entire first page with details.

Winslow would be lionized upon his return to the United States and promoted to commodore. For Semmes, nonetheless, defeat did not signal the end of his "personal" war. He had lost nine killed, ten drowned, including the British surgeon, Llewellyn, together with twenty-one wounded. Only one was killed on the *Kearsarge*, two wounded. Courtesy of the scarcely neutral *Deerhound*, Semmes along with 114 other officers and men was landed in England, leaving but fifty prisoners of war for the Federal navy.

"Old Beeswax" spent the summer and autumn busily editing his journals for a London publisher. He then left England late in 1864, returning to America by way of Havana and Shreveport. Playing cat-and-mouse with General Sherman's armies in Georgia, Semmes arrived in Richmond the last week in January 1865, to be commissioned admiral and handed the dubious honor of command of the James River Squadron. It wasn't much, consisting primarily of converted tugs and other river craft.

Near Petersburg, he spent an evening with General Lee, the two at least tacitly concurring on "the approaching downfall of the cause." He learned in the morning that even as the two senior officers had talked "160 men deserted in a body!"

The end was near. On April 2, Lee ordered the evacuation of Richmond. Semmes had no alternative but to blow up his squadron, starting with his flagship, the ironclad *Virginia* (II) which atomized herself "like the shock of an earthquake . . . the air was filled with missiles . . . the explosion of the magazine threw . . . shells with their fuses lighted into the air. The fuses were of different lengths, and as the shells exploded by twos and threes, and by the dozen the pyrotechnic effect was very fine. The explosion shook the houses in Richmond and must have waked the echoes of the night for forty miles around."

"The spectacle was grand beyond description."

Thus the second ironclad *Virginia* had gone the way of her predecessor.

Semmes well knew, of course, that wars were not won by "grand spectacles" when they involved the destruction of your own side's weaponry. Yet, with his "squadron" immolating itself under the night skies, the old warhorse remained full of fight. He commandeered one of the last railroad trains he could find in the Richmond yards, tore down fence posts for fuel and pounded westward with a singular passenger list of generals, colonels, ordinary soldiers, sailors, and a few civilians who refused to be thrown off. Some riders on the car roofs ducked for tunnels; others hanging onto the coaches' steps would draw themselves tighter in for the same transits.

His "railroad cruise" ended at midnight April 4, at Danville, Virginia, about 130 miles southwest of the fallen capital of the Confederacy, having narrowly missed a raid by General Sheridan who had torn up the tracks only an hour and a half after Semmes's unusual trainload had passed.

With a command of 250 soldiers, sailors, and marines, Semmes helped "hold" Danville, the temporary seat of the Confederacy after Lee's surrender at Appomattox on April 9. When that city became untenable, he moved on to Greensboro, North Carolina, where, on May 1, he signed formal surrender and parole papers for representatives of Sherman's army.

Semmes returned to Mobile and the practice of law. In spite of his parole, he was arrested later in the year and held for several months on open charges. Under the "rules of war" Raphael Semmes had proven an honorable and chivalrous warrior. Not even the most biased judge or jury could find him guilty of any charges that a spiteful post-bellum administration could conjure. Semmes was released and sent back home once more.

He died in Mobile in 1877. Four years before, when Winslow slipped his anchor for the last time, a mellowed Semmes had observed of his erstwhile nemesis, "He was the Christian gentleman."

The Confederate cruisers, of which *Alabama* was the most devastating, had left their mark. It would require seven years and an international tribunal before it was conceded that England owed and must pay the United States fifteen and a half million dollars for the cruisers' depredations. All-told, these raiders, greater and lesser, had burned or sunk 110,000 tons of the American merchant fleet (rated at 5.5 million tons in 1861, exclusive of the considerable whaling fleet) and inspiring owners to sell another 800,000 tons to foreign owners and thus sail under neutral flags. Changing registry as an intended temporary measure turned out in most cases, however, to be permanent.

While the federal government's war fleet had built to formidable proportions, the merchant marine would persist as crippled as the veterans themselves now bedding in the newly established, somberly spreading hospitals around the nation. Rebuilding and modernizing would be tedious, lengthy, and costly.

Yet in these turbulent years the "mystique" of the Blue Riband had not lain dormant. The *Scotia*, for example, the last of Cunard's paddle steamers, had swept eastbound during 1863 in just eight days, three hours. Great Britain especially, with her divided interests in North and South, hung on daily word of the war's progress. And her newspaper readers learned of latest developments some two days sooner than their counterparts in the United States and in the Confederacy were made aware of European news. Eastbound mail ships paused at Cape Clear on the southeast Irish coast, where waiting correspondents ravenously devoured their cargoes of newspapers, then spewed the contents on the telegraph to London, Liverpool, Southampton, Manchester, and other great cities across the Irish Sea.

The transatlantic cable did not become reality until July 1866, more than a year after Appomattox. The Massachusetts merchant, Cyrus Field, had made several unsuccessful attempts to lay a cable in the 1850s, and one message actually had flickered across the Atlantic before the cable parted. Now Field, as a director of the Anglo-American Telegraph Co., purchased the *Great Eastern* for $125,000. The huge ship finally justified the herculean efforts to build, operate, and maintain her by successfully laying 2,300 miles of sheathed electric wire between Heart's Content, Newfoundland and Valentia, Ireland.

The historic feat proved the *Great Eastern*'s swan song. She was thereafter anchored in the Mersey, off Liverpool, as a floating museum, concert hall, gymnasium, pub . . . what have you. She was finally broken up in 1889, that task proving at least as difficult as her birth pains.

Speed, meanwhile, remained in the forefront of skippers', if not passengers' minds. While there was speculation whether the even one-week crossing would be reality, the Inman Line's *City of Brussels*, in 1869, plowed from New York to Queenstown in seven and three-quarter days.

New names, too, were being heard on New York's waterfront—the "Ismay Line" for one, the brainchild of the gruff if competent Thomas Henry Ismay. In the dying months of the 1860s and the swaddling years of the '70s, he launched successively six handsome six to ten day steamers: *Oceanic, Baltic, Atlantic, Adriatic, Republic,* and *Celtic*. They looked more like the liners of the coming century. Their hulls were longer, less box-like, closer to yacht lines. Masts were shorter, less essential as steam engines became more reliable. There were one or two decks with open railings instead of one vast promenade beneath the funnels and the soot. Protruding deck houses, serving various functions, were gone.

On March 1, 1871, the line (officially Ismay, Imrie & Co., of Liverpool, later to become the White Star Line) ran this advertisement in the Liverpool Daily Post:

"Sailing on Thursdays from Liverpool, and calling at Queenstown on Fridays to embark passengers.

"Will sail as under for New York, via Queenstown, *Oceanic,* 4,500 tons, 3,000 H.P., Capt. Digby Murray, to sail to-morrow, Thursday, March 2nd, 1871.

"These steamships have been designed to afford the very best accommodation to all classes of passengers, and are expected to accomplish quick and regular passages between this country and America.

"The State Rooms, with Saloon and Smoking Rooms, are placed amidships, and the passengers are thus removed from the noise and motion experienced at the after part of the vessel.

"Passengers are booked to all parts of the States, Canada, and Newfoundland, Nova Scotia, etc. at moderate through rates. A Surgeon and a Stewardess carried on each ship. Drafts issued at New York for sums not exceeding £10 free ($50).

"Parcels will be received at the Company's Offices until 6 P.M. of the day before sailing.

"Bills of Lading to be had from Messrs. Benson & Home, and Mawdsley & Son. Shipping notes at the Company's Office. Loading berth, South West corner Bramley Moore Dock."

Ismay offered ten cubic feet of luggage space for each adult passenger, "provision of all food," plus the luxury of oatmeal served in the evening, before retiring. Saloon or first class fare was $100, steerage, $25. At that price, immigrants had to supply themselves with knife, fork, spoon, tin mug and plate, also bedding. Gas lighting, instead of oil lamps, was tried, with indifferent success because of the gas lines' tendency to split.

With all the refinements of the new liners, iron hulls and continually more powerful engines, the steamships, along with their masters, were not quite ready for the swift crossing so passionately desired by competition. Progress continued to have its price. For example, in the decade commencing with 1858, 2,110 lives were lost in 35 steamship disasters, 29 of them of British registry. Speed had its part in the majority. As the vessels became larger, so did the casualties.

On the last day of March, 1873, the *Atlantic* was a few days from New York with nearly a thousand passengers. Gales had so slowed her crossing that Captain James A. Williams decided he'd have to put in to Halifax to replenish dwindling coal supplies. He almost made it. Instead, he crashed at twelve knots onto rocky ledges off the mouth of Halifax Harbor. It was 3:15 A.M. on Tuesday, April 1—All Fools Day.

More than half of those aboard perished this cold, starry night simply because the captain was going too fast and had neglected to take soundings.

In November of the same year the French *Ville du Havre* luxury steam packet, slightly larger than the ill-fated *Atlantic,* also pounding along at twelve knots under auxiliary sails, collided in calm, clear waters off the Azores with a sailing vessel, the *Loch Earn.* Some 80 percent of the 300 souls aboard, including the wife of the captain, died.

Speed stabilized, not surprisingly, in the '70s. With memories of the two disasters freshly in mind, captains allowed the Blue Riband to gather dust. The Atlantic crossing stuck at somewhat more than a week (by a few days, rarely by a few hours), depending on the power of the ship and the expertise of the engineers. Far better vessels, meanwhile, slid off the ways, following the trend of the Ismay "—ic" liners, more resembling steamships than clippers.

For example, there were the Guion Line's "United States Mail Steamers" sailing the Hudson every Tuesday from "Pier New 38" for Queenstown and Liverpool. They ranged from the *Wisconsin,* 3,400 tons to the *Alaska,* 7,500 tons, and were all advertised as:

". . . built of iron, in watertight compartments, furnished with every requisite to make the passage across the Atlantic both safe and agreeable, having bath-rooms, smoking-room, drawing room, piano and library; also experienced surgeon, stewardess and caterer on each steamer.

"The staterooms are all on deck, thus insuring those greatest of luxuries at sea, perfect ventilation and light."

New spectrums of magnificence included stained glass skylights above the grand saloon, the brilliance of which not even clouds of black smoke belching from the several furnaces could measurably dim. The Guion's *Oregon,* too, offered her own bonus—the first transatlantic steamship to advertise electric lights, in 1879.

As in the preceding '70s, the United States that year continued to focus its attentions on peace. President Rutherford B. Hayes had proven a more able, honest and progressive president than his Democrat opponents had predicted or still cared to admit. Wiping out lingering, hateful vestiges of the war, he had removed occupation troops from the last Southern states (South Carolina, Louisiana and Arkansas), established an effective civil service, and plumped for the rights of the black man. The Treasury continued to count a surplus—eight million dollars—even though it had shrunk from twenty-one million dollars the previous year.

There were positive stirrings in Central America of a new day in international transportation as Ferdinand De Lesseps, in 1879, commenced preliminaries for an isthmian canal. It was the tenth anniversary of the opening of the Suez Canal, which the same octogenarian Frenchman had successfully engineered.

More and more, in the brittling months of the 1870s, the United States was going out into the world. The clipper ship captains and daring raiders such as Raphael Semmes had already shown that the seven seas were no more than distant extensions of Main Street, in peace or in war. And the very fibers of the American people would be woven of the many racial stocks borne to the New World's shores on homeward voyages.

Thus, in the *New York Times* of July 9, 1879, a short item buried down in page five attested to the now matter-of-factness of what in truth was not commonplace: "OFF FOR THE ARCTIC SEAS."

The preceding day, a Tuesday, under sunny skies the *Jeannette* had dipped her flag to San Francisco's Golden Gate and set course toward the North Pole. The diminutive unpretentious size of the three-master, 420 tons and only 142 feet long, was complemented by the inexperience of the 33-man crew and, indeed, of her commanding officer, Lieutenant Commander George Washington De Long. The 35-year-old De Long had been able to convince both the U.S. Navy Department and his sponsor, James Gordon Bennett, playboy publisher of the *New York Herald*, that slim credentials would be outbalanced by all-consuming enthusiasm and ambition to penetrate the frozen hell of the polar regions. These extremities had already claimed other more knowledgeable explorers, including Sir John Franklin and his elaborately planned quest, involving two ships, just four decades earlier.

George's parting with his 28-year-old wife, Emma, in the Palace Hotel the night before sailing had been especially disturbing to both of them. As she sat on his lap, clad in his favorite black velvet dress, arms about his neck, he had urged her not to "smother" herself in mourning should something happen, then added, "There is only one thing that could have made me any happier than I have been . . . if I could have felt that you depended on me for everything and in every way. . . ."

Pretty little Emma could see only loneliness ahead—the long winter, or winters, in Burlington, Iowa, where she would stay with her sister and the De Long's only child, five-year-old Sylvie. Yet, she had expected just such a moment for nearly all of the eight years of their married life.

De Long, only child of a Huguenot family, was raised in Brooklyn by an over-solicitous mother who had dreamed of a career for him in the priesthood, or at least the law. George, studious, solemn, somewhat introverted, wanted the Navy instead. To his disappointment he spent the war years at the Naval Academy, temporarily located in Newport, Rhode Island.

Along the way De Long had become obsessed with the Arctic. In fact, his honeymoon was barely over before he was en route to Greenland waters on the old steam sloop *Juniata*, searching for the lost exploration vessel *Polaris*. His continuing "Arctic fever," by his bride's diagnosis, led him in search of a wealthy sponsor, James Gordon Bennett.

Bennett, currently dividing his time between London and French residences, was receptive, and for several reasons. As one consideration, his *Herald* had reaped a financial harvest when his reporter, Henry M. Stanley, had located the lost missionary Dr. David Livingstone in Africa, in 1871. For another, Bennett had himself been thinking of northward voyages. This was inspired at least in part by a desire to place greater distance between himself and a man, Fred May, with whom he had dueled. The duel had involved the honor of May's sister.

Exploratory conversations resulted in the purchase of the small *Pandora,* which drew but thirteen feet, thus making her peculiarly adapted for coastal work. She had logged previous polar duty, including the discovery of bones and other relics of the Franklin expedition. She was refitted in the Thames and renamed *Jeannette* in honor of the publisher's sister.

Before she sailed for San Francisco with Emma and little Sylvie on board, Henry Stanley had sped De Long on his way. He offered the oblique speculation that he might be writing a companion to his book on the finding of Livingstone, "How I Found De Long." The serious-minded George discovered no humor in the remark.

His crew, meanwhile, was being put together, starting with Master (lieutenant junior grade) John W. Danenhower, 29, moustached, handsome, six feet tall, fresh from the sloop U.S.S. *Vandalia* cruising in the Mediterranean with the former president, General Ulysses S. Grant, and Mrs. Grant. He would be navigating officer.

Bennett also furnished two experienced seamen from his yacht *Dauntless,* diminutive Jack Cole, Irish boatswain, "worth his weight in gold," and Alfred Sweetman, who underscored his exactness of mind as he listed his age, "38⅚ years."

Jeannette arrived at Mare Island Navy Yard, San Francisco, two days after Christmas, 1878—18,000 cold, stormy miles from England, six long months, yet representing to Emma "the happiest period of my life."

Extra deck housings were added at this major yard, the bow and other portions of the ship strengthened, new boilers, new pumps, and a steam winch installed, while bunkers were enlarged to accommodate a total of 132 tons of coal. Supplies were trundled aboard, including two conversation pieces: an electric generating machine from a young inventor, Tom Edison, and a talking device, the gift of a Scottish voice instructor, Alexander Graham Bell. De Long, attributing no practical use to the generator, figured he'd put the sole light bulb atop the mainmast to "cheer the men" on dark days.

The talking gadget seemed wholly frivolous to the commanding officer. He did plan to use its wire for telegraph keys, already aboard, to link the ship with Siberia should the need arise. However, he never checked on the existence of telegraph stations along desolate, ice-locked coastal Siberia.

The crew reported aboard one by one, ranging in age from 21 to a solitary grizzled veteran of whale ships, pressing 50, Bill Dunbar, the ice pilot. The oldest officer, at 39, was Chief Engineer George Wallace Melville, a gruff, capable man whose Civil War service had been distinguished. Endowed with a high forehead, bald dome, and flowing beard, he appeared to be a cross between a Biblical prophet and a wrestler.

Dr. James Markham Ambler, of Fauquier County, Virginia, became expedition surgeon. Lieutenant Charles Chipp, former shipmate of De Long on the *Juniata,* who bore a marked resemblance to General Grant, left naval duty in China to become the executive officer.

Two civilians were given the rating of seamen: frail, quiet Raymond Lee Newcomb, of Salem, Massachusetts, a naturalist; and big, burly Jerome J. Collins, a meteorologist-reporter and James Gordon Bennett's special emissary. The versatile and brilliant Jerry Collins was musically inclined. In fact, he was at the small pump organ in the wardroom piping out the rollicking notes of the new musical *Pinafore* as the *Jeannette* sailed.

While the departure was cheered by many along the shores of Vallejo, host community to the Navy Yard, the absence of offiical well-wishers either from the Navy Department or from Publisher Bennett did not go unnoticed by De Long. In fact, the Navy tug *Monterey* sloshed across the *Jeannette's* wake without, as the expedition's commander would observe, "even a blast of her steam whistle."

After two weeks of generally calm sailing, the little ship poked into northerly fog banks, feeling her way through rocks and shoals. She arrived on August 2 at Unalaska Island, a pinpoint on the stepping stones of the Aleutians. Its only inhabitants were employes of the Alaska Fur Company and a few shabby Indians. All pitched in to load a waiting cargo of deerskins, sealskins, blankets, furs, 150 tons of coal, and 6 tons of dried fish for dog food.

The next stop was St. Michael's in Norton Sound, another desolate trading post of the Alaska Fur Company, still mounting ancient cast-iron cannon in testament to its recent Russian ownership. As one was fired in smoky salute to the *Jeannette,* the very gunners appeared amazed anew that it did not fragment itself into shards.

Forty snarling and fighting sled dogs, more wolf than domestic canine, were strong-armed aboard, together with two young Indians, Alexey, logged as a "hunter," and Aneguin, hunter/dog handler. There the *Jeannette* met the *Fanny A. Hyde,* a chartered coal and provision schooner. However, since the supply ship held more coal than the exploration vessel could bunker, De Long decided she should follow him as consort a little farther on after he quit the "miserable place," St. Michael's.

On August 25 *Jeannette* arrived at St. Lawrence Island, where final coal and provisions were loaded and last letters to home posted on the *Hyde.* Collins wrote a final dispatch to the *Herald:*

"Feeling that we have the sympathy of all we left at home, we go north trusting in God's protection and our good fortune. Farewell. . . ."

Also aboard the schooner was a Chinese cabin boy who had decided he had no taste for the polar regions. Remaining were two others of like ancestry, Ah Sam, the cook, and Charles Tong Sing, the steward. The *Jeannette* crossed the Bering Straits on August 28, pushed northward . . . and into ice. On September 4, De Long wrote in his meticulously kept journals:

"The day opens calm and with a thick fog. Still at anchor to the floe. We observe a gradual closing in of large floes around us . . . the rigging is one mass of snow and frost, presenting a beautiful sight . . . the pack ice surrounding us seems to have a uniform thickness of about seven feet, two feet being above water."

A clammy film of moisture soon covered all bulkheads and overheads, defying removal even by determined scrubbing. Worse, the *Jeannette* was already being punished by the ice, shaking "very badly," according to Danenhower, as she smashed into the larger floes. Melville's experienced eye observed something yet more alarming; the manner in which the ice "set in behind" as though heavy prison gates were closing in the explorers.

With steam winch, tackle, and anchor, De Long attempted to haul his command ahead. The engines pounded as if in extremis, clouds of spent steam cloaked the groaning ship, and the crew stood on the floes and pushed until red-faced and breathless. But the *Jeannette* scarcely budged. On September 6, Danenhower wrote, " . . . we banked fires, secured the vessel with ice anchors and remained. The ship was frozen in."

At first, the experience of being ice-locked was not only unique but rather pleasurable. The men exercised on the ice and organized polar bear hunts, "a most exciting sport," as Melville wrote, the snow "flying like feathers," as the dog pack went yelping off after a sighted bear. Bear steak was also a treat.

The first hunt, however, brought about an unpleasant revelation. Collins, the expedition photographer, had forgotten all his developing chemicals. Although the chief engineer had brought along a camera of his own, his type of developer, involving the "Beachey" process, was of no use to Collins's plates.

De Long, as it now became evident, was not one to readily forgive or forget. From this time on his relationship with Mr. Bennett's personal representative deteriorated rapidly. Others, inevitably, were already beginning to wear on one another's nerves. Melville, irritated by naturalist Newcomb's dissecting of birds and the attendant mess and odors, referred to him openly as "Ninkum." And Chipp, the quiet executive officer, annoyed the chief engineer by his tendency to go off to "mope by himself." Even someone's cough or facial twitch could elicit a "stop that!"

Tantalizingly in sight of the *Jeannette* was Herald Island, named not for Bennett's paper but for a Royal Navy expedition which found it in 1849. At one time a sled party, headed by Melville, attempted to reach it only to be frustrated by open lanes of water. However, reaching it would have meant little reward. Rocky, perpetually frozen Herald supported no life. Besides, the ice pack was inexorably carrying *Jeannette* past it.

Then, seeming salvation, on November 24. De Long could write, "It has come at last; we are broken adrift from our floe!" The unpredictable pack was alive again. As it moved, it emitted crushing, crashing sounds which reminded Melville of "distant artillery," almost "tortured" in its overtones and implication.

"Huge floe-bergs," the engineer officer wrote, "as large as churches bobbed up and down like whales," soon becoming so menacing that De Long considered abandoning. "The poor ship began to creak and groan with the immense strain ... the decks bulged upward, the oakum and pitch were squeezed out of the seams, and a bucket almost full of water, standing on the quarter deck, was half emptied by the agitation."

Finally, the pack loosened its grip, leaving *Jeannette* in a little canal, with no place to go. And even these waters froze within hours, causing De Long to observe wryly, this was "no place for a ship."

The weather worsened, driving the temperature far below zero. It brought cruel winds and snow flurries. The nights were so abominable that even the cold-loving dogs padded up the gangplank after their evening meal "as methodically," according to the commanding officer, "as we do when it strikes two bells."

Christmas arrived, celebrated with a minstrel show arranged by the innovative Collins, three quarts of whiskey distributed by the ship's surgeon, and a dinner featuring "Arctic turkey" (roast seal). But it wasn't enough. Hours after the others had retired, De Long sat in the tomb-like damp of his cabin, penning, "this is the dreariest day I have ever experienced in my life. . . . we tried to be jolly but did not make any grand success of it."

January 1880 arrived, with scant harbingers of anything better. Melville described "giant blocks" of ice "pitched and rolled as though controlled by human hands" building up in some places to fifty-foot high mountains. All this pressure told on the *Jeannette,* which finally opened up in several places. For more than two weeks the pumps were worked, bailing lines passing upward from the bilges while bulkheads of cement, plaster, wood, oakum, tallow, anything "to stop the rush of the incoming water" were constructed.

Finally, the dark, cold streams were dammed. The ship had been saved.

Tempers worsened. Collins and Melville fought verbally. When the chief engineer called the former "that damned Irish cow," Collins complained to De Long. In mildly reprimanding his chief engineer, the commanding officer told him he swore too much anyhow and that "won't do!" Collins's organ playing finally upset even the long-suffering Newcomb, who bluntly advised, "You give me an earache!"

There was, by the same token, real sickness. The worst was an infection which threatened to take Danenhower's left eye. Dr. Ambler was powerless to control it.

However, able to take sights with his right eye, the navigating officer reported early in March that the *Jeannette* had drifted fifty miles with the pack since September "in an uncertain manner." A few days later De Long took his own bearings and came up with a sobering conclusion. *Jeannette* rested in "almost identically the same position" as on November 30, 1879.

If Danenhower's own readings were accurate or relatively so, this meant that the ship had been moved in a wide, aimless, and conceivably fatal circle. In June De Long wrote:

"The absolute monotony. The unchanging round of hours, the awakening to the same things and the same conditions that one saw just before losing one's self in sleep; the same faces, the same dogs; the same ice; the same conviction that tomorrow will be exactly the same as today, if not more disagreeable; the absolute impotence to go anywhere, or to change one's situation an iota . . . all our books are read, our stories related, our games of chess, cards, and checkers long since discontinued."

The winter turned into spring, spring into summer, the seasons demarked only by the calendar. Perhaps the sole scientific accomplishment, aside from Newcomb's bird studies, was Chipp's galvanometer recording of the electric properties of auroras. None had been able to make Mr. Bell's or Mr. Edison's inventions so much as whisper or glimmer. When the telegraph lines were stretched over the ice, they gnarled and cracked.

With September, De Long was asking of his journals, "Is this always a dead sea? Does the ice never find an outlet?"

A year in the ice passed, another Christmas, and continuing deterioration of morale and tempers. While De Long did not much care for Newcomb or Dunbar, the ice pilot, he saved his special spleen and vindictiveness for Collins, who he thought was shirking his duties. The latter, as Bennett's emissary, protested that he should not be classed as an enlisted man, asserting, "You follow me and treat me like a dog!"

Finally, the commanding officer relieved Collins of all duties and started preliminary notes for a court-martial when, as, and if the expedition returned to the States.

De Long, aided by Dr. Ambler, at least had kept his men alive and free of the seafarer's historic shipmate, scurvy. Not so with the dogs. One by one they had been perishing, from disease, accident, or wounds from their own brawling. Plug Ugly, the largest and strongest of the pack, had been accidentally shot during a bear hunt. Others had been so badly clawed by polar bears that they had to be put away. Even with the pack cut approximately in half, however, dwindling dog food was, in De Long's words, "a serious consideration."

Then, in May 1881, nearly two years since the expedition had hauled out of San Francisco Bay, land slowly hove through the mists into sight, with the continual drifting of the pack. De Long named it Henrietta Island, in honor of Bennett's mother. Yet it was two more weeks before a party could attain its rocky shores.

It provided a forlorn place of glaciers and gorges, 1,600-foot high mountains with an enamel-like sheathing of ice, hospitable to nothing edible with the possible exception of lichens. Melville, for one, found "the silence awful . . . confounding and the loneliness of our situation indescribably depressive."

During a raging blizzard the *Jeannette*'s explorers planted the United States Flag on this foreboding bit of rock and ice, then left a zinc case describing the visit and the purpose of the expedition.

The spirits of De Long, who had remained behind, were elevated by the discovery, as bizarrely pleasing as though he had come upon "an oasis in the desert." He was also heartened by the audible cracking of ice beneath the ship's keel, causing him to theorize that at last the prison doors of the ice pack were to be thrown open. On June 10, *Jeannette* actually was afloat again.

Time, however, was running out.

That very night, Melville sat up to calculate the amount of water being pumped out of the hold. He checked and double-checked his computations, only to conclude that the *Jeannette* was shipping fifteen tons of water a day! For a vessel of only 420 tons that could be fatal. Even as the chief engineer was about to confront De Long with this disturbing information and "just before the bell struck eight for the midnight hour" there came a sharp report, much like that of a cannon being fired, awakening all who were asleep.

"The floe," he wrote, "had split fore and aft on a line with our keel and the ship, oscillating for a few minutes, came to rest with her starboard side close to the ice, the other floe pieces, on which were the dogs, observatory and a few small articles, moving off to a distance of a hundred yards or more. Our situation was now full of peril."

Knowing that his command was doomed, De Long ordered all stores unloaded onto the ice: more than two tons of pemmican, 1,120 pounds of hard bread, 260 gallons of alcohol, 150 pounds of Liebig's extract of beef, 252 pounds of canned chicken, chocolate, cheese, whiskey, brandy, 2,000 rounds of ammunition, and much more. It seemed sufficient, and yet, by De Long's observations, the men were 500 miles from the Siberian mainland at the nearest point, some 750 miles south of that Lorelei, the North Pole.

Dr. Ambler, taking inventory of his medical supplies, was less than sanguine about the health of the crew: Danenhower's eye still aflame with pain; Chipp, feverish, in bed; Jack Cole showing signs of mental crackup; others with head colds; almost everyone afflicted by muscular aches, cramps, and overwhelming fatigue.

On Sunday afternoon, June 12, Newcomb noted a "humming sound" throughout the vessel. Her list increased to such an extent that all hands were ordered to their sleeping bags on the ice. About 4 A.M. Monday someone whispered to Melville, "There she goes!" He sat up sleepily to observe the *Jeannette* right herself almost onto even keel, "the floes that had crushed her slowly backing off; and as she sank with slightly accelerated velocity, the yardarms were stripped and broken upward parallel to the masts; and so, like a great, gaunt skeleton clapping its hands above its head, she plunged out of sight!"

Newcomb later wrote, "She was gone, her requiem being the melancholy howl of a single dog."

Part II

"... I am resigned and bow my head in submission to the Divine will."

IN BURLINGTON, IOWA, Emma De Long continued her letters, which she posted via the Navy Department in the thin hope they would, somehow, be sailed the infinite, improbable distance to the *Jeannette.*

" ... the house reminds me so much of you, all the time. At 5 o'clock every afternoon I have a feeling that you will soon be home and I must be all ready to receive you."

Sylvie, now eight, with straight-combed hair, high-button shoes and a solemn expression, added a postscript: "My Dear Papa, how are you? I am taking music lessons. I like them very much, we miss you very much and want you back soon. I pray for you every night and ask God to bless you and make you successful and bring you home safe to Mama and your loving daughter."

In Washington, concern mounted for the expedition—so much so that the navy purchased the old, creaky New Bedford whaler *Mary and Helen,* renamed her U.S.S. *Rodgers,* and shooed her north along with the revenue cutter *Corwin* in search of De Long. The quest would prove immeasurably more difficult than Stanley's for Dr. Livingstone.

On June 19 the stores and tents plus two cutters and a whaleboat were loaded onto four sleds. Men beside dogs, the survivors of the *Jeannette* expedition slogged south for Siberia. In their own improvised harness-straps, the crewmen discovered that hauling their dead weights must have been comparable to moving blocks for the pyramids. Their feet, not equipped by nature with the sled dogs' broad pads, sank in the morass of snow. Sometimes the men plunged waist-deep into pools of water.

"We reached one of the black flags that had been planted by Ice Pilot Dunbar," Danenhower wrote, "but seeing that he had planted another one ahead of us, we pushed on with the first cutter to reach that too. This goal reached, we found that we were a mile and a half from the starting place, and that it had taken us three hours to make the distance."

Walter Lee, the heavy-set machinist, suffering severe leg pains, stumbled constantly. Old Civil War wounds were acting up. Worse, in one fall he shattered the crystal and hands of a massive pocket watch. Lee had spent many long hours in Union hospitals just listening to the timepiece's reassuring tick-tick-tick.

"Throw it away!" Melville suggested. Then, when he saw tears welling in the big man's eyes, the chief engineer ordered Alfred Sweetman, the methodical English carpenter, to fashion new hands out of a tin can and to encase the whole in a protecting clamshell-like cover.

Both Sweetman and William F. C. Nindemann, the German-born rigger and quartermaster, had already been recommended by De Long for Congressional Medals of Honor for their heroic efforts to shore up the leaking *Jeannette*. Nindemann, on an earlier voyage, had been rescued from an ice floe in Baffin Bay.

Lee's pains were but one manifestation of the miasma of hurt and suffering shared by all. Stomach cramps were as common as muscle aches, and there was little relief, since Dr. Ambler's supply of brandy, whiskey, and opium was almost exhausted. Through it all, nonetheless, De Long was determined to maintain his "ice journals," burdensome as their ever-accumulating bulk had become.

"Twenty-eight men and twenty-three dogs," he wrote, "laying back with all their strength could only start our 1600-pound sled a few feet each time, and when sliding down a hill it would plunge into a snow bank . . . though the temperature was between 20 and 25 degrees, we were in our shirt sleeves and perspiring as on a hot summer day."

Cold summer rains drenched the men during hours of light. They froze by night, unable to start a fire. The tents leaked. Winds blew without cessation over a lonely, white wasteland that was inhospitable to any form of life and which a twentieth-century chronicler would label "hell on ice."

The miserable men became increasingly irritable. Danenhower, half-helpless with his bad eye, criticized the whole plan and organization of the southward "retreat." Further, he could not understand why he was kept on the sick list, protesting he was "one of the strongest men in the party." Collins, still in the limbo of one facing court-martial, and preparing his own defense in writing whenever he had the chance, confided to James Bartlett, a fireman, "If anything happens to me you will find letters on me for Mr. Bennett and the *Herald.*"

Newcomb himself was added to Collins's court-martial "club" for "using insolent and insubordinate language" and for allegedly trying to "produce discontent among the men." For a time Newcomb's shotgun "Betsy," for collecting bird specimens, was taken away from him. Chipp, however, successfully interceded for "Betsy's" return.

Seaman Cole, showing worsening signs of mental aberrations, was relieved of all duties. This action, if indeed it were wholly necessary, transferred his burdens to others.

On the Fourth of July, De Long ordered little flags flown from the tarpaulin-topped sleds. By the end of the month, the survivors came ashore on a mass primarily of basalt, which De Long named Bennett Island. He planted in the ice a little silk flag Emma De Long had sewn and took possession in the name of the president of the United States. As a matter of fact, he had no idea who that person was, Hayes having been succeeded by James A. Garfield, and the latter now hovering between life and death from an assassin's bullet.

They pushed off from the barren bit of land in about a week. August moved ahead.

During this month and the next, Lieutenant Robert W. Berry, a friend of De Long's who was commanding the converted whaler *Rodgers,* sniffed along the northeastern shores of Siberia and the Kamchatka Peninsula without finding any hint of the lost expedition. Another vessel financed by Bennett, the 1,375-ton sloop, U.S.S. *Alliance,* under Commander George H. Wadleigh, was farther off the scent yet in Icelandic waters. From its handsome, comfortable cabins, the publisher's correspondent, "Mac" MacDonna, was able to write travelogue-like dispatches for transmitting back to his city room as the occasion presented.

By September, De Long had led his emaciated, immensely wearied band close to the New Siberian Islands. On the fifth, they reached one of the outer group, Kolteny, where, at long last, there appeared signs of previous, if not recent, habitation. There were half-ruined huts, a wooden drinking cup, wooden spoon, fork, an elephant tusk and a Russian coin with the date 1840. On the eleventh, at another island, Semonovski, De Long left in a small tin case the record and position of the *Jeannette's* loss and the dismal log of the ice trek:

"We are all well, have had no scurvy and hope with God's aid to reach the settlements on the Lena River during the coming week."

The next morning, September 12, wholly in green water, gray-flecked by gale winds of 60 knots, the survivors in their three small boats, at last removed from the sleds, set sail for Cape Barkun, a promontory buttressing the eastern deltas of the Lena River. The two cutters were commanded by De Long and Chipp, the whaleboat by Melville. The three rode up on the giant combers and plunged dizzily down into the troughs as though they would never again level out.

De Long had ordered the boats to stay close together. But that really was not possible. Under low, leaden skies and blinding spindrift, the three soon separated. Melville brought his cutter somewhat into control by trailing a "drag," or sea anchor, impro-vised from rope and canvas and weighted with firepots. De Long, whose cutter had lost its mast, used a water cask for the same purpose, but this quickly followed the mast into the howling, watery vortex. A second anchor was fashioned from an oar, employing a pickax as ballast.

"During the midnight," Nindemann, in the commanding officer's cutter, wrote, "it seemed as if there were two seas running from different directions, which made it very bad for the boat. The sea was pretty choppy and broke into the boat over both sides and stern . . . three or four men bailing all the time."

And Ambler declared, "God knows where we went that night." By dawn, however, the winds somewhat moderated and the seas became less angry and "confused." Yet, the ordeal was telling on all of the cutter's occupants, especially De Long, as Dr. Ambler added, "the captain complained of cold feet and hands, and had a nervous chuckle in his throat."

By the end of the week, September 16, Melville made land—the sand spits of the Lena River, "as big as the Mississippi," it appeared to Bartlett, the fireman. Three days later (September 19, 1881, the day on which President Garfield died in Elberon, New Jersey, to be succeeded by Chester Arthur) the chief engineer touched shore at a fishing village, where the eleven weary, half-frozen, icicled survivors were treated to a dinner of cooked goose, venison, and fish.

One of the natives, Vassili Koolgork, was persuaded to pilot the cutter to another settlement, Geeomovialocke, farther up the river, still some 3,000 miles from civilization as the Americans knew the meaning of the term. This would be the city of Irkutsk, near the Mongolian border.

De Long's cutter, containing twelve persons in addition to himself, came ashore a day later than Melville, but in another part of the Lena Delta, the Osotok River. Nindemann, however, had to construct a raft to ferry the men over the slush and mud to firm ground. By this time, only one dog remained, "Snoozer". The others had run off, drowned, or died of sickness. And Snoozer was almost too tired to drag his paws over the ice.

The men were equally listless, and dispirited at not having found any habitation. The health of all was fast deteriorating. On October 1, the surgeon was compelled to amputate the frosbitten toes of Hans Ericksen, a Danish seaman. It was too late. He died within the week. His shipmates then made a sobering discovery. They were too weak to move his body, much less bury it in the hard ice.

"What in God's name," De Long wrote, "is going to become of us?"

They were too tired to move even themselves. Everything was a disproportionate challenge requiring exertion to the point of and, frequently exceeding collapse—walking, standing up, sitting down, eating what little there was to eat, hauling their supplies even though a trail of jettison now stretched behind their route of torturous progress. The heavy "ice journals" caused especial discontent among those who had to carry them, but De Long was adamant, snapping, "These records have to go with me!"

When De Long reprimanded Nindemann for lightening his own load by discarding some clothing, the latter barked back, "I would sooner be along with the devil than be along with you!"

Finally, alcohol became the staple, after the survivors had been reduced to slaughtering Snoozer, to chewing the leather in their boots and even attempting to find sustenance in sweet oil, washed down with watery willow tea. The men now only inched forward. Thus, De Long became convinced that the strongest must move on and attempt to find help. It was decided that two, Nindemann and Louis P. Noros, a seaman, probably possessed the capability of making it, even though the latter admitted his feet hurt, his legs were sore, and his trousers "dried up like a board, more of a hindrance than anything else."

Explaining that it was useless to give him written instructions in Siberia, where surely none could speak English, De Long told his quartermaster, "I want you and Noros to go south to a place called Ku Mark Surk ... where there is a settlement and probably you will find natives there. If you should not find any go as far as Ajaket, a place farther to the south, and if you should not find natives there go to Bulun. ...."

However, the commanding officer concluded, if he could not find assistance anywhere, to attempt to return. Nindemann realistically replied that he entertained "very little hope."

On October 9, they set out, sped on their way by Collins's wistful, "remember me when you get to New York," and Dr. Ambler's more oblique, "Nindemann, I will see now what kind of man you are." Collins had himself been denied permission to accompany the pair, De Long having asserted, "Mr. Collins, you would not get five miles away from camp."

With them, Nindemann and Noros took a rifle, forty rounds of ammunition, two ounces of alcohol, blankets and spare underwear, which was Collins's gift.

Those left behind kept painfully on. De Long wrote:

"Underway again at 10:30. Lee breaking down ... halt for dinner—1 oz. alcohol. Alexey shot three ptarmigan. Made soup. We are following Nindemann's tracks, though he is long out of sight ... high bluff. Ice running rapidly to northward in river. Halt at 4:40, upon coming to wood. Find canoe. Lay our heads on it and go to sleep. Half ounce alcohol, supper."

It was the last of the alcohol. The glycerine was almost exhausted. The men were so weak they could not raise their legs to break through the slush ice, being compelled to push through it. The surface of this Siberian earth was a "vast morass," spongy and wet by day, frozen and often snowcovered by night.

"We are in the hands of God," De Long wrote on October 13. "We cannot move against the wind, and staying here means starvation. Afternoon, went ahead for a mile, crossing either another river or a bend in the big one."

When they missed Lee, they turned back to find he had lain down, waiting to die. At that point, "all united in saying the Lord's Prayer and creed." A new snowstorm howled that night over the wastes. The Indian guide, Alexey, and Lee were faltering as though their hours were numbered. Smoke wisps on the horizon taunted the men. Were they mirages?

De Long did not miss divine service on Sunday, the sixteenth. On Monday Dr. Ambler baptized Alexey into the Christian faith. Prayers for the sick were read on this, Collins's fortieth birthday.

At sunset Alexey breathed his last. He was placed on the frozen river the next day, Tuesday the eighteenth, and covered with slabs of ice which were at once his shroud and his tomb.

The tent was cut up the next day for new footgear. Heinrich Kaack, a German seaman, died on Friday, the twenty-first. Lee died a few hours later. Again prayers for the sick and then those for the repose of their souls were read in a hoarse, faint monotone.

Dr. Ambler commenced a letter to his "dear brother," Edward Ambler, of Fauquier County, Virginia, "in the faint hope" that it would actually reach him through "God's merciful providence." Confessing that he possessed "very little hope of surviving," the expedition's surgeon continued:

"We are growing weaker, and for more than a week we have had no food. We can barely manage to get wood enough to keep warm, and in a day or two that will be passed.

"I write to you all, my mother, sister, brother Cary and his wife and family, to assure you of the deep love I now and have always borne you. If it had been God's will for me to have seen you all again I had hoped to have enjoyed the peace of home-living once more. . . .

"As for myself I am resigned and bow my head in submission to the Divine will. My love to my sister and brother Cary; God's blessing on them and you. To all my friends and relatives a long farewell. . . .

De Long was scrawling his own entries:

"Saturday, October 22, 132nd day. Too weak to carry the bodies of Lee and Kaack out on the ice. The doctor, Collins and I carried them around the corner out of sight, when my eye closed up.

"Sunday, October 23rd, 133rd day. Everybody pretty weak. Slept or rested all day, and then managed to get enough wood in before dark. Read part of divine services. Suffering in our feet. No foot gear.

"Monday, October 24th, 134th day. A hard night.

"Tuesday, October 25th, 135th day.

"Wednesday, October 26th, 136th day."
It was as though De Long barely had the strength to record even the days, Tuesday and Wednesday. Then, for the next four days, the expedition's leader resumed his notations:
"Thursday, October 27th, 137th day.   Iverson broken down. (Nelse Iverson, coal heaver)
"Friday, October 28th, 138th day.   Iverson died during the early morning.
"Saturday, October 29th, 139th day.   Dressler died during night. (Adolph Dressler, seaman)
"Sunday, October 30th, 140th day.   Boyd and Gortz died during night.   Mr. Collins dying.   [George Boyd, fireman, Carl Gortz, seaman]."

Nindemann and Noros reached Bulun, the little Lena settlement, on October 29.   This feat was accomplished by finding huts, firewood, and game along the way, by their own physical condition and determination and, of course, luck. The last days they were sped on their way by native reindeer sleighs.

On November 2, Melville and the pair were reunited when one of the engineer's guides received a note from Nindemann. Melville then prepared a telegram to the secretary of the navy:

"The steamer *Jeannette* was crushed in the ice June 11, 1881. Latitude 77 degrees 15 North, longitude 157 East. With sledges and boats made good to 50 miles northwest of the mouth of the Lena River where the three boats were separated in a gale."

The telegram did not arrive in Washington until four days before Christmas. The navy could not do much, expecially since the search vessel *Rodgers* had just caught fire in St. Lawrence Bay and burned to the waterline. Lieutenant Berry, however, had started overland with a picked group, continuing his mission to find De Long.

To James Gordon Bennett, this was another Stanley Livingston quest in embryo. He dashed off a cable to the chief of his European bureau in Paris, a bearded, flamboyant habitué of the Left Bank, John P. Jackson. Jackson was ordered to get himself to Moscow as fast as he possibly could and find De Long. The publisher then put the *New York Herald*'s best editorial writer to work on a special apologia:

"The brief but startling story of the loss of the *Jeannette* . . . adds another memorable chapter to the annals of Arctic adventure . . . however deplorable the disaster which arrested the movements, he [De Long] returns home with tidings of a large area of the polar ocean never before seen by man."

In its mingled excitement and sense of responsibility, if not guilt, the *Herald* published one dispatch entirely in its original French, forgetting to translate it.

By early February, 1882, at least four distinct groups were on the prowl for De Long: Melville, assisted by Nindemann and others; Lieutenant Berry plus a second Navy group led by Lieutenant Giles B. Harber; and Jackson, the correspondent now joined by A. Larsen, artist for the *Illustrated London News.* Lavishly entertained en route by Russian officials, drenched with vodka, the journalists finally met Danenhower in Irkutsk in late February. He was in command of a small band of survivors heading westward toward Europe and transportation home.

Almost forgetting his initial assignment—to find De Long— Jackson interviewed Danenhower over a period of three weeks, in a shabby hotel room filled with cigar smoke and the stale reek of beer and alcohol. Word by word, sentence by sentence, the whole sordid story came out: the jealousies, suspicions, corrosive hatreds that undermined the expedition even before the *Jeannette* sank. Danenhower was bitter at Melville, at De Long. In the event De Long was found alive, his navigating officer planned to "spend every dollar I had in the civil courts" to fight his erstwhile commander.

Not until March 23 did Melville finally come upon De Long's last encampment and the mute, frozen amen to an expedition: eleven corpses. Oddly enough, according to Melville, they "looked first rate. Their faces were a little flushed, their hands black from the fire, and their faces a little burned, but they looked quite natural. The color was frozen in their faces, they were not the color of dead men."

The ice journals, all the weighty, scrawled, heart-breaking volumes were there, the last will and testament of one more man obsessed with "Arctic fever." The last entry had been made on October 30.

There were some mysteries in the final positions of the bodies. De Long had "his left hand partially raised in the air," making searchers wonder if he were shielding himself from a blow, especially with reference to the journal entry of October 22, "... when my eye closed up." Had someone struck him?

Collin's face was covered with a pair of red flannel drawers, "his fists clenched ... his expression ... very bitter."

The surgeon was lying atop a pistol that belonged to De Long, a pool of dark, half-frozen blood beneath his face. There existed also a bite mark by his thumb as though Dr. Ambler had sought to drink his own blood.

Not until early May did word of the finding of De Long's party finally reach the United States, and Emma De Long, in Burlington, Iowa. It would be nearly two more years before George Washington De Long's earthly remains and those of his companions would be returned home, some to be buried beneath an heroic monument in Woodlawn Cemetery, north of New York City.

Yet, interment did not quite bury the story itself.

William Bligh, at 34, in the context of the rough-and-tumble nautical fraternity, was "no more arrogant or unusually distinguished as a martinet from his fellow commanders." Devoted and sometimes sentimental family man when not parrying the thrusts of mutineers, he was the adoring husband of "Betsy" and father of six daughters.

—National Portrait Gallery, London

The 320-ton *Savannah* introduced steam to the North Atlantic in 1819. Her single cylinder was rated at only 72 horsepower, comparable to a compact car of today but far less efficient. The voyage to England consumed a month, and at that her engines wheezed their tortured raspings but three of those many days.

—U.S. Navy photograph

(Above) Nemesis of the Confederate raider C.S.S. *Alabama*, U.S.S. *Kearsarge* at 1,031 tons was a powerful steam sloop whose formidable armament was built around two 11-inch smooth bore Dahlgren pivot guns. Chain armor dropped over her sides rendered her invulnerable to most enemy shells.

(Left) "Old Beeswax," Raphael Semmes, appears uncharacteristically relaxed on the deck of his *Alabama,* which embodied, to him, the "grace of a swan." The famous privateer ("pirate!" the North scored him) was "vain, arrogant . . . hot-tempered and opinionated." Behind him is his "exec." John McIntosh Kell.

(Below) "Graceful even in her death struggle," the *Alabama* "disappeared from the face of the waters," as her executive officer, Kell, described the end of the famous cruiser, weary and depleted after nearly two years' raiding around the globe. Her grave was 4½ miles off Cherbourg, France. This lithograph of an oil painting by Xanthus Smith hangs in the Franklin D. Roosevelt Library, Hyde Park.

(Above) The ill-fated Arctic steamer *Jeannette* in Le Havre, France, before her departure for San Francisco. The former *Pandora* with some history of polar probing, she was registered at 420 tons, 142 feet long, seemingly well pedigreed and proven for northerly climes.

(Below) "... and so like a great gaunt skeleton ... she plunged out of sight." This handsome woodcut of the sinking of the *Jeannette* after being crushed in the ice is taken from the 2-volume book published by Emma De Long in 1884 and based on the "ice journals" of her late husband and expedition commander, George Washington De Long.

(Above) The 32,000-ton *Lusitania,* in 1907, swept transatlantic travel into the 20th century. Nearly one-sixth of a mile long, she relied on the newest concept in propulsion—steam turbines—to drive her at phenomenal speeds approaching 30 knots. The big Cunarder pampered her passengers with hot and cold running water, cabin telephones, individual bathrooms, elevators, roof gardens, and an ancestral sort of air conditioning. Her only flaw, in spite of boasts to the contrary: she was not unsinkable.

(Below) She "quivered her whole length" as she poised for her final plunge and, then, a survivor turned in his lifeboat to exclaim, "My God—the *Lusitania's* gone!" Torpedoed May 7, 1915, within sight of a sun-bathed Irish coast, the "lovely" *Lusitania* abruptly stopped the clocks of complacency and naivete in America. Although many of the passengers carried cameras, not one photograph ever surfaced to record the torpedoing (by the U-20) or the events immediately following.

(Above) Jinxed sisters? This is a very rare photograph of the 48,000-ton *Britannic,*
sister of another ill-starred steamship, the *Titanic.* In November, 1916, in the
Aegean, she was lost either through mine or torpedo. The photographer caught
Britannic in this picture leaving the harbor of Mudros, Greece, possibly on her last voyage.

(Above) *Kaiser Wilhelm II,* 19,000 tons, was considerably luckier than the
somewhat smaller *Kaiser Wilhelm der Grosse* which, as an armed auxiliary, was
sunk early in the war. She remained in neutral U.S. waters until America's entry in
April, 1917, when she was seized as a transport and renamed *Agamemnon.* She
could carry half a division and was capable of 23½ knots.

(Below) The mighty *Vaterland,* 58,000 tons and, in 1914, the world's largest liner,
had been in service less than three months when war's outbreak caught her in
Hoboken. Seized by the U.S. Government in 1917 and renamed *Leviathan,* she was
our biggest troop carrier, taking nearly 100,000 doughboys to France and England
and bringing the Yanks back again after the Armistice.

33 SUB SURVIVORS SAVED

26 Others Believed Dead in Squalus Disaster

Diving Chamber Makes Four Tri

Rescue Device Jams Last Ascent, Hang Suspended For Hour

By NAT A. BARROWS

PORTSMOUTH, N. H., May 25 (Thursda Back to comforting fresh air and an ocean th danced and sparkled in friendly welcome, survivors of the lost submarine Squalus—h gard ghosts of "Pigboat" men—returned fr an underwater tomb today in an ingenious rea "elevator" which on its fourth and last asc caused almost four hours of anxious waiting its cables fouled.

Behind them, in flooded compartments, t left 26 shipmates for whom, an official annou ment early today indicated, the Navy had gi up all hope. Not the slightest sound had ce from those four compartments since the Squa went down yesterday morning, disabled by watery inflow from an open induction valve.

Another tragedy was averted when the ing chamber in which the last group of e was being raised jammed for hours betw

AS FIRST MEN FROM THE SQUALUS REACHED THE SURFACE (Wide World Photo)
Members of the crew of the Falcon are helping Lieut. J. C. Nichols (in blue uniform) out of the rescue chamber. Six more survivors followed him out of the device.

Ex-Gov. Al Smith Presents New Archbishop to Laity
By JOSEPH F. DINNEEN | the back lots of Whitman, spiritual

TAX REVISION HASTENED BY TALK WITH F. D

Charlestown Man Tells Exclusive Rescue Story
By a Globe Staff Reporter

PROBABLY DEAD
OFFICER
Patterson, J. H., ensign, appointed from Oklahoma.
CIVILIANS

It read like the reporting of a miracle when banner headlines on metropolitan dailies from coast to coast announced that the majority of the crew of the sunken submarine *Squalus* had been snatched from the depths and almost certain doom. The day was Thursday, May 25, 1939.

—U.S. Navy photograph

How were trapped crews of disabled submarines rescued? With the McCann Rescue Chamber, developed in the mid-1930s by Lt. Cdr. Allen R. "Mac" McCann. Weighing 9 tons, it was guided down by a mother ship, or tender, via a cable that had been attached to the crippled submarine. Winches inside and controllable water ballast tanks regulated the rate of ascent or descent.

(Above) After almost four months of unremitting salvage operations, the submarine *Squalus*, buoyed by pontoons and air pumped into her hull, surfaced in September, 1939. Once during the operations she "porpoised," as shown in this remarkable picture. She then had to be brought to the surface again, in proper trim for towing. On September 14, 1939, nearly four months after she sank off the New Hampshire coast, the *Squalus* was returned to the Portsmouth Navy Yard and the bodies of trapped crewmen removed.

(Left) This little excursion boat went off to war. *Tigris One*, from Teddington on the upper Thames, had been a favorite between the World Wars for honeymooners seeing landmarks along the river from Windsor Castle to Waterloo Bridge and beyond. She was among the hundreds of "little ships" that contributed to the success of Operation Dynamo, the evacuation of Dunkirk. Badly damaged and stranded on the beach, she was salvaged by a group of French soldiers who sailed her back to Dover.

(Below) " . . . the never-ending stream of weary men . . . sometimes hurrying into a tired run, sometimes plodding blindly on towards safety, sometimes packed up stationary on the narrow parapet waiting for the next ship to berth . . . " This was Dunkirk for nine nightmare days in May–June, 1940. Yet Britain rescued her army in what correctly came to be known as a "miracle"—just under 339,000 troops including some of her allies.

The French destroyer *Bourrasque* goes down after striking a mine on May 30. Minutes before she had sucessfully evaded German shore batteries. All destroyers engaged in the evacuation were prime enemy targets. To compound the tragedy, many of the nearly 1,000 soldiers who had jammed her decks died in the water when the sinking destroyer's own depth charges exploded.

The "little ships" of Dunkirk return up the Thames. More than 200 were sunk or abandoned.

Home from the sea—Cecil Wynne-Edwards and Bee Mary at their home, Hayling Island, near Portsmouth, England. In the kitchen is an object that mutely attests to "the memory of a nightmare"—the primus stove from H.M.S. *Keith*.

5

Return of the Mammoths

"The main saloon . . . entirely free from columns."

OF THE THIRTY-THREE who had sailed bravely northward past the Golden Gate, only twelve had returned. The Indian guide Aneguin died in Siberia of smallpox. Cole, the English seaman, was incurably insane. No trace was ever found of Chipp's boat.

An investigation was demanded by the family of Jerry Collins, whose debasing treatment was now a matter of record. The Navy, all too anxious to forget the whole miserable debacle, convened and in relatively short order concluded a court of inquiry with these words:

". . . the court finds no occasion to impute censure to any member of the party . . . the general conduct of the personnel of the expedition seems to have been a marvel of cheerfulness, good-fellowship and mutual forebearance."

The condition of the *Jeannette* upon sailing was adjudged "good," if "unavoidably deeply loaded." To Dr. Ambler "great credit" was accorded, especially so for keeping the crew free of the dread scurvy. Bennett, the powerful publisher, himself breathed a sigh of relief when he found his major role in the expedition was quite over-looked. It seemed to some more than coincidence.

Largely through the importunings of lawyers representing Collins's survivors, the Committee on Naval Affairs of the House of Representatives held its own inquiry—which would ultimately speak from 1,046 pages of small type. The committee's report set forth a saga which was invariably bitter, always tragic, often venomous, and occasionally explosive. But the committee drew no conclusions.

Scientifically, the expedition had established one bit of intelligence: the westward drift of the icepack, which would be of value to explorers of succeeding generations. Were there any further meaning, or lack of meaning, it would lie in the irresponsibility of journalism in the nineteenth century and the destructive potential of a proud, stubborn man whose qualifications lay mostly in his all-consuming ambition.

If Arctic exploration had been dealt a temporary setback by the *Jeannette* expedition, transatlantic communication was flourishing in speed, luxury, dependability, and size. In these waning years of the Victorian Era, liners were becoming so handsomely outfitted and comfortable in comparison to what they used to be that doctors without hesitation now recommended ocean voyages for their patients' health. Much water had surged beneath many keels in a short 40 years since the gravest apprehensions and solicitude were tendered the Atlantic passenger.

The last hints of the great days of canvas or of the hermaphrodite steamship carrying masts for sail disappeared with the new breed of liner. The vestigial outcroppings had rather abruptly become as extinct as the great auk and as useless as its wings.

Along with the new Guion Line, the American Steamship Co., offspring of the Pennsylvania Railroad, showed Old Glory on its four "fine" iron steamships, including the *Ohio.* This line was boosted by none less than President Ulysses S. Grant, who chose its ships for his 'round-the-globe tour after leaving office in 1877.

The year in which the survivors of the *Jeannette* returned home, in 1882, the one-week or longer "jinx" was broken. The pride of Guion's fleet, the big *Alaska,* pounded in to Queenstown six days, 22 hours out of New York. Two years later, S.S. *Oregon,* recently purchased by Cunard, raced from Queenstown to Sandy Hook in six days, nine hours, and 42 minutes, clocking eighteen and three-quarters knots.

Records continued to tumble. In 1889, the twin-screw *Paris,* of the International Navigation Co., clipped a full day off that record, becoming the "first five-day ship," although the run, during which she averaged nearly twenty knots, was actually 22 hours and 30 minutes in excess of five days.

Along with her sister, *New York,* at some 10,500 tons gross, she was the largest liner since the *Great Eastern. Paris* was endowed with a then unheard of indicated horsepower of 20,600, so powerful that she blew an engine, sending her to dry dock for several months. The accident did not mar her reputation as "the world's first unsinkable ship."

By now, however, with the twentieth century but a decade distant, American businessmen were asking Congress why the government didn't help the merchant marine to compete with subsidized foreign steamship companies. After all, the railroads, with not a whit of reticence, were demanding—and obtaining—handsome Federal largesse in thé form of land grants, postal contracts, and military business.

In 1891, the legislators passed a subsidy law, providing for special payments to mail-carrying vessels in relation to speed and size. The law made possible a more regular schedule of transatlantic mail. This favor from Uncle Sam directly inspired the *St. Louis* and *St. Paul,* of the International Navigation Co., forebear of the United States Lines. The beautiful young Mrs. Grover Cleveland, with the corpulent president at her side, christened the *St. Louis* on November 12, 1894 in Philadelphia.

Only slightly smaller than the Cunarders *Campania* and *Lucania,* which had entered service the previous year, the 12,000-ton steel (*not* iron) American-built liners featured steel bulkheads with no openings below main deck. The competition facing the new American contenders was formidable. Capable of sustained speeds of nearly 22 knots, first the *Campania,* and then her sister *Lucania* almost effortlessly snatched the Blue Riband. The latter crossed the Atlantic westbound from Queenstown, the year the *St. Louis* was launched in an unbelievable five days, seven hours, 23 minutes, a record that would stand for a decade and a half.

The Old World and the New were being drawn ever closer together, with all the inherent social, cultural, and political implications. Europeans not only could emigrate in mass but with considerably increased likelihood of actually reaching their destination—usually Ellis Island.

But speed and capacity, if readily comprehensible, were only two factors. Another phenomenon, manifest just before the turn of the century, had been foreshadowed by the *Great Eastern* decades earlier—monster size. The very goal of bulk and weight seemed to transcend considerations of speed, economy, efficiency, or safety.

The appearance on the seven seas of gargantuan steamships would prove epic in itself—and somehow evocative of the evolutionary process of living species long ago.

Unlike the mammoths, however, whose hulking silhouettes would plod through an entire era—the Ice Age—the ocean monsters would steam through an ephemeral lifespan measured in decades. In their very size lay the seeds of their obsolescence and extinction.

A prototype of the superliner was North German Lloyd's *Kaiser Wilhelm der Grosse* which shoved her Teutonic bulk out of Hamburg in 1897. Not "big" by future standards, she was nonetheless, at 14,349 gross tons, the largest on the Atlantic at that time. Her four funnels were themselves a selling point since the myth had been fostered—surely by steamship agents—that the number of towering, ugly stacks was in direct ratio to the vessel's safety. The four were busy enough, raining soot without surcease over all who dared the boat deck. The liner's 30,000 horsepower triple expansion engines made her a glutton for coal—250 tons a day!

Wagnerian in mood, her heavy decor was reminiscent of Charlottenburg Castle. The *Kaiser's* gilded, plush, carpeted grandeur extended to the cabins and even the bathrooms, on which were lavished brass and mirrors that would have challenged the glitter of an Oriental house of prostitution. For the first time a saloon was designed exclusively as a nursery, with Hansel and Gretel smiling out blandly at the Kinder from wooden wall panels.

Dumplings, game from the Black Forest, sauces that hitherto could be savored (and gulped) only at Unter den Linden's best, Rhein wine, Munich beer—the great ship served a heaping, caloried Gemütlichkeit worthy of the table of Frederick the Great or, indeed, Kaiser Wilhelm the Second. But for those who preferred not to rub shoulders in the capacious main saloon there were four private dining rooms, all named with a nod toward nostalgia: Wilhelm der Grosse, the Empress Augusta, Prince Bismarck, and General von Moltke, four fat *Essenzimmers* set to a noble person's taste and inclination to prosit.

Music, too, there was aplenty. A stiffly uniformed ensemble could toot or fiddle a repertoire ranging from Mozart to a march capable of starting the most phlegmatic noncom goose-stepping. Little was wanting to complete the traveler's giddy illusion of an afternoon in the Tiergarten, the Opera, or a royal review in Potsdamer Platz.

Theoretically the fastest afloat, rated at a possible 22.5 knots, *Kaiser* never did beat the fleet *Lucania* for a sustained crossing, though she claimed the Blue Riband on her maiden voyages, both west and eastbound. She was, in truth, fifteen hours behind the recent record. But what admiralty court would listen to charges of perjury involving an entity which did not even exist—a Blue Riband?

Aside from her nursery, the great austere ship possessed another first, the latest electronic curiosity, a wireless. The experimental set, however, measured a range of only about six miles.

And even as *Kaiser Wilhelm* waddled back and forth across the Atlantic with ponderous regularity, two new challengers were being groomed: the rival Hamburg American Line's *Deutschland* and White Star's *Oceanic*. The former was but a slightly larger (by some 2,000 tons) and faster model of the *Kaiser*. The *Oceanic* (launched in 1899) was, on the other hand, hailed as "the crowning success of the nineteenth century."

Somewhat in excess of 17,000 tons gross, she was about ten feet longer than the *Great Eastern,* but deficient in tonnage by some 7,000, even though, in "displacement" they were comparable. Featuring private cabins, complete with baths, "for millionaires and star actresses," she seemingly had been designed to out-*Kaiser* the *Kaiser Wilhelm der Grosse*. The correspondent for the *Liverpool Post,* at the launching in Belfast, for which a general holiday had been declared, wrote:

"State-rooms in scores to the right and to the left; now mahogany; now oak; now satinwood; now a mixture of any two or three of them, until the lavishness of everything became surfeiting, notwithstanding that the Louis Quinze style succeeded the Queen Anne and the Queen Anne gave way to something 'too utter' in decadent sumptuousness. Three decks of these apartments, with lavatories of costly marble, suites of baths, and every other appurtenance of physical comfort placed conveniently here and there."

The reporter also thought of her as "huge," but "not elephantine," and described the lifeboats as "big as barges." He forecast that *Oceanic* would cross the Atlantic "with the speed and certainty of an express train," all, to him, adding up to "the conquest of the mighty force of matter by the mighty force of mind."

The *Oceanic*'s was the most photographed launching yet, with box and bellows-camera fans complemented by ancestral newsreels, the "cinematographs" and "biographs." Yet with all the high hopes and excitement attending the birth of this graceful, two-funneled liner, she would never take the Blue Riband, being appreciably slower than the two new Germans or the twin Cunarders. She would also prove a jinx ship. She was struck by lightning the next year, 1900. In 1901 she collided with an Irish coastal steamer, *Kincora,* which plunged to the bottom with loss of life. In 1905, her officers fought back a mutiny.

If there was only one way (up!) to go in size, the same was true of corporate expansion. In 1902, with unabashed greed J. P. Morgan established the International Mercantile Marine Co. He bought up transatlantic steamship lines as a collector might buy period furniture. Included, in addition to White Star, were the American, Red Star, Atlantic Transport, Inman, Dominion, and Leyland lines, some 120 vessels.

There was even an "understanding" with Holland-American, Hamburg-American and North German Lloyd lines, making the grab almost complete—the sole, noteworthy exception being Cunard. For her "ransom," however, Cunard would pay a price.

In return for a Royal Exchequer low-interest loan of more than $12 million, the fastest Cunard ships would be registered as naval auxiliaries. In other words, not only would there be provisions for gun mounts, but the liners must be readily convertible to transports. The first to take advantage of this governmental largesse was the 19,524-ton *Carmania,* also the first of the fleet to be fitted with steam turbines: a ship of conservative Edwardian decor.

Her appearance, in 1905, would be followed two years later, by two of the largest, finest, fastest liners ever built, the 32,000-ton, 790-foot long *Lusitania* and *Mauretania.* The most impressive creations afloat, the beautiful, sleek twins, nine decks tall, with their four funnels, revealed new horizons in marine transportation. Everything was a superlative.

Four powerful steam turbines in each produced an unheard of

72,500 horsepower, turning four towering propellers capable of driving the superliners at nearly 30 knots, like thoroughbreds of the seas. Electric controls expedited such operations as steering, closing 175 watertight compartments, and detecting fire, while electric-controlled lifeboat davits powered quick "push-button" launching.

The liners' luxuries included such refinements as elevators, cabin telephones, hot and cold running water, individual bathrooms, complete electrification, an ancestral sort of air-conditioning, plus roof gardens with their potted palms, nurseries, kennels, even fireplaces.

The double-decked first class dining saloon, in glistening white and gold, with a high-domed balcony section, seating 500, was blessed with paintings of the nine muses, modified Corinthian columns, and an immense mahogany sideboard. All contributed to the ships' regal aspect, making travel aboard either one of the "lovely sisters" something special. They were outdecorated only by their German competitors.

If the *Paris,* two decades earlier, had been touted as the first "unsinkable" ship, then surely the *Lusitania* and *Mauretania* must be the second and third. Praising the five-foot deep double-bottom hull and watertight compartmentation, the *Scientific American* wrote that the claim of her builders seemed well established that "she [the *Lusitania*] is unsinkable by any ordinary disaster."

Records cracked like fragile china when these liners raced into service, ushering in the four-day crossing. In 1909 *"Maury"* stroked to Sandy Hook in just four days, ten hours from Daunt's Rock, averaging more than 26 knots. She would hold the Blue Riband for about a quarter of a century, by her example making reciprocating steam engines obsolete.

"Seafaring men," wrote *The Era* magazine, "now look forward to the 1,000-foot long ocean steamer which will have a speed of at least 30 knots. It is certain to come. . . ."

It was, and sooner, perhaps, than anyone could have guessed. In October 1910, the 882-foot White Star *Olympic,* 45,000 tons, was launched in Belfast. Again hyperbole was the norm as steamship lines vied both in ostentation and bulk. The first class dining saloon, again a show place, was decorated in Jacobean English. The seventeenth century English homes, Hatfield and Haddon Hall, were among the models. The first class lounge was in Louis Quinze, directly mirroring Versailles, the reading and writing room, Georgian. There was the first transatlantic swimming pool, or "swimming bath," plus Turkish baths, in Arabian mood, and so on and so on.

Those who might have labeled her a *ne plus ultra* in transatlantic mammoths were partly mistaken. Even as she plowed into schedule in 1911, her sister, some 5,000 tons larger and yet more ornate, was being launched in the same yards: RMS *Titanic.*

There was scant wonder that her maiden sailing on April 10, 1912, evoked only mild interest in the press or in public curiosity. After all, even *Titanic* wasn't that 1,000-foot ship, although she was within about 120 feet of the magic fifth-of-a-mile length.   Dockside watchers along the Mersey, the Solent, the Elbe or the Hudson were already used to floating mammoths: "When you've seen one, you've seen 'em all."

Rated at 21 knots, her three propellers driven by a singular combination of turbines and reciprocating engines, *Titanic* could never be the fastest on the North Atlantic. But she had attracted, among her 1,316 passengers, an assemblage of first voyage notables: names including John Jacob Astor, Isidor Straus, Henry Widener, Major Archie Butt, and others, reading like random tear sheets from a social register.

The liner, the world's largest, sailed through generally flat seas and into fairly crowded sealanes. By Sunday evening, April 14, about 1,000 miles east of New York, off the Grand Banks, she also approached spotty icefields, the annual spring drift south from Greenland, including actual bergs and growlers, which were especially hazardous since most of their bulk lay under the surface. Most vessels, large or small, had slowed down; others had stopped altogether.

Arthur Rostron, the captain of one such vessel, the aging, 13,600-ton Cunarder, *Carpathia*—Mediterranean-bound—had surmised that the *Titanic* would probably have to make a long southerly sweep to avoid the field. This he considered a bad bit of luck for Captain Edward J. Smith of the *Titanic,* since he would then have no chance for even a moderately fast crossing. It would be "Smitty's" last voyage before retiring at 60.

Meteorologically, Rostron tagged this "a fine clear night . . . very cold and every star in the heavens shining bright, the sea quite calm and no wind."

Harold Cottam, the lone "sparks" or wireless operator aboard the

Carpathia, called it quits about midnight. Although his transmitter had an effective range of only 130 miles, he could hear Marconi stations on either side of the Atlantic. Tonight there was an inordinate amount of traffic from Cape Cod and Cape Race, Newfoundland, to and from the *Titanic,* whose call letters were "MGY." Most of it was the idle chit-chat from passengers who considered they were making history. It kept the two operators on the big White Star Liner so inseparable from their keys that Jack Phillips, the first wireless man, had snapped earlier to Cyril Evans, "sparks" on the *Californian,* to "shut up!"

The small Leyland Liner, hove to after being surrounded by ice, had been trying to advise the *Titanic* of this urgent act, since Evans believed her position to be near the *Californian*'s.

Cottam, on the *Carpathia,* dozed in his chair without turning off power, his shoes only half unlaced. When he opened his eyes again the brass clock over the *Carpathia*'s transmitter indicated 12:30 Monday morning, April 15. Something inspired him to put back his headsets and say hello to MGY, or "GMOM" (good morning old man!) to the *Titanic* before stretching out on his bunk. Instead of an acknowledgment, Cottam picked up this message:

"Have struck an iceberg. Come to our assistance at once. Its CQD, OM (old man) Position Lat. 41–46 N Long. 50–14 W."

Phillips had been transmitting the plea for half an hour, although the *Titanic* had struck the iceberg at 11:40 P.M. Sunday night. She was then steaming at 22.5 knots, her fastest speed of the voyage. Captain Smith, who had not steered to the south of the icefield as Captain Rostron surmised, had wasted almost 30 precious minutes before calling for help, so firm had been his faith in the indestructibility of his command.

Sometimes Phillips used, and for the first time, the newer distress signal, "SOS," adopted simply because of its series of three dots, three dashes and three dots again, but not having any other meaning. It was not an abbreviation, as popular notion had it, for "save our souls," any more than "CQD" meant "come quick danger." "CQ" had been a general call up, like "hello" used by the British Post Office; then "D," being the first letter in the word "distress," was added in 1904. Five years later, January 23, 1909, "CQD" was flashed into the air the first time in the collision and sinking of the White Star Liner *Republic* off Nantucket Island. Only two of her 440 passengers were lost.

Rostron, at first incredulous when advised of the SOS, nonetheless was convinced after visiting the radio "shack" in person. He ordered, "Tell him we are coming as fast as we can!"

The *Carpathia* swung around in her course, some 58 miles of ocean stretching between her and the stricken giant. Rostron summoned the chief engineer and ordered another watch of stokers to get the fires roaring and to "make all possible speed to the *Titanic*." Lifeboats were readied to be swung out, dining rooms would be converted by the surgeons into emergency wards, hot food was prepared, the purser staff would be stationed at gangways to assist survivors aboard, while lookouts were doubled up to spot icebergs by the telltale glint of stars from their pinnacles.

Soon, according to Second Officer James Bisset, "we were belting along at 16 knots, the greatest speed that old lady had ever done." Meanwhile two more messages from the *Titanic*. One was to the *Olympic*, 600 miles to the east, advising that boats were ready to be filled. This in itself shocked the captain of the *Carpathia* since he realized, now, the great liner's plight must be hopeless. The second asked when the Cunarder expected to reach the scene.

"In about four hours," he instructed Cottam. "That would be 4:30 A.M."

Still, *Carpathia* should be the first, according to the desperate cross-current of messages from other ships. There was, for example, the 6,600-ton Canadian Pacific *Mt. Temple*, 50 miles to the west, but hemmed in by an exceedingly thick icefield, so awesome a barrier in fact that Captain Henry Moore kept stopping his ship and, at one time, hoisted a man by bowline to the masthead in the hopes he could pick out a channel from his vantage point.

The North German Lloyd *Frankfurt* was 140 miles to the southwest, half a day's steaming, the Allen Liner *Virginian*, 170 miles east. So incredulous in fact was the officer of the watch when the *Virginian*'s Marconiman had brought the first distress message that he had shoved him away, advising against further such "jokes." The slow Russian tramp *Birma* was close by, but nonetheless could not make it until hours after dawn. The *Baltic*, among those which earlier had conveyed ice warnings, was also under a full head of steam for the *Titanic*, but she was 370 miles to the east. And there were still others, including the *Californian*, with her Marconiman Evans sound asleep, hove to in the ice.

Seemingly, the little Leyland liner was just on or over the horizon from the *Titanic* as Second Officer Herbert Stone had been watching rockets and lights after midnight.

At 1:25 A.M., Cottam picked up a message from the *Titanic* to the *Olympic:* "We are putting the women off in the boats." Ten minutes later, *Titanic* called the *Carpathia:* "Come as quickly as possible. Engine room filling up to the boilers . . . TUOMGN ("Thank you, old man, good night.")

When Rostron was shown these two messages he became convinced that the *Titanic* was doomed. Remembering as he did that the 5,147-ton *Arizona* of the Guion Line had survived a collision with a berg in 1879, he had hoped that this far more massive ship could also limp to port even with a gash in her side or keel. What Rostron did not know at that moment was the great length of the rip: 300 feet.

Then another intercept; "We are sinking fast. . . ."

Soon, Cape Race was advising the *Virginian:* "We have not heard the *Titanic* for about half an hour. His power may be gone."

At 2:05 A.M., however, Cottam again picked up *Titanic's* CQD signals, as he logged, "His power appears to be greatly reduced."

At 2:30 A.M., when the *Carpathia* should have covered nearly two-thirds the distance to the *Titanic,* Rostron noticed a green flare just off the port bow. At the same time, a berg was reported dead ahead, causing the Cunarder's helm to be swung hard a-starboard. Rostron ordered his own rockets to be fired regularly.

At 3:15 A.M., within twelve miles of the now silent *Titanic's* position, green flares continued to be sighted at intervals. Yet no masthead lights of the 15-story-high liner could be seen. This absence in itself became increasingly ominous to those on the bridge of the *Carpathia.* Finally there came hints of daylight, for which Bisset was "longing." He knew dawn was at last coming when he began to make out the holes in the deck grating. The night's gravest hours now had passed.

At 4 A.M. four bells were rung for the changing of the watch. The lookout in the crow's nest sang in his long-drawn-out wail, "A-a-all's well and lights burning brightly."

The *Carpathia,* in a record three and a half hours, not the four estimated, had arrived at the spot where the *Titanic* should have been. All engines were stopped as a huge berg loomed.

And just then a lifeboat was sighted rising and falling in the swell. A slight chop had risen with the dawn breeze. As it neared the starboard side, an officer, standing, shouted, "We have only one seaman in the boat and cannot work very well!"

Rostron called through a megaphone, "All right. I'll bring the ship alongside the boat." He sent Bisset and two quartermasters over the side on rope ladders to grab the boat and guide it to an opened side door on "C" deck. When Bisset made a count, he found there were other men besides Fourth Officer Joseph Boxhall, plus 25 women and ten children. What at first he took to be a woman nursing a child turned out actually to be a woman with a small dog.

On the bridge, Rostron asked, "The *Titanic* has gone down, I suppose?"

"Yes," and Boxhall's voice broke. "She went down about 2:30." (The exact time was to be determined at 2.20 A.M.).

"Were many people left on board when she sank?" Rostron persisted.

"Hundreds and hundreds . . . perhaps a thousand! Perhaps more! My God, sir, they've gone down with her. They couldn't live in this icy cold water. . . ." Then, as if in afterthought, Boxhall added, "She was hoo-doo'ed from the beginning."

The loss of this "palace afloat," which some had dared label "unsinkable" with all but 703 souls out of more than 2,200 aboard did nothing to discourage transatlantic travel. In fact, there was an almost morbid rush to book aboard the *Titanic's* slightly smaller sister, *Olympic*.

Nor had the push for more and bigger ocean behemoths abated. They kept stirring, then appearing like reawakened creatures long extinct, ghostly apparitions from millions of years ago, a seeming reversal of the entire mysterious process of evolution. Still they came, steaming, with their deep throaty, lonely howls.

Launched the very next year, in April, was the 901-foot-long, 47,000-ton *Aquitania,* supreme creation of Cunard. Her steely bulk inspired the author E. Keble Chatterton to muse:

"I asked myself whether it was true that I was standing on a ship, whether it was not an enormous town hall or some new Houses of Parliament that they were building firmly to the ground. There was the width of the broadest highway on her deck with ample room for footpaths and the busiest vehicular traffic to pass and repass. I climbed higher still to the next deck, and the first obvious suggestion was that this vast space would be ample for two first-class football teams to decide a cup tie. And then I reminded myself, and had to keep on remembering, that the whole of this amazing structure was only temporarily sojourning on land, that it was being built to float on water, that, excepting for the rare occasions when the hull needed attention in dry dock, the *Aquitania* would never again rest her weight on mother earth.

"It seemed like a page from Gulliver. . . ."

Certainly there was a Gulliver-like unreality, so much so that the *London Economist* questioned the entire *raison d'être* of the "monster ships," writing of them:

". . . so huge that they can not be properly managed and supervised by a single man . . . like a small town with no cohesion, different languages spoken, the west-end quarter composed of millionaires and the east-end quarter composed of slum dwellers."

No matter, Hamburg-American was garishly splashing advertisements in the world's carriage trade periodicals and metropolitan newspapers, hawking its newest, "World's Largest Ships," the *Imperator,* 52,000 tons gross, already in service, the mighty *Vaterland,* at 58,000 tons and 950 feet long, beyond dispute the largest anywhere upon the seas:

". . . the great liner with its paintings, sculptures, and decorations affords an interesting study of the decorative arts. The grand dining saloon, which seats 800 guests, is finished in white and gold, its ceiling being supported by Ionic columns. In contrast to this the Ritz Carlton is carried out in mahogany and walnut, decorated with heavy garlands in bronze. The smoking-room is paneled in Flemish oak in low tones, while the main lounge, which may be converted into a ballroom, is decorated in warm red tones. The art treasures include paintings by old Italian masters, as well as work of many notable contemporary artists. On the main staircase hang two landscapes by the Venetian artist, Giovanna Battista Pittoni (1690 –1767). . . ."

Trumpeted with special pride was the Pompeiian swimming pool, while structurally, the designers of the huge vessel took pains to point out that "the main saloon . . . is entirely free from columns." The same architects had also provided for a miniature rail line within her holds to haul the 8,000 tons of coal needed to bunker the cavernous bins. It wasn't too much, considering the *Vaterland* burned 1,000 tons a day.

When she arrived in New York on May 21, completing her maiden voyage with considerably more success than her hapless White Star predecessor, newspapers took creative satisfaction in comparing *Vaterland*, upended, to the Woolworth Building. It turned out that the German contender won by 200 feet over the supreme edifice of the five-and-dime store founder.

The gambit in contrasts was just beginning. When RMS *Aquitania* premiered the very next month, the usually restrained *New York Times*, caught up in the madness of the moment, had its artist superimpose an eight-car Twentieth Century Limited on the liner's boatdeck, between the four towering funnels. And to think, the caption confided in its readers, there were "92 feet to spare!" British illustrators were more fanciful yet, depicting their own trains chugging out of the funnels' enormous diameter.

Now, with three superliners, Cunard could offer sailings every Saturday, meaning a seventeen day turnaround: approximately six days each way and five days in port provisioning and coaling.

Even the sinking in the St. Lawrence of the 14,000-ton *Empress of Ireland*, after a collision on May 29, with more than 1,000 dead, had failed to dampen the welcoming huzzahs for the *Aquitania*. Indeed, the echoes of the *Vaterland*'s arrival had barely died out.

And there was excitement ahead, since two more behemoths were straining to be born, the 48,000-ton *Britannic* on English ways (in Belfast), the *Bismarck* in German waters.

It was a singular July, that year of 1914. In spite of manifest preparations for war in Europe following the assassination of Archduke Francis Ferdinand in Sarajevo, Serbia, June 28, it was proving a boom travel summer. All steamship lines, advertising lavishly for business, were heavily booked. In fact, passengers, luggage in hand, were streaming down for the Hudson River docks early on a hot, humid Saturday morning, August 1, when the blow struck.

Germany had declared war on Russia, following Austria-Hungary's similar action against Serbia. Sailings were abruptly canceled, catching the largest liner of them all, *Vaterland*, at her Hoboken pier. At sea, the always popular *Olympic*, inbound, was blacked out through the impromptu stuffing of pillows against portholes as she raced for Ambrose Channel at flank speed, safety valves "tied down." She was met by the cruiser H.M.S. *Essex* to escort her the last some 1,000 miles.

Mauretania and *Cedric*, radioing that a German warship was after them, rolled through summer thunderstorms for Halifax. Cunard's first turbine liner, the 19,000-ton *Carmania*, was in mid-Atlantic, homebound, when advised that the midnight hour was at hand.

Curiously, perhaps, the Atlantic was filled with German liners. Hamburg-American's *President Grant*, primarily a cruise ship, was called back to New York. North German Lloyd's 14,000-ton *Kronprinz Wilhelm*, outbound, without passengers, hammered south. Opening top secret orders, her youthful, moustached captain, Paul Thierfelder, was advised to rendezvous with a warship to be armed for a swashbuckling new role: merchant raider.

His immediate concern, however, was far less epic, since the *Wilhelm* had been commandeered by hordes of huge, ferocious rats that had sent the ship's cats and a couple of ferrets scurrying for cover. Half of Thierfelder's crew, wearing tennis shoes so they could walk quietly, had been mobilized with clubs, baseball bats, and large hammers to hunt out the vermin.

The *Kronprinzessin Cecilie*, also of North German Lloyd, bearing millions in gold bullion, was four days from Plymouth, England, when she received the prearranged radio code from Nauen radio: "Siegfried Tod!" Since none of the officers of the "Crown Princess" wished to be dead like the unfortunate Siegfried, the liner was hauled about, Bar Harbor-bound—a three days' wild, panic-fraught voyage to the Maine coast.

The conflict spread with pandemic speed. On August 3, Germany declared war on France, the ally of Russia. The next day, Britain was herself committed even as German armies marched across the Belgian border. The same day, August 4, *Lusitania* sailed boldly from New York for Liverpool, on schedule, blacked out, betting on her great speed to sweep past anything the enemy could hurl astride her course.

Now, it was indeed the "European War." Whatever the opposing passions, purposes, objectives, and ideals (if indeed there were "ideals"), none could readily dispute Kaiser Wilhelm II's pronouncement, "a fateful hour has fallen for Germany!"

6

Why Did They Sink the *Lusitania?*

"Submarines active off south coast of Ireland."

WHILE THOUSANDS of American tourists besieged European steamship and travel offices for passage home, the belligerents were pondering how best to utilize the giant liners, which all at once appeared far less desirable than they had the past giddy decade. They were not readily maneuverable, and they presented targets which even the most myopic gunner or torpedoman could scarcely miss.

However, the *Olympic* and *Aquitania* were at first armed, with the intent of a dual use as auxiliary cruisers and transports.

Lusitania and *Mauretania* were already registered as "Royal Navy Reserved Merchant Cruisers ... at the disposal of His Majesty's Government." They were, further "in receipt of an annual subvention (or allowance) and permitted to fly the blue ensign." The latter flag denoted a naval auxiliary vessel, contrasting with the white ensign of the Royal Navy itself or the red ensign of the merchant marine, with no naval connection—that is, unarmed, not fitted or suited for carrying troops, or the like. While fast, the "lovely sisters" were almost as unwieldy as the *Aquitania*, with a comparable craving for coal.

"*Maury,*" even so, was earmarked as a transport-hospital ship, depending on the needs of the moment, while *"Lusy"*, unarmed, would remain in transatlantic service. This made her the only superliner now running between New York and England, although the neutral American ships, *St. Louis* and *St. Paul*, were almost as fast.

The *Vaterland* stayed right where war had trapped her, in Hoboken. There her remaining crew settled down to a pleasant limbo of beer, pinochle, and socializing with the large German population, a sort of little Hamburg across the Atlantic Ocean. Her sister, the *Imperator*, was snug in the real Hamburg. Unfinished *Bismarck* remained in the same city at the Blohm and Voss works.

Britain's largest merchant liner, *Britannic* (originally listed as *"Gigantic"* until the *Titanic* made such names unpopular) was still in Belfast at Harland and Wolff's great ship spawning yards.

However, other liners already had their papers, were being mobilized and hurried off to the colors. The *Carmania*, for one, impressed the Royal Navy as an ideal auxiliary. Not too large, and at eighteen knots fast enough, she was converted in one week, with her main battery consisting of 4.7-inch naval rifles, supported by machine gun nests. Armored plates were riveted against exposed areas, reinforced with bags of coal and sand. Captain Noel Grant, R.N., commanding, she sailed August 14 for Atlantic patrol.

During the same period the brand new Hamburg-South American Liner *Cap Trafalgar*, about the same tonnage as *Carmania* but two knots faster, had rendezvoused off the Brazilian coast with the gunboat *Eber* and a supply ship, to hurry aboard 4.1-inch cannon, machine guns, and other war, fuel, and food supplies. One of her three funnels was removed, the remaining two painted in Union Castle Line colors.

Meanwhile, *Kaiser Wilhelm der Grosse*, painted gray, already fitted out as an auxiliary cruiser, had enjoyed some success operating in waters between her home base and the Spanish coast. She sank a trawler and captured four other vessels, none large. Two were allowed to proceed since they were neutral and their passenger lists included women and children. The chivalrous behavior of her captain was reminiscent of Semmes and the *Alabama*.

Then, on August 26, after an unequal battle with the British cruiser *Highflyer*, she was sunk off Rio d'Oro, Spain. She was gone, pride of the North German Lloyd, plush carpeted saloons, shiny brass bathrooms, private dining saloons, nursery and all—early blood drawn in the war at sea.

On September 3, *Cap Trafalgar*, under Commodore Julius Wirth of the Imperial Navy, put to sea off Brazil. She was a fully registered privateer. *Carmania* was in the same sub-equatorial waters, seeking to join Sir Christopher Cradock's creaking old squadron on patrol to sever the Kaiser's lifeline to South American bauxite, phosphates, and other essential ores and minerals.

Off rocky, mountainous Trinidade Island, 500 miles east of Espirito Santo, Brazil, *Cap Trafalgar* was coaling on September 14 when surprised by *Carmania*. Driving south for Cradock's squadron, Captain Grant was merely making a landfall. Coming upon his enemy was "a fortunate accident."

A fight was inevitable even though the faster *Cap Trafalgar* at first attempted to make for the open sea. But Grant outmaneuvered Julius Wirth, forcing action. At about a mile range the two heavy liners began slugging at one another. They continued to do so for an hour.

Carmania's guns were slightly heavier, the construction of the ship somewhat sturdier. Yet the carnage to each combatant was devastating. Soon, according to a young lieutenant on the former North German Lloyd liner, Otto W. Steffan, "Enemy shells and shrapnel tore to bits the flowers in our elegant Wintergarten. Marble was torn from the walls. Rubble was heaped on rubble. . . . water gushed over the deck, steam billowed up in clouds from the broken pipes."

The *Carmania* herself, by the appraisal of one seaman, was "a medley of destruction." Both blazed furiously, with all central gunnery control knocked out. Fire lines were ruptured, leaving bucket brigades the only alternatives. Bathtubs were filled as handy reservoirs until even their pipes went dry. Flames on both the *Carmania* and *Cap Trafalgar* leapt higher than the erstwhile luxury liners' funnels.

For the German, however, help appeared to be near. Thierfelder's *Kronprinz Wilhelm,* having picked up *Cap Trafalgar's* distress calls, was steaming under forced draft, less than an hour away. His counterpart had radioed Wirth, "Hold out, I am coming!"

But *Cap Trafalgar* couldn't wait even a few more minutes. Two explosions shook her, she lay over on her beam ends until her funnels were parallel with the water, and then as abruptly righted.

Her bow dipped under, her stern up, and she took the final plunge, as the waters of the South Atlantic extinguished with billowing clouds of steam the erupting volcano that once had been a handsome steamship.

She had lost twenty dead including her captain, while nine perished on *Carmania*. The casualties were remarkably light on both sides considering the furious tempo of the longest "single" naval engagement of the war and the only one involving two auxiliary cruisers.

Kronprinz Wilhelm's mast tips actually had been sighted on the horizon by Captain Grant of the *Carmania*. Thierfelder, who could easily have finished off the staggering, flaming British liner, turned away, perhaps thinking it a trap, not knowing the strength of the Royal Navy in these lonely waters. One factor was real and omnipresent—there were many more rats still to be hunted down and exterminated.

With all navigation aids destroyed, Captain Grant extinguished fires, trimmed his battered ship (she had been hit more than 300 times) and succeeded ultimately in limping into Pernambuco for temporary repairs. *Carmania* was fortunate in being unable to join Cradock's squadron. The admiral, along with his two old cruisers, *Good Hope* and *Monmouth*, and all aboard (1,600 men) were lost on November 1 off Coronel, Chile, when surprised by Count Maximilian von Spee's Far East Squadron.

The blow had been almost too devastating for Britain to bear. It came short weeks after the loss in one night of three other old cruisers, the *Aboukir, Cressy,* and *Hogue*, on North Sea patrol, destroyed by a single U-boat. More than 1,400 Britons, mostly "weekend sailors," Royal Navy Reserves and Fleet Reserves, had drowned within sight of the Dutch coast and the Maas lightship. That one small submarine could exact such shocking toll boggled the battleship minds of the Admiralty.

Four days before the annihilation of Cradock's ships the battleship H.M.S. *Audacious* struck a mine in Irish waters and soon sank. Her crew was rescued by the mighty *Olympic*, serving as a troop transport, even as the old naval hands plucked from the waters worried irrationally that her lofty silhouette might attract a submarine.

On December 8, Cradock was avenged. First Lord of the

Admiralty Winston Churchill had helped assemble an overwhelming squadron led by the 17,000-ton battle cruisers *Invincible* and *Flexible*, then sent it at flank speed to the east coast of South America. Vice Admiral Charles Sturdee, in command, met the Germans off the Falkland Islands, where, in a blazing engagement of some nine hours, Von Spee and almost his entire squadron were destroyed —four ships, 2,300 men. Only one destroyer, the *Dresden*, escaped.

The losses were wildly disproportionate. The British suffered but ten killed, fifteen wounded.

The gods of sea warfare, however, remained fickle. On New Year's night, in brilliant moonlight over the North Sea, the battleship H.M.S. *Formidable* belied her name as she succumbed to two torpedoes. Only one-fourth of her crew of 800 was saved. Even they would have been lost had it not been for the presence in the area of a trawler which happened to be dragging her nets.

Three weeks later, off Dogger Bank, English east coast fishing grounds, the battleship *Blucher* was sunk by units of the Home Fleet. A spectacular photo of the crew scrambling like ants over the upending keel was printed widely in Great Britain and subsequently throughout the world. The photo had the undesirable effect of imbuing His Majesty's subjects with overconfidence in the Royal Navy.

February and March marked the beginning of the debacle of the Dardanelles—an effort to relieve the sagging Russian lines by opening up the southern, or Turkish, front. Among the mounting Allied losses were those of the battleships *Majestic* and *Triumph* (victims of one submarine, the *U-21*) and the French cruiser *Provence*, which carried 930 men with her to the bottom of the Mediterranean.

The outrageously costly effort to force the historic straits was Britain's first reverse of magnitude. She could point with pride to the fighting qualities of her Expeditionary Force on the western front where, after battles such as Mons, the Kaiser's onslaught had at least been blunted and, at Ypres, stemmed. Even London trams had been ferried across the Channel to hurry troops against Germany's initial stab at Paris, halted only at the Marne.

In March came the death of the first American citizen in the war at sea, Leon Thrasher, 31, lost with 103 others aboard the torpedoed British steamer *Falaba*.

The war in Europe produced mixed reverberations in the United States. Sentiments were pro and con the Allies or the Central Powers. England was not alone Americans' "mother country." Many Americans were of German or Middle European ancestry. It wasn't easy to be "neutral in thought as well as in act," as Wilson had counseled. There was also the confusing but welling tide for "preparedness," compounded by yet another factor, the good business and good times generated by burgeoning war orders to American manufacturers from Great Britain and France.

Another echo was as understandable as it was inevitable; the emotional and nostalgic tug at the hearts of a number of those newly emigrated to the United States. One such was 52-year-old Elizabeth Duckworth, of Taftville, Connecticut, who found the urge to return to the mills of Blackburn, in Lancashire, irresistible.

On Friday, the last day of April, 1915, straw suitcase and brown paper bag (containing a ham sandwich) in hand, she said goodbye to her daughter, son-in-law, and grandchildren and stepped onto the electric inter-city trolley for New London. There she would take the train (after paying a fare of $3.04) to New York, where she would take passage on RMS *Lusitania*, sailing the next morning for Liverpool.

Nearly 2,000 others were also preparing to embark on the great ship, advertised by Cunard as the "Fastest and Largest Steamer now in Atlantic Service." They encompassed a whole spectrum of age, affluence, and fame, and each had his or her own purpose for venturing onto imperiled seas in wartime. In fact, this very Saturday morning, May 1, New York newspapers carried a notice inserted by the German Embassy in Washington, underscoring the peril:

Travelers intending to embark on the Atlantic voyage are reminded that a state of war exists between Germany and her allies and Great Britain and her allies; that the zone of war includes the waters adjacent to the British Isles; that, in accordance with formal notice given by the Imperial German Government, vessels flying the flag of Great Britain or of any of her allies, are liable to destruction in those waters and that travellers sailing in the war zone on ships of Great Britain or her allies do so at their own risk.

The stark message drew reporters and newsreel cameramen to Pier 54 in the Hudson to elicit comments from the great and less-than-great. They interviewed Alfred Gwynne Vanderbilt, for one, worth perhaps one hundred million dollars, en route to inspect his London stables. The handsome 38-year-old international playboy scoffed, "Why should we be afraid of German submarines? We can outdistance any submarine afloat."

He happened to be standing beside the liner's captain, 60-year-old William Thomas Turner, a Commodore Captain and Number Two skipper in the whole Cunard fleet. His firm hand had guided and bridled the mighty *Aquitania* on her maiden voyage. Turner, a squat, bulldog sort of figure, veteran of the days of sail, rested a hand on Vanderbilt's shoulder as he added, "Do you think all these people would be booking passage on board the *Lusitania* if they thought she could be caught by a German submarine? Why, it's the best joke I've heard in many days, this talk of torpedoing."

While he alluded to her top speed of 27 knots, the master knew better, since six of her 25 boilers had been shut down the previous November when she resumed regular transatlantic service. This was necessary to conserve coal and also manpower, since Britain wanted her own, first, in the trenches. *Lusitania* now could make but 21 knots at the very best—still about half again the speed of a surfaced U-boat.

Not all, however, were as flippant over the German Embassy's "joke" or about mysterious telegrams signed "Morte" received by Vanderbilt and other notables, urging the recipients to "cancel passage immediately!" Mrs. James H. Brooks, 41, of Bridgeport, Connecticut, wife of a chain company representative, en route to London to try to sell some of his wares, speculated in conversation to a friend, "Is Jay [as she called her husband] crazy?"

If he was, so were lots of others, also England-bound on RMS *Lusitania*—people like Charles Frohman, the Broadway producer and mentor to such stars as Ethel Barrymore, Ellen Terry, Maude Adams, Otis Skinner, John Drew, and William Gillette; or Elbert Hubbard, the "sage of East Aurora (New York)," also known as "Fra Elbertus," author of many "Little Journeys" to the famous and of the "Message to Garcia," founder of a cult or commune in East

Aurora known as The Roycrofters, a professional eccentric with his
floppy slouch hat, oversized bow tie and long hair. Laughing with
reporters about a little essay, "Who Lifted the Lid off Hell?" which
said uncomplimentary things about Kaiser Wilhelm II, the "Fra"
wondered aloud if the latter would try to get even with him before
he progressed as far as Berlin, which was his ultimate objective.

His wife, Alice, the second Mrs. Hubbard, did not think he was
very funny.

There were well-to-do but less known personages, too, including
Charles A. Plamondon, of Chicago, president of a machinery
manufacturing company, and Mrs. Plamondon; Allen D. Loney, a
New York socialite now driving for the Red Cross who had returned
to bring his wife and fourteen-year-old daughter, Virginia Bruce
Loney, back with him; George A. Kessler, New York wine merchant, burdened with stocks and securities; Paul Crompton, a
director of Booth Steamship Co. Ltd., with his family, recently of
Philadelphia, which included four sons and two daughters as well as
Mrs. Crompton; Theodate Pope, of Farmington, Connecticut, archi-
tect, Progressive party leader, psychical researcher, who would be
the guest in England of Sir Oliver Lodge, the spiritualist; D. A.
Thomas, Liberal Member of Parliament, champion of 50,000 Welsh
coal miners, and Lady Mackworth, his young daughter, a suffra-
gette, who had already done time for her militant beliefs; Albert L.
Hopkins, president of the Newport News Shipbuilding and Drydock
Company; Oliver P. Bernard, scenic director of the Boston Opera
House and Covent Garden, London; two playwrights, Charles Klein,
author of *The Lion and the Mouse,* and the less known Justus
Forman; English cotton merchants Robert J. Timmins and Ralph
Moodie, who made their headquarters in Texas; Marie de Page, wife
of Dr. Antoine de Page, who had been seeking contributions for her
husband's hospital at La Panne, Belgium (the busy doctor also ran a
nursing school in Brussels directed by the Englishwoman, Edith
Cavell); Charles Lauriat, proprietor of a popular Boston book store;
a number of men of the cloth, including the widely- read Roman
Catholic Chaplain of Oxford University, Father Basil Maturin, and a
Scotch-born Episcopal minister from Calgary, Alberta, the Rev. H.
L. Gwyer, and his bride of three weeks; and a moderate number of
Canadians and Australians en route to join the war effort in one
capacity or another.

The cargo was as mixed as the passenger list: 111,762 pounds of copper, 217,157 pounds of cheese, 43,614 pounds of lard, 17 packages of dental goods; 205 barrels of Connecticut oysters, among many other items in modest quantity including 4,200 cases of small-caliber rifle ammunition and approximately 100 cases of empty shrapnel shells. The total value was manifested with the Collector of the Port of New York as $750,000.

"Lusy" had relatively little cargo space. After all, she had not been designed as a freighter. Impossible to confirm was the persistent rumor that six million dollars in gold bullion was also aboard.

The *Lusitania's* 10 A.M. sailing was delayed two and a half hours, in part because of a more or less routine wartime search of the ship and luggage for bombs or incendiary devices, and also because passengers from the *Cameronia* had been transferred at the last minute. The Royal Navy had decided only this morning to exercise its prerogative to call *Cameronia* to the colors and operate her at least this voyage as an auxiliary.

At 12:30, aided by three tugs, *Lusitania* backed from her pier. Newsreel cameras were cranked. On the boat deck a small group known as the Royal Welsh Male Singers sang "The Star-Spangled Banner." Elbert Hubbard, the friendly extrovert, waved his hat to those on the pier. Even gruff Captain Turner grimaced at the lenses.

As she passed the Battery, a mist and drizzle which had dampened the morning hours gave way, suddenly, to sunlight which glinted off the gold lettering on the great liner's bows. Saturday afternoon strollers in Battery Park took off their caps and waved at the towering liner. Along with the Woolworth Building and the *Vaterland,* still a prisoner by choice in Hoboken, the great Cunarder was one of the most impressive spectacles along the New York skyline.

In moments, she had passed the Statue of Liberty, then the Narrows, between Staten Island and Brooklyn. Soon there was little to remind the watchers on shore that a superliner had sailed away, other than a faintly shimmering wake and a nostalgic hint in the air of coal smoke.

That same afternoon, on the other side of the Atlantic, off the Scilly Islands, the U.S. tanker *Gulflight* was torpedoed by the German submarine *U-30,* with the loss of three American lives including that of her captain, who died of a heart attack. Although towed to port, she became the first United States ship to be violated in Germany's proscribed zone.

There were at this time about half a dozen U-boats in waters surrounding the British Isles. Although the Kaiser's underwater fleet was fast building up—about 30 launched since the beginning of the war, augmenting the 28 in commission—not many more than fifteen could be kept at sea at any one time. Obviously, the maximum concentration was astride the lifeline to the United Kingdom. Without continual importation of food and supplies, the English must soon be depleted and compelled to sue for peace.

Just two days out of Emden, making her first landfall—lonely Fair Island, between the Shetlands and the Orkneys—was *U-20,* en route to relieve *U-24* and *U-32.* Youthful *Kapitanleutnant* Walther Schwieger, blue eyed, rather baby faced, starting on his first cruise aboard this particular *Unterseeboote,* had received the sort of orders that were issued to other submarines making sorties at this time:

"Large English troop transports expected starting from Liverpool, Bristol (south of Liverpool), Dartmouth . . . get to stations on the fastest possible route around Scotland; hold them as long as supplies permit . . . submarines are to attack transport ships, merchant ships, warships . . . ."

Verbal orders, too, there must have been, but by their nature they would not become a matter of record. Schwieger, however, would log the presence of one Helmsman Lanz, a "pilot," not a regular member of the crew, who "knows all English ships by their build and can also tell at once at what speed they generally run."

Just 650 tons, *U-20,* like other U-boats, had horrible living conditions. *Kameradschaft,* however, compensated for the almost total absence of civilized comfort. The 35 crewmen, along with pet dogs and cats, slept by their torpedoes, which they named affectionately, "Bertha," "Shining Emma," "Yellow Mary," and the like. Each cylindrical messenger of sudden doom carried 290 pounds of a new explosive, trotyl, and possessed a range of nearly four miles. Accuracy was another matter. Too often, the torpedoes circled back toward the U-boat which had launched them.

Below decks the men played tinny recordings on their little wind-up gramophones, for example, "The Rose of Stamboul" or *"Die*

Lorelei." If someone could pump the accordion, so much the better. When the submersible might surface safely—and it had to for charging batteries as well as replenishing foul air—the sailors were able to smoke cigars, which by then tasted like nectar.

Hunting was good in late April and early May. In addition to *Gulflight,* several trawlers and small freighters and colliers of varying nationalities had been bagged between the east coast of Scotland and the Scillies by the U-boats which had preceded Schwieger.

On Wednesday, May 5, Schwieger arrived on station off the Old Head of Kinsale, a prominent Irish landfall about fifteen miles west of Cobh, or Queenstown. There he overhauled and sank the schooner *Earl of Latham,* carrying a cargo of Irish bacon, eggs, and potatoes for Liverpool, 270 miles to the northeast, in the Irish Sea. The crew barely had time to take to boats.

The same evening he fired a torpedo at what he identified as a 3,000-ton Norwegian steamer. The torpedo missed, and Schwieger dived when it appeared that his intended quarry was about to ram the *U-20.*

By Wednesday the *Lusitania* was nearing Ireland, less than 48 hours west of Cape Clear and the Fastnet Rock, on the southwest tip. The crossing had been calm and uneventful, in fact so much so that Dorothy Conner, a young Red Cross volunteer from Medford, Oregon, had complained, "It's been such a dull, dreary, stupid trip. . . ."

Dorothy was accompanied by her brother-in-law, Dr. Howard Fisher, of Washington, D.C., who hoped to set up a hospital somewhere in France.

For Captain Bill Turner, dullness was welcome. To his direct way of thinking it presupposed freedom from danger. Also, despite the fact that his command still could fly the blue ensign of the Royal Navy auxiliary fleet and thus was fair game, Turner remained convinced that the enemy would not attack such a large liner, especially since it carried many women and children as well as men above fighting age.

Turner, who had filled in for *Lusitania's* regular master, the ailing Daniel "Paddy" Dow, had failed to show much concern over memoranda issued before he left Liverpool. For example, one "Confidential Daily Voyage Notice" read:

"German submarines appear to be operating chiefly off prominent headlands and landfalls. Ships should give prominent headlands a wide berth."

A companion advisory urged, although it did not order, zigzagging "in an area known to be infested by submarines." Turner received no other war instructions until Thursday, May 6, at 8:50 P.M., when Marconi Operator Stewart Hutchinson copied from the British Admiralty: "Submarines active off south coast of Ireland."

The captain, puzzled by the terseness, asked for a repeat. It tapped back identically. However, half an hour later the Admiralty transmitted from its high, powerful towers on Valentia Island on the southwest coast of Ireland:

"To all British ships 0005 (Greenwich):

"Take Liverpool pilot at bar and avoid headlands. Pass harbors at full speed. Steer mid-channel course. Submarines off Fastnet."

Lusitania herself was only about 12 hours due west of Fastnet Rock. Turner ordered lifeboats swung out, the principal watertight bulkheads closed, lookouts doubled, and a check made to ascertain that all portholes were tightly closed and blacked out.

On board there was the traditional ship's concert, final social event of the voyage, with parties preceding it in the cabins of such as Hubbard, Vanderbilt, and Frohman. Charles Plamondon, a meticulous diarist, would record:

"Thursday, May 6, *Lusitania,* 488 miles. Pleasant weather, sunshine all day. Evening concert for sailors' and seamen's homes."

One by one the passengers returned to their cabins and to bed. None was unusually concerned for his or her safety. The very magnitude of the liner inspired confidence.

Lusitania steamed through the night at 21 knots, her top speed with the six boilers "locked up." Aside from the short wireless warning, repeated with monotonous regularity, the night passed uneventfully. The doubled-up lookouts had only the empty sea, the ship, and themselves to look at.

For Schwieger Thursday had been a good day. He had sunk two 6,000-ton Harrison Liners, the *Candidate* and the *Centurion,* torpedoed without warning off Waterford, on the south coast of Ireland, east of Queenstown and near the entrance to St. Georges Channel and the Irish Sea. All aboard both steamers safely made the lifeboats.

The *Kapitanleutnant,* however, who had now expended all but three torpedoes and two-fifths of *U-20's* fuel oil, decided against continuing to Liverpool, "the real field of operations." Instead he would patrol the mouth of the Bristol Channel, to the south of his original area. He spent the night largely drifting on the surface, resting and waiting.

Friday morning, May 7, passengers on the Cunarder were awakened by the deep blast of her fog horn. After dawn the liner had run into intermittent banks of fog 75 miles off Cape Clear and the Fastnet. Turner ordered speed reduced to eighteen knots, not only because of the fog but also because he wished to steam the final miles through the Irish Sea in the dark and arrive at Liverpool Bar at 4 A.M. Saturday at high tide.

By 8 A.M. the fog was so thick that the captain slowed his command down to fifteen knots.

To the east, Schwieger too was in "the soup." He logged, "since the fog does not abate, I now resolve upon the return journey, in order to push out into the North Channel (between Scotland and Ireland) in case of good weather."

However, Schwieger did not do what he had asserted he would do. He turned west and started cruising at approximately *U-20's* maximum twelve knots towards Queenstown. He did not confide in his log. Why?

In mid-morning Turner estimated he had passed Fastnet Rock, lost off the port beam in swirling, opaque mists. Finally, a few minutes after 11 A.M., the fog dispersed, leaving a warm, clear day and flat seas, with a hint of a ground swell lazing in from the Irish coast. Turner ordered speed upped three knots to eighteen, as lookouts strained their eyes for the first landfall. All they saw were the expected dirty gray seagulls, joining the liner as if in escort. At 11:25 A.M., another message arrived from the Admiralty:

"Submarine active in southern part of Irish Channel, last heard of twenty miles south of Coningbeg Light Vessel. Make certain *Lusitania* gets this."

Before noon a hazy hint of land materialized off the liner's port beam. Captain Turner figured it must be Brow Head, a medium-high promontory fifteen miles northwest of Fastnet Rock, almost on the western coast of Ireland. Yet this was confusing, since *Lusitania* should already have passed Fastnet and be well on her way toward

Queenstown. While trying to resolve this question of position and bearing, he asked his officers to check on the boilers for emergency steam pressure and to be sure the portholes were tightly dogged down.

The passengers, one by one, commenced lunch in their various dining areas. The sun, always welcome after a dark night and foggy morning, glinted off the bright colors of the murals of the Muses in the dome of the first class saloon. In third class there was plain food from common, pub-like tables—and no Muses.

At 12:40 A.M., Turner was handed another radiogram:

"Submarine five miles south off Cape Clear, proceeding west when sighted at 10 A.M."

At 1 P.M. a good landfall, Galley Head, was logged. Yet, this promontory was 60 miles to the east of Brow Head. Surely, *Lusitania* could not have covered 60 miles from Brow Head in approximately one hour, not even in two hours at reduced boiler capability. The earlier landfall, then, could *not* have been Brow Head.

In any event, since Turner was looking at Galley Head, he felt secure in that the submarine off Cape Clear must now be well astern of the *Lusitania*. He puffed on his pipe as he determined to bring his mighty command yet closer to shore where he could obtain an unmistakable identification of landmarks along the green Irish coast. Then he'd know where he was for sure.

Those passengers still on deck and not eating watched the white, foaming wake curve to the left, or north, as the master set course on 67 degrees, toward Ireland.

At about the same time Schwieger had surfaced his *U-20* off the 256-foot-high Old Head of Kinsale and was studying it through binoculars. Jutting three miles seaward, just west of the Bandon River, the Old Head was a distinctive and perfect landmark for a bearing. Houses could be seen here and there on the bluff, also fishing shacks along the shore. What Schwieger couldn't see, however, even through his powerful binoculars, were the school children gathered around the base of Kinsale Light. They, along with the light keeper and coast guardsmen, had seen the *Earl of Latham* sink on Wednesday.

What might happen today?

Certainly no patrol was in evidence, even though there was a decrepit makeshift Irish Coast Patrol responsible for War Area XXI, extending from the west coast of Ireland up to St. George's Channel and into the Irish Sea. In addition to some old cruisers and destroyers, the flotilla consisted of four armed yachts and sixteen armed trawlers, commanded by Rear Admiral H.L.A. Hood. The command itself was in the nature of a reprimand, since Hood was considered to have done a "not wholly effective" job in organizing the Dover Patrol. On the other hand, the Admiralty could not spare any first class units from the east coast or the great anchorage at Scapa Flow. Germany's High Seas Fleet was much in being a few short miles across the North Sea, and, indeed, powerful units periodically were unleashed to raid East Anglia.

By 1:30 P.M. passengers on the *Lusitania* could discern the outlines of trees, rooftops, and church steeples along the lush shores. The spectacle sweeping past was at once friendly and reassuring. Ten minutes later Turner picked up a familiar landmark: the Old Head of Kinsale.

Now, he knew *where* he was, but not precisely, within yards, how far the liner was steaming offshore. This would have some bearing on his arrival off Liverpool Bar. If he speeded up, he would arrive there too soon and have to heave to until the tide crested. If he slowed down or zigzagged, he'd miss the tide; and, anyhow, it was Turner's impression that the zigzag procedure applied only *after* a U-boat was sighted. He was, however, in error, since he had on his desk a memorandum suggesting such a procedure "in an area known to be infested by submarines."

What the veteran Cunard master did resolve upon was a four-point bearing on Kinsale, meaning that the *Lusitania* would have to be held for some 40 minutes at a fixed speed (eighteen knots) on an undeviating course (which was now 87 degrees east) within easy view of the coast and, in turn, by all other eyes ashore or on the ocean. Again, Turner was mistaken, if not acting directly in violation of Admiralty orders: "Ships should give prominent headlands a wide berth."

At 1:50 P.M. Junior Third Officer Albert A. Bestic commenced his four-point bearing. Below, late as well as hearty eaters lingered in the saloons. In first class, the orchestra was whining through "The

Blue Danube" waltz. There, Timmins and Moodie, the cotton brokers, were laughing at an incident of the morning—a frightened Greek passenger, lifejacket strapped securely about him, had entered one of the lifeboats and, still, adamantly was refusing to leave.

Timmins thought it was the funniest sight he had ever seen. A big man, the cotton merchant laughed until the sweat ran from his jowls. Finally, he called a steward to order a second dish of ice cream.

"We've got time," he observed to Moodie, leaning back and wiping the perspiration off with his napkin.

In second class, the Rev. Gwyer and his bride were also laughing—at a table companion, Lorna Pavey, of Saskatchewan, a Red Cross nurse-to-be, who was eating a grapefruit. Since this item was something less than the national fruit of Canada, her choice of dessert struck the minister as quite droll.

On deck, passengers such as Theodate Pope, the architect/spiritualist, Oliver Bernard, and James Brooks were taking brisk laps, working off their lunches. The water, it appeared to Theodate, was a "marvelous blue."

During this time, approximately between 2 P.M. and 2:09 P.M. *Kapitanleutnant* Schwieger had sighted the "four funnels and two masts of a steamer . . . ship is made out to be a large passenger steamer."

He ordered *U-20* into a crash dive, down to some 30 feet, easy periscope depth, and kept watch on the "steamer." Submarine and liner converged rapidly. Since *Lusitania* was on a steady four-point bearing, Schwieger hardly had to turn his 'scope a millimeter to right or left.

What was this "steamer?" German intelligence surely knew that the Allies counted only six four-stackers. *Mauretania,* it could be no secret, was transporting troops and wounded at the Dardanelles. *Aquitania* was on the same run, which, inbound to or outbound from England would keep the pair toward the Bay of Biscay and far from Irish coastal waters. *Olympic* lay in the Mersey being fitted for this same hot, wasting duty. *Britannic* remained at her Belfast yards. The *France,* flying the Tricolor, was not in service at this time.

This "steamer" was obviously inbound from the western Atlantic, either the United States or Canada. With Helmsman Lanz aboard, who "knows all English ships by their build," there seemed no reasonable doubt that Schwieger quickly recognized the identity of the "large passenger steamer" materializing in his sights to giant proportions. She could be none other at this time and place.

Finally, at approximately 2:09 P.M., at a range of less than half a mile, Schwieger gave the order. "Fire!"

One torpedo arrowed away from *U-20*.

Part II

"They did not want to kill anybody."

ON THE FORECASTLE WATCH, Seaman Leslie Morton, eighteen, looked, looked again, then sang out through a megaphone to the bridge, "Torpedoes coming on the starboard side!"

Jay Brooks, standing on the Marconi deck, the loftiest eminence of the towering liner, saw the wake at the same time, 100 feet off the starboard side of the ship. He grasped the rail and shouted, "Torpedo!"

He leaned over until the sizzling white streak of water disappeared inside the hull far below him. He waited, one foot off the deck, like a ballet dancer.

Captain Turner started for the starboard bridge wing. He never got there. He was halfway when an explosion rocked the *Lusitania.* Brooks watched a geyser of steam, water, coal, smoke and other debris gush through the large air ventilator nearest the starboard side of the bridge. The water knocked him onto the deck. The steam choked him. The noise, like that of an avalanche, deafened him.

At the first jolt, Marconi Operator Robert Leith, finishing lunch in the first class saloon, raced up stairs and ladders to his post and was tapping out, in seconds:

"Come at once. Big list . . . 10 miles south Old Head Kinsale."

He didn't know really how far the ship was from Kinsale. The definitive four-point bearing had only begun. He was guessing.

There existed, however, no doubt in anyone's mind that the liner had been torpedoed. Only their reactions and impressions differed. On the promenade deck, Charles Lauriat, the Boston book merchant, perceived the impact as a "heavy, rather muffled sound." Nearby were the Elbert Hubbards, whom he urged to hurry to their cabins for lifejackets. But the sage of East Aurora merely stood there, "affectionately" holding his wife, Alice, by the waist.

Lady Mackworth, the suffragette, had lost no time in fetching her belt, although she couldn't locate her father, D. A. Thomas, champion of the Welsh coal miners. She made her way through crowded passageways and staircases to the boat deck. Already aware of a marked list, she walked uphill to the port, or "high," side,

where she encountered Dorothy Conner and Dr. Fisher standing
rather calmly in the bright sunshine.

Lady Mackworth, recalling Dorothy's comment about the "dull"
voyage, observed wryly, "Well, I guess you've had your thrill."

The Rev. Gwyer, no longer laughing but still in the second class
dining saloon where people were screaming and tumbling off their
chairs, stood up to his great height and observed in the hearing of
most:

"Let us quieten the people!"

He urged the passengers to move without panic to the doors and
assured that "everything's going to be all right!" While he did not
really believe that himself, in a very few moments he had the diners
filing more or less quietly out "like a regiment of soldiers."

Timmins, who never received his second dish of ice cream, went
with Moodie to their cabin for lifejackets. When they made their
way to the starboard boat deck, they found George Kessler, the wine
merchant, smoking a cigar and helping women into the boats.
Kessler casually confided that he was doing this only "in a spirit of
convention" since he did not believe the *Lusitania* would sink.

The list was so bad that the port side was useless. The boats
simply lay against the metal plates of the liner. They banged against
the big protruding rivet heads. When deck hands attempted to
lower them on their falls (or, ropes), the same rivets tore gashes in
the bottoms.

As a matter of fact, there was doubt as to whether Captain Turner
ever passed an order to lower boats. A few, including Brooks, would
swear he ordered them *not* lowered. Certainly, ample opportunity
existed on the bridge for confusion.

Lusitania would not answer her helm, swinging to port in a slow,
wide arc. The engine room would respond to neither full ahead or
astern, inspiring the inevitable conclusion that the liner was without
power. Her major steam lines doubtlessly were ruptured.

Thus, Turner abandoned any hope of beaching his stricken
command. The list, only a few minutes after the liner was hit, had
increased to a dizzy 25 degrees, meaning that she was gulping in cold
seawater at a far faster rate than had the *Titanic.* Marconi Operator
Leith, hanging onto his transmitter table to maintain his balance,
sparked out:

"Send help quickly. Am listing badly."

The message was picked up by several ships, including the British tanker *Narragansett,* 35 miles southeast of the big Cunarder; the freighter *Etonian;* and the steamer *City of Exeter,* both of which flew the Union Jack and were near the *Narragansett.* All started for the *Lusitania's* position.

It was heard, as well, by various shore stations, including that on the Old Head of Kinsale itself, and relayed to Rear Admiral Sir Charles Coke, commanding the naval station at Queenstown. He started four small tugs readying for sea: the *Julia, Flying Fish, Warrior,* and *Stormcock.*

Admiral Hood, of the Irish Coast Patrol, ordered steam up on his old cruisers, the *Juno, Isis, Sutley,* and *Venus.* Word spread throughout the harbor and adjacent coast, sending to sea tenders, fishing boats, and other rescue craft not equipped with radio, the *Bluebell* and *Lady Elsie* among them.

None, however, knew exactly the position of the *Lusitania* or what would be its own individual fate in these troubled waters.

Schwieger, watching in disbelief through his periscope, could second the sense of urgency. He would log:

"She has the appearance of being about to capsize. Great confusion on board, boats being cleared and some of them lowered to the water. They must have lost their heads. Many boats crowded come down bow first or stern first in the water and immediately fill and sink. . . . in front appears the name *Lusitania* in gold letters."

Watchers on the Old Head of Kinsale had seen the liner approaching, then heard "a sort of heavy rumble like a distant foghorn." They could discern the steam and smoke shoot up and then the huge ship list and begin to settle.

If the passengers had not all "lost their heads," as it appeared to the U-boat commander, some were acting in a most peculiar manner. One man stripped the clothing off his wife down to her stockings and underwear, then tied a lifejacket snugly about her. He told her to wait while he assisted other men in loosening the straps around the collapsible boats—something which should have been done long before. They weren't much better than rafts, anyhow, possibly not even as efficient.

Others were not waiting for the boats or for the ship to sink. A fireman, begrimed and wild-eyed, climbed onto a rail, stood poised a second, then executed a dive which appeared worthy of a professional. A seaman discovered a cowering group of six men and women huddled in an improbable place—on the awning above the veranda cafe. When he tried to help them down, the awning's spars broke and the lot fell in a struggling heap onto the deck.

Several boats, as Schwieger observed, had dumped their occupants into the water because one set of falls had been lowered faster than the other set. Those who had clung to the vertical seats and gunwales struggled up the ropes or the netting which had been draped in some places over the sides.

Men such as Oliver Bernard were trying to find enough lifejackets for the women, making repeated trips below decks fighting the list and milling crowds. At one point he almost ran into Alfred Gwynne Vanderbilt. Bareheaded, dressed in a pin-stripe suit, he was holding what looked like a lady's large jewel case. He grinned at the scenic artist "as if amused by the excitement."

Then a woman, spying Bernard with a lifejacket in hand, screamed, "where did you get it, where did you get it?" She snatched it and raced away, leaving him to hunt for yet another woman to assist.

By now, however, Oliver Bernard realized that there was an onrushing urgency. The *Lusitania* could not last much longer. He climbed to the Marconi deck, where he removed his coat, waistcoat, collar, and necktie. He folded them neatly and placed the little bundle at the base of one of the big, tilting funnels, thinking even as he did so that his act of habit was preposterous.

He sat down to untie his shoelaces in a strangely detached mood and seized by an "awful sadness." Most of his shipmates, however, were more determinedly trying to save their lives. Some, such as Elizabeth Duckworth, of Taftville, Connecticut, were already in boats. She had watched one improperly launched, spewing its occupants into the cold, churning waters. One occupant was a little boy who had been among her table companions.

Charles Lauriat, the Boston bookseller, stepped into a lifeboat to find it already afloat while hanging from its davits—the *Lusitania* was sinking that fast! Lauriat hacked at one of the rope falls with a pocket knife—too late. The boat swamped anyway, dumping out its 60 or 70 occupants. He shouted to them to put their hands on each other's shoulders to keep in a group. A strong swimmer, he stroked out until he was some 100 feet from the liner, then paused to watch a spectacle of frightened, desperate passengers and crew clawing ever higher to keep away from the ever-nearing waters, onto railings of successive decks, onto stanchions, davits . . .

Those such as Jay Brooks decided not to wait for a boat. After having assisted many ladies into the life craft, however, and watched some being thrown into the sea, he himself dived in, not bothering so much as to remove his shoes. To Jay, who had swum in the Androscoggin in Maine as a boy, the Atlantic felt "mild."

The sea and the foundering liner made up the minds of those such as Margaret Mackworth, Theodate Pope, and young Dorothy Fisher, who had debated what to do. It simply reached out for them and gathered them into its wet amplitude.

Yet others either did not appreciate the critical nature of the situation or contemplated death with magnificent indifference. Vanderbilt was one who totally ignored a steward's shouts to "hurry—or it will be too late!" He merely lit another cigarette. As a matter of fact, one skill in particular had never been mastered by this otherwise athletic young man—he could not swim a stroke.

Frohman, the producer, lit a fresh cigar after having casually removed his lifejacket and assisted a woman into it. A young actress, Rita Jolivet, would quote him as saying, "Why fear death? It is the most beautiful adventure in life."

She recognized the words from *Peter Pan,* by Frohman's friend and favorite author, James Barrie.

The Elbert Hubbards adamantly refused to be helped into a boat. Looking "very gray," according to a passenger who had vainly argued with them to save themselves, they stood there calmly, holding hands. Another who recognized the pair thought he saw them turn and head below decks as if returning to their cabin.

On the *U-20, Kapitanleutnant* Schwieger logged, "It seems as if the vessel will be afloat only a short time. Submerge to 24 meters and go to sea. I could not have fired a second torpedo into this throng of humanity attempting to save themselves."

She had in truth "only a short time." The stern raised high in the air as the bow struck bottom. Here the depth was relatively shallow, less than 300 feet, while *Lusy* was 790 feet long. Captain Turner, fully uniformed to his golden-visored cap, had remained on the bridge until swept from it. Now stroking for his life, he rolled over onto his back to observe the great ship, as she "quivered her whole length."

Within, furnishings, cargo, machinery, anything not firmly lashed or bolted down tore loose and went crashing towards the bow, as if a big hardware store had been somehow turned upside down. Then, with increasing ominous rumblings, the liner began to right herself and settle lower by the stern. For those who had been caught aft, it was like riding an elevator down again.

For a moment it appeared that miraculously, *Lusitania,* pride of the Cunard Line, had survived her crisis and was once more on even keel. But her death thrashings were not yet finished. Next she lay over on her starboard side, her masts, antennae, rigging, davits, ventilators, other protrusions striking and killing or maiming those struggling in the water. Some, such as Timmins, the cotton broker, were able to dive deeply and escape the new menace.

Somehow, he thought he was riding Niagara Falls into an abyss until the depths around him were "black as the inside of a cow" and his head felt like a "steel plate" from the increasing pressure. Methodically, he counted—one stroke, two strokes, three strokes, until he surfaced after thirty-one strokes. From this great number of strokes he estimated he must have been at least fifty feet below the surface.

At least two passengers, including Margaret Gwyer, had the bizarre experience of being sucked into one of the funnels and as quickly blown out again. Turner himself observed a friend, William H. Pierpont, of Liverpool, swallowed by one of the huge stacks, then belched forth with "a terrible hissing sound."

Pierpont was so scared, understandably, that he swam off as fast as "ten men," by the captain's measure.

George Kessler, the wine merchant, lucky to be in one of the few successfully launched boats, turned to see a foaming, flotsam-flecked vortex, then pronounce an obituary of the liner, "My God—the *Lusitania's* gone!"

In eighteen minutes, perhaps even less, the Cunarder had been utterly destroyed. Nothing remained but a clutter of boats, debris, and people. Those who had managed to survive did so in various and often unusual ways.

Theodate Pope, after fighting off a man who tried to perch on her shoulders, managed to grab and then straddle an oar. She was somewhat cheered by a group floating nearby chanting "Tipperary."

Lady Mackworth supplemented her lifejacket's buoyancy by clutching a thin piece of board. Soon she was joined by others grasping or atop a hencoop and chairs to form a "large, round floating land." Later her refuge became a wicker chair, creating the illusion in other observer's eyes that she was rocking in it across the waters.

Turner himself clutched a small chair, while from time to time beating off seagulls which dived on him.

As many as five men at various times struggled for finger room about the perimeters of a small keg.

Scores clung to the keels of overturned lifeboats or imperfectly assembled "collapsibles," which proved to be aptly enough named. The strong hung on; the weak and the elderly dropped off one by one and vanished.

Whether in lifeboats, clinging to bits of jetsam, or merely stroking for shore (as some preferred, refusing aid) the *Lusitania* survivors made slow progress toward the Irish coast. By late afternoon the tanker *Narragansett,* and steamers *Etonian* and *City of Exeter* had actually arrived near the scene, in fact were sighted by some of those who had been aboard the doomed liner. However, the *Narragansett* dodged a torpedo attack while the latter two ships sighted periscopes. The three decided they could not linger in such imperiled waters.

The first rescue vessels to reach the human backwash of the *Lusitania* were the naval auxiliary *Indian Prince* and the trawler *Peel 12.* Elizabeth Duckworth, who had proven a powerful rower and, in fact, had dragged aboard an exhausted swimmer, helped deliver the first load onto the *Peel 12.* When a lifeboat directly behind hers called for volunteers to row back in search of others still in the water she heard an officer reply, "I can't spare anyone."

Standing up in the boat and stepping onto a gunwale, she shouted, "You can spare me!"

And she leaped into the other boat, calling for an oar.

Many, not so fortunate to be in the relative security of a boat or to be sought after by those as determined as Elizabeth Duckworth, remained in the chill waters until dusk. Margaret Mackworth and

Theodate Pope were among this number. However, by nightfall, the living and the dead from the lost Cunarder were coming ashore. At Queenstown, U.S. Consul Wesley Frost wrote:

"We saw the ghastly procession . . . under the flaring gas torches along the Queenstown waterfront. The arrivals began soon after 8 o'clock and continued at close intervals until about 11 o'clock . . . bruised and shuddering women, crippled and half-clothed men and a few wide-eyed little children . . . women caught at our sleeves and begged desperately for word of their husbands, and men with choking efforts of matter-of-factness moved ceaselessly from group to group, seeking a lost daughter, or sister, or even bride. . . ."

Oliver Bernard, who had come ashore in the relative luxury of a lifeboat, had many of the same impressions as he roamed the charnel house which was, suddenly, Queenstown.

"Nude, semi-nude, innocents, trophies of war—babies so discolored that it was difficult to believe that these effigies had ever lived. Mothers, wives and daughters lay in a row all round the shed, in sodden garments, not believably human persons of the day before. . . . poor Charles Frohman alone was undisfigured; he must have died without protest before the sea could do its worst. . . . .

"The most appalling impression . . . was that in death all human beings were alike, shapeless, inanimate clay; death masks of those victims would have revealed no individualities, nothing but a horrible, lifeless uniformity. What happened to all those images and likenesses of God?"

The list of the dead read like something snatched through macabre and morbid impulse from an international Who's Who. In addition to Frohman, his two compatriots of the theater had joined him in eternity: Justus Miles Forman and Charley Klein. Lost, too, were Elbert and Alice Hubbard, Alfred Gwynne Vanderbilt, Marie De Page, Albert L. Hopkins shipbuilder and a giant among industrialists, the Charles Plamondons of Chicago.

The roster of the not so well known, including Father Basil Maturin, Allen D. Loney, and the entire Crompton family of eight, went on and on, part of the staggering total of 1,198 dead (including 785 passengers) out of the 1,959 who had sailed aboard *Lusitania* the Saturday before. The 1,198 represented but 300 less than had been lost on the *Titanic* three years earlier.

Of the 159 holding American passports, 124 were dead. There were many children in that number.

News of the disaster reached the United States quickly even allowing for the time difference. Consul Frost telegraphed Ambassador Walter Hines Page in London, whose cable reached the State Department at 3:30 P.M. the same Friday.

The stock market plummeted. Businesses up and down the east coast and as far west as Chicago closed early, whether or not they claimed any connection with any part of the passenger list. To Broadway, it was the torpedoing of Charles Frohman. Marquees would be dark that night. Philadelphia, which had lost all of the Cromptons, was stunned, and in East Aurora, the Roycrofters simply refused to acknowledge that Fra Elbertus was other than immortal. He could *not* be dead, he could *not*.

Reporters, knocking on the door of the German Embassy in Washington, were first met by a counselor, Prince Von Hatzfeldt Trachtenberg, who became the spokesman for Count Von Bernstorff, the ambassador.

"They did not," he asserted, "want to kill anybody."

But his ultimate in understatement did not satisfy the American people. Cartoonists mirrored the fast swelling outrage. The *New York Sun,* for example, depicted the Kaiser fastening a medal around the neck of a mad dog as a small flag labeled *"Lusitania"* disappeared beneath the sea. The *Philadelphia North American* caricatured this helmeted Hohenzollern as a roaring monster drowning a woman with his hands. In some cities German-American stores were pillaged. Resulting hysteria was vented even against such food as sausage and such pets as dachshunds.

Long after the last funerals were solemnized, diplomatic notes continued to crisscross the Atlantic between the United States and Germany. Berlin's justification pivoted around the contention that the Cunarder not only carried war materiel but was armed. Wilson would reiterate his dissatisfaction with official replies, which were something less than apologetic, or promises of preventing a recurrence.

The *New York Herald* would point out a year later that the Kaiser had not yet "atoned" in any manner. In addition, his machine continued acts of provocations by sinking American vessels with the resultant loss of further lives under the protection of that flag.

"Unrestricted submarine warfare" became Imperial Germany's policy.

The culmination came on Good Friday, April 2, 1917, when President Wilson stood before a hushed Senate chamber to ask that the existence of a state of war with Germany be declared. He expressed his personal belief that "America has found herself."

Whether she had or had not, the nation's road to war, which beyond dispute had commenced with the torpedoing of the *Lusitania,* had been muddy and would continue to be so. The debate on whether the *Lusitania* was a legitimate prize of war would not ever be entirely stilled.

Yet, whatever the great liner carried or did not carry was in itself irrelevant. Schwieger could not have known whether there was a regiment of troops on board or several orphanages chaperoned by scores of frocked, elderly nuns. Below decks there would have been trench mortars and heavy caliber ammunition or tons of bandages and food for the babies of Belgium. Schwieger *did* know, as did anyone else familiar with Brassey's, Jane's, and other marine registers that *Lusitania* was authorized to fly the Blue Ensign.

That made her a proper target for sinking, by the curious "rules" of sea warfare, even though the U-boat had failed, first, to give warning.

Manifestly bent on torpedoing anything that moved across the seas, Schwieger was guilty, above all, of consummate naiveté and of a total lack of understanding of human emotions and international public relations. Since the Cunarder was inbound from New York, he might have guessed that some Americans were aboard.

While a young naval commander in an infant, brash, and murderously effective weapon of war, Walther Schwieger was quite old enough to appreciate the neutrality of the United States and the advantages to the German Homeland of keeping that nation out of the war.

Skeptics would come to speak darkly of the *"Lusitania* plot," perhaps involving even British leaders themselves, desirous of a new ally. Such was manifestly nonsense, since England, in the spring of 1915, was not yet hurting and needed the United States only as an arsenal and, for the most part, as a friend.

A plot to sink the liner? No. Incomparable Teutonic stupidity, as demonstrated by one U-boat captain? Yes.

For a postscript on the *Lusitania,* the so-called mystery surrounding her, and attempts to probe the wreck, see Bibliography.

7

U.S.S. *Squalus*—The
Nineteenth Dive

"... the awfulness of the men's situation ..."

AT A COST OF 203 U-boats, Imperial Germany had, by Armistice Day, (November 11, 1918), destroyed slightly more than seven million dead-weight tons of enemy and neutral shipping. Even so, through replacements supplied largely by the United States, the Allies ended the European war—"The Great War"—with but three million tons of shipping capacity less than they had had in the summer of 1914.

Most of the behemoth liners survived that vast and terrible conflict, reprieved for another incarnation. Only three were gone: *Lusitania, Oceanic,* and *Britannic.* Long a jinx, *Oceanic* stranded off Scotland early in the war and was scrapped. The new *Britannic,* which had never entered passenger service, became by far the largest merchant loss of either combatant.

Operating ostensibly as a hospital ship in the Aegean Sea in November, 1916, *Britannic* struck a mine or was torpedoed. It was never firmly established which. Unlike the debacle of the *Lusitania,* only 21 lives of the some 2,100 aboard were lost. Unclarified was the status of the troops she carried: whether some or all were "invalids" as defined by the Geneva Convention.

(It was not until 1975 that the wreck of the 48,000-ton intended

129

replacement for the *Titanic* was located and photographed. She was 345 feet deep in the Aegean, lying on her side. Among the team that found her was Dr. Harold E. Edgerton of M.I.T. A pioneer in underwater photography and in the perfection of the strobe light, Edgerton also had taken part in finding the U.S.S. *Monitor* off Cape Hatteras two summers earlier.)

That so few of the superliners, truly "super targets," were sunk was in part tribute to the convoy system, in part a result of blind good fortune. Such giants as the *Leviathan* (the *Vaterland* before her seizure by the United States), *Aquitania, Olympic,* and *Mauretania* plowed through several seas and oceans as transports or carriers of the sick and wounded. *Olympic* rammed and sank a U-boat; the *Mauretania* proved far more nimble than her hapless sister as she eluded a torpedo sizzling hard abeam.

The *Bismarck* and *Imperator,* however, languished throughout the war in their snug harbor, Hamburg. As war reparations, the *Bismarck* became the *Majestic,* of White Star, and the *Imperator* the *Berengaria,* of Cunard.

Leviathan, named by Wilson and meaning literally "sea monster," was the greatest transport of them all, with a capacity to carry an entire division, upwards of 12,000 troops, in addition to a wartime crew of 2,240. Sailing for the U. S. Lines after the war, she was reconverted to carry about 2,000 "paying guests."

All of these prewar ships, however, had outlived their days. Far too much fuel was required to propel their dead weight through the water. *Leviathan* was the worst, a financial nightmare to her owners even with continuing governmental subsidies.

Sleeker, faster, more efficient liners were sliding off the ways in Great Britain, France, and even in Germany, already rebuilding from her attrition of the war. During the presidency of the latter nation's war immortal, Field Marshal Paul von Hindenburg, two 50,000-ton modern liners were introduced to the North Atlantic: the *Bremen* and the *Europa.* Both claimed the Blue Riband, since either one could hit 28 knots almost effortlessly. *Europa* did so first in 1930.

The elapsed time, however, still did not beat *Mauretania* at her best. A basic quibble had remained unresolved for nearly a century: from what landfall to what landfall, and just *how many* nautical miles was the route traversed? Thus, the 51,000-ton Italian pride,

Rex, streamed a long, prefabricated Blue Riband when she raised Genoa in 1933, four days, thirteen hours, and 58 minutes out of New York. No doubt she was at least as fast as the *Bremen* or *Europa,* but comparing the route to the Mediterranean from Ambrose Channel with the shorter to Bishop's Rock or another British Isles landfall was like comparing apples to eggs.

Then came *Normandie,* at 82,799 tons, 1,029 feet overall, the largest steamship ever conceived, the ultimate in elegance. Movie theater, chapel, hospital complete with X-ray machines and an operating amphitheater, a 100-foot long grand saloon plush and silent with Aubusson carpeting, Algerian onyx paneling and a series of glasswork depicting the mythology of the sea, bronze doors—all contributed to the French Line's boast: "the finest ship ever launched." And on her maiden voyage in 1935, she proved herself the fastest: four days, three hours, and two minutes, Bishop's Rock to Ambrose, averaging 29.98 knots.

Curiously, the fatal, febrile years prior to 1914 were being repeated, not only in crumbling world rapport, but in the race for behemoths of the sealanes. In 1936, the *Queen Mary,* of Cunard (which had merged with White Star), ushered in the "three-day" crossing, three days, 23 hours, and 57 minutes from Ambrose to Bishop's Rock, averaging 31.65 knots. A single day's run was 737 nautical miles at 32.04 knots. Within 2,000 tons of the *Normandie*'s bulk, *Queen Mary* appeared to embody the last word in practically everything. Her motor-driven lifeboats, for example, were kept electrically warmed at all times. Each one of them could carry more people than the *Britannia,* nearly 100 years earlier. For those tired by walking upstairs, 21 elevators maintained communications between the many decks.

Then, early in 1938, occurred a drama in *sotto voce* that recalled memories to many a middle-aged American who had sailed off to war aboard the *Leviathan.* The old ship steamed under her own power to the ship breakers in Scotland. John W. Binks, former master of the *Olympic* and the *Majestic,* was recalled from a British snug harbor to command her skeleton crew. He would write of the journey:

"One day the steering gear went out of order. Through the man at the wheel keeping it over too long one way, the liquid ran out over the side so that she wouldn't steer, so we tried to turn her round the other way, but nothing doing—for over an hour she wanted to go back to New York. Then everything got all right, and back on our course we went. The same night the fog whistle started blowing for some reason every minute, although it was a clear night, and we searched round to find out what happened; but it stopped on its own, so we never really knew what was going to happen next.

"We had no observation all the way across, but picked up the Butt of Lewis Light all right, so were quite pleased after the steering we had. . . .

"We anchored Thursday, February 3, passage seven days, seventeen hours. Average speed 17.1 knots. Distance 3,164 miles from Ambrose Channel Light Vessel to Inverkeithing Island on the Firth of Forth.

"Next morning it was blowing a gale, and although all hands were still on board no work was done, as they were all packed up, waiting for their money; no steam in the main engines when the ship dragged her anchors, and we drifted nearly on the rocks of a small island named Haystack. A few British engineers ran below and got a little steam up so that we were able to weigh anchor and just managed to save the ship, and in time had enough to steam up to the anchorage again."

As a postscript, Captain Binks concluded she was "a hoodoo ship all right."

The next year, 1939, in the late spring, a sea drama of an entirely different type was enacted, this one off the New England coast. It involved the U.S. Navy's newest and best submarine, the four and a half million dollar U.S.S. *Squalus.* At 1,450 tons, 310 feet long (comparable to some of the freighters of the World War), she belonged to a class that was the most modern and possibly the deadliest in the world. This was no coincidence since naval architects ever since 1917 had been bending over their drawing boards to perfect this weapon of demonstrable and awesome destruction.

In so doing, the U.S. Navy had taken its losses. Among the worst was that of the *S-51,* sunk east of Block Island in September 1925 after colliding with the coastal steamer *City of Rome.* Only three of her crew were saved, and those because they happened to be in the conning tower. Thirty-four were lost. If any good were to emerge from the disaster, it was the expertise gained from raising the hulk the next spring—the knowledge of how to work at 132-foot depths with air hoses and pontoons.

In December 1927, the year Lindbergh flew the Atlantic, the nation was shocked anew by the loss of *S-4*, only a few miles from Provincetown, on the sandy tip of Cape Cod. The submarine had collided with an escort, the Coast Guard cutter *Paulding*. The agony was prolonged, hour after hour, day after day, while divers from the salvage tug *Falcon* "talked" with crew members trapped inside the *S-4* by hammering out Morse code against the cold, slippery hull. She was only 102 feet down, easy diving range.

A newlywed, Lieutenant (J.G.) Graham N. Fitch, of Washington, D.C., used a lug wrench to communicate from his dark, eerie prison. On the fourth day he tapped out, "Last oxygen gone. Is there any hope?"

There was not. When the *S-4* was hauled to the surface three months later, the bodies of all 40 of her crew were removed for final burial. In Graham Fitch's dead hand still was clutched the wrench that had evoked response, if not salvation. Friends of the craft's dead radioman recalled a poem recently scribbled by him:

> We all come back, come back for more
> And there friends is the rub,
> We like the life beneath the sea
> Life in a damned old tub!

This tragedy had assumed a personal aspect for Americans, from the Northwest to the Florida Keys. The heartbreaking messages from an underwater steel tomb had torn at the emotions of plain people like the final, gasping entreaties of a dying child. It was too much.

Inevitably there arose a welling outcry: "Do away with the submarines!" The *Philadelphia Inquirer* editorialized, for example:

"The Navy has lost something priceless in public confidence and esteem that will be difficult to regain."

Navy Secretary Curtis D. Wilbur was pilloried as an "incompetent." Indeed, could President Calvin Coolidge himself be held blameless, irrespective of whether the silent Vermonter was able so much as to differentiate a submarine from a canoe? Legislators on Capitol Hill, disarmament-minded anyhow, introduced bills to ban such craft and found unqualified endorsement in the person of the pacifist Secretary of State Frank B. Kellogg. The latter recommended ". . . that all nations of the world should unite in prohibiting the use of submarines and discontinuing construction thereof in every country."

Representative Louis A. Frothingham of Massachusetts echoed that "submarines, like poisoned gas, are a menace to non-combatants and to civilization."

Somehow submarines survived as an item of military hardware. The surprising sum of $175 million was provided for 35 additional such "boats." Their rehabilitation was obviously influenced in part by the decision of Great Britain, France, Italy, and Japan to keep on launching these underseas "raiders." In a few years, Nazi dictator Adolf Hitler, in defiance of the Treaty of Versailles, would be recreating for Germany a fleet of even more deadly U-boats.

Instead of banishing its submersibles, America began building even larger ones, in 1930 the 2,730-ton *Narwhal* and *Nautilus,* each mounting a powerful six-inch gun. At the same time, the navy had not turned a deaf ear to the criticisms. It wasn't enough to pump water out of a submarine on the bottom and haul her up with pontoons. This salvaged boats but not lives. Submarines must be made safer. If this were a goal not completely attainable, as it was not, then there must be more advanced provisions for rescuing trapped crewmen.

The first breakthrough was the invention of the Momsen lung, inspired in great measure by the loss of *S-4.* Its namesake, Lieutenant Commander Charles B. Momsen, a personal friend of Graham Fitch, the officer with the lug wrench, had asserted then in mingled grief and frustration: "God damn it, we've got to do something!"

Momsen, a dynamic if rather deadpan submarine commander, was the man to do it. "Swede," as all his friends knew him, entertained no illusions about submarines or diving. If anything went wrong under the water, which happened more often than not, he tended to blame it on the "ganomes," little creatures, as he explained it, which "come out of the bottom of the sea to tangle lines, disconnect hoses, steal the diver's tools and perpetrate all sorts of deviltry to foul up the poor diver's work."

By the same token he was convinced that it was none other than the ganomes which also put sand in submarine engines, punched holes in pipes, started little fires, and drank all the sulphuric acid out of the batteries so that the electric motors would grind to a halt. The ganomes were anathema in many diabolical exasperations.

However, determined to outwit the ganomes, Swede stuck to his sketching and experimenting until the "something" evolved into the "Momsen lung." It was a special oxygen-charged breather bag which would allow a man to reach the surface from depths of scores of feet. It was sort of a grandfather of skin-diving equipment, except that the Momsen lung was not fitted with oxygen flasks.

While Swede Momsen's device became standard in the Navy in the early 1930s, there remained two signal deficiencies. A person still could get "the bends," or nitrogen bubbles in the blood, from too rapid ascent, and he might literally freeze to death in 30- or 40-degree water on his way up.

The second development was the "McCann Rescue Chamber," named for Lieutenant Commander Allen R. "Mac" McCann, of Massachusetts, one of several who sculptured with considerable devotion a nine-ton diving bell. Designed exclusively for saving lives from submarines that wouldn't surface, the chamber accommodated upwards of a dozen persons, including a crew of two. Its air remained at surface pressure, replenishable through hoses to the mother ship, with discharge valves for exhausted air. Watertight suction seals were provided on the bottom for attachment to the submarine's escape hatches.

In practice the bell worked so well that five were constructed by the mid-1930s and distributed along the east and west coasts, with one at Pearl Harbor. Off this major Hawaiian base the *F-4* had been lost in 1915, claiming 21 lives.

Also, submarines were equipped with buoys which ran a telephone line to the surface, other markers with brightly painted lettering announcing such alarms as "Submarine in Distress!" together with quantities of yellow, orange, and red smoke floats. All-in-all, when the Japanese *I-63* sank in Bungo Channel, 400 miles southwest of Tokyo on February 2, 1939, with the drowning of all 81 aboard (the worst yet in history), U.S. Navy submariners had reason to take comfort in the fact that such heavy casualties probably could not happen to their own numbers again. The irony was that the McCann chamber had been offered to Japan and other navies of the world, and turned down.

It seemed especially improbable that such fate might befall the U.S. Navy's newest, handsome *"Sargo"* class boats, the latest of which were *Sculpin* and *Squalus*. Admiral Karl Doenitz would have heartily welcomed all of them to the *Unterseeboote* arm of the rapidly building *Reichs Kriegsmarine.*

After her more or less routine builder's trials, *Squalus* (named for a species of shark) was commissioned on March 1, 1939. The officer who would "con" her was Lieutenant Oliver F. Naquin, Annapolis '25, whose earlier underwater assignments had included World War vintage "O" and "R" boats and, most recently, the command of *S-46.*

A native of Alexandria, Louisiana, "Ollie" or "Nake" Naquin was slender, prematurely balding, warm, gregarious. Off-duty, he was a cornetist of recognized skill, whether rendering jazz or Taps. Unlike Captain Nemo, however, he did not play the organ.

One of the Navy's most able engineering officers, Naquin had watched as No. 192 grew from so much steel, tubing, rubber, wiring, and other structural members at the Portsmouth Navy Yard into something that could "swim," and surely dive. He came to love her as a personal possession. His crew of 55, the majority of whom had seen previous underwater duty, was handpicked for dependability and instant response to command. On a submarine, any less would not be enough.

In early May *Squalus* appeared among the lobster haulers and other fishermen who butted out from Portsmouth, Kittery, York, Newburyport, and still other harbors along the New England coast. She was so fresh that she had a "new car" smell of paint blending with a more characteristic heavy scent of diesel fuel. Naquin led her with firm bridle, as horse trainers would a colt, from the Navy Yard (actually located in Kittery, Maine) down the Piscataqua River toward the Isles of Shoals.

This was a familiar run for submarine trials and training dives. Just twelve miles southeast of Kittery or ten miles due east of Rye Beach, the grubby little island outcroppings, hospitable only to gulls and occasionally seals, formed both a reference point and a slight but rocky buttress against winds howling in from the austere Atlantic. The sea floor remained some 250 feet down, which was quite sufficient for underseas craft with a pressure depth of nearly 400 feet.

By May 23, *Squalus* had logged eighteen dives, the first few of which had been at dock, nearby or in the harbor. She was credited officially with but eleven days' sea time, during which there had been only two seemingly minor malfunctions. Once a main motor bearing had overheated; then the main induction valve wouldn't lock open. In fact Naquin had requested a special check of that wide, 31-inch diameter valve during builder's tests.

The valve was sort of an aorta for the deep-breathing diesels, needing to gulp thousands of cubic inches of air to feed their 6,140 horsepower. When the submarine dived, the valve was shut hydraulically by a piston closing off the seawater, which could otherwise roar in, cataract-like. A somewhat smaller companion valve, eighteen inches, admitted the crew's breathing air via ducts to the six principal compartments of the submarine. One lever—forward, open; back, closed—actuated both.

The big valve leading to the four diesels had been designed by the Bureau of Construction and Repair, the "mother" of this particular vessel. Others of the *Sargo* Class had been produced under contract to the Electric Boat Co., of Groton, Connecticut, which held some differing mechanical points of view—the exact design of the induction valve, for example. Its experts maintained in effect that the Navy version of the valve was not wholly failsafe. Yet these differences were not considered grounds for concern, since there had always been contrasting opinions by engineers on almost anything, even, or perhaps especially, the rear ends of automobiles.

Too, *Squalus's* architects could point out that there was a double-check against accidental flooding through these two large valves: four "stop valves" inside the submarine which could close off these pipes manually in anywhere from seven to fifteen seconds. However, neither induction valve should be closed while the diesels were running or a lethal vacuum would be established within the submarine, caused by the immense suction power of the big engines.

At 7:30 A.M., Tuesday, May 23, 1939, *Squalus* cast off moorings and pushed out from the Navy Yard dock. No. 192 was "fully booked" this trial—59 souls in all. The number included three civilians; Harold Preble, veteran naval architect, attached to the Portsmouth yard; youthful Don Smith, representing General Motors, builder of the diesels; and Charles M. Woods, Navy Yard electrician.

To Charlie Woods and, in fact, all on board the hum of the diesels was reassuring. They could not have been operating more smoothly to drive the twin propellers and ease the *Squalus* into midstream. Work crews ashore barely looked up as she glided down the Piscataqua, leaving a slight cloud of bluish exhaust in her wake. For what was so unusual about a submarine throbbing off for trials?

Not even gulls circled or cried overhead as they did in escort for most moving river craft. The birds seemed to know that nothing was *ever* thrown overboard from a submarine, so distinguishable by its blunt, protruding conning tower and little else.

The early morning was bright but with high clouds and a whine of wind that hinted of blustery weather to come. And it did, very quickly, at river's mouth. Ahead, in these most often inhospitable waters, lobstermen were already thrashing seaward in the white-flecked coastal chop.

At 8 A.M., the quartermaster logged, "Whaleback Light abeam to port, distance 1 mile."

Now the salt spray slapped against the conning tower and into the faces of Naquin and the handful of his command crowded into its scant space. Seawater streamed down the sleek tower's black sides and onto the gratings of what little deck was exposed. Soon none of the crew would inhabit topsides.

At 8:10 A.M.—"rigged ship for diving."

This was to be a "fast dive"—60 feet in 60 seconds, then about twenty feet below that to a level-off depth of 80 feet, or wherever twenty seconds more would take them. In testament to the gunning for its run, the diesels emitted new clouds of exhaust. Although rated at twenty knots, *Squalus* would probably hit no more than sixteen knots before plunging below the surface.

There was a seemingly infinite number of checks to be made before the submarine was finally "rigged": levers; indicators; valves including special conical kingstons; "Christmas trees" of red and green lights; RPM counters; gauges for depth and pressure; voltage, and other meters; even such mundane and seemingly obvious necessities as the securing tightly of the eight torpedoes and of galley plates, cups, saucers, and utensils. When each compartment could report that everything was rigged and the many instruments were indicating as they should be, then and only then the diesels could be shut down, the far weaker electric/battery motors switched on and the air intake vents tightly closed.

The submarine was "buttoned up," no longer a surface ship —ready to dive like a shark or, in this case, her fast-swimming namesake, the dogfish. In charge was the executive/diving officer, Lieutenant William T. Doyle, Annapolis '30. The handsome Baltimorean, as a reservist, had once served on the old *Cheyenne,* the last of the famous, if not especially seaworthy, *Monitor* class.

By the time Doyle was satisfied that the ballast tanks in the keel were ready to take in seawater then expel it on command through air pressure and that the stern and bow planes, the equivalent of fish fins, were working, it was just 8:25 A.M.

Squalus was one mile abeam of the Isles of Shoals Light.

Still atop the conning tower, Naquin received word between this time and 8:30 A.M. that the ship was "rigged for diving!" He thereupon ordered the radio operator to advise the Navy Yard that 192 was going down for about an hour. Position, course, and approximate speed were also wirelessed to shore.

Now the harsh, rattling blasts of the diving horn echoed from the steel walls, or "bulkheads," of the submarine, while the equally familiar command/announcement "Dive! Dive!" shrieked from the loudspeakers. Inherent in both messages, one mechanical, the other more personal, was a singular mix of excitement, anticipation, and latent foreboding.

As any submariner knew, the boats did not, invariably, come up again.

Those who *had* diving duty stations waited there for the next order. Those who *did not* were surprisingly casual, and that did not seem to conflict with regulations. For example, Robert Washburn, a seaman, second class, from Greenwich, Ohio, suffering from a head cold and wishing he were back at the base hospital, had wandered to the diminutive sick bay in the after battery room. He asked Pharmacist's Mate First Class Raymond F. O'Hara of Elmira, New York, for some medicine.

To most aboard the submarine these moments were alive with a series of commands, replies, and simple statements of fact snapped lightning-fast back and forth between officers and non-commissioned or petty officers. Naquin and all who were in the conning tower more or less literally slid down the ladder and into the control room, seconds ahead of the resounding slamming shut of the hatch.

Doyle, easily the most tense man in the *Squalus,* advised his captain that there was "pressure" and a "green board." Harold Preble, at his side, matched what he saw against a quarter of a century of being "taken down" to second with his own professional enthusiasm, "Perfect board!"

Increasing barometric pressure (assuming that sensitive instrument was registering properly and being read correctly) meant that there was no way at the moment for air to leak out of the long hull. Thus, the pressure would build up inside. The "green board" spoke electrically the same message—that all openings were tightly shut and that the red lights of the "Christmas tree" control panel had winked out, glowing only a friendly green, synonymous from childhood with safety.

However, the pattern possessed a subtle, built-in defect. One could not be absolutely sure at a quick glance if *all* of the green lights were shining. Nor were the little electric switches at the valves, hatches, and various vents so sensitive as to preclude the red light from going out when they were partially shut, if only by a hair.

"Kingstons open" announced a planesman, indicating that the valves were opened to flood the main ballast tanks in the keel. This would reduce buoyancy sufficiently both to accelerate and regulate the depth of the dive.

At 8:40 A.M., at sixteen knots or slightly better, on a southeasterly course, some five miles seaward of the Isles of Shoals, No. 192 plunged under. The man-made underwater creature was responding nimbly to the electrically controlled levers which put the bow and stern planes in a diving position in further emulation of her finny counterparts. Manually, the same operation could be effected by spinning wheels.

Doyle ordered the planesmen to level off at periscope depth, approximately 62 feet.

One minute later the gauge registered 50 feet and it looked to Naquin, Doyle, and Preble as though the big craft were indeed making a "fast dive." In fact, Naquin was about to congratulate Doyle on his handling of this test when a yeoman (second class) "talker," Charles J. Kuney, of Tulare, California, beside him, suddenly pressed the headpiece against his ears as his mike dropped from his hand and swung by its cord. He shouted, "The engine rooms are flooding, sir!"

Another talker in the after compartment had passed this message of doom.

As if to punctuate the cry, *Squalus* at once assumed a sharp angle by the stern, throwing many of the crew off their feet, causing others to grab stanchions, levers, anything to steady themselves.

Washburn never got his medicine. Pharmacist's Mate O'Hara watched as "bottles started to drop out of *the medical cabinet. I started to try to catch them, then the water came in the exhaust forward near the medicine cabinet. . . . "

To Francis Murphy, quartermaster first class, one of the control planesmen, "she went down slowly, but it seemed fast enough." As a matter of fact, the resident of Charlestown, Massachusetts, had been so worried about the *Squalus'*s earlier difficulties, that he had asked his mother to pray for him.

From aft, a terrified scream through Kuney's headset, "Take her up! The induction is open. . . . "

The voice dwindled off and would not be heard again. As one man, Naquin and Doyle chorused, "Blow main ballast!"

Then Doyle added, "Blow bow buoyancy and safety tanks!"

Next, "Full power!" on the electric engines.

" . . . attempting to surface ship, diving planes hard rise, put bow planes on hard dive, attempting to raise stern. Large up angle. . . . " was the way, in expressive understatement, the next few seconds would be logged.

Machinist's Mate Alfred G. Prien, also at the controls, believed that application of the "horizontal rudders" was aiding the stricken craft to "level off." And Gerald C. McLees, engineer's mate third, of Richmond, Kansas, "didn't think it was going to be serious."

Prien's assessment was true enough for a moment. *Squalus* hung at about 70 feet in relatively normal trim.

"Close watertight doors . . . ventilation flappers!" rang through the speakers. In an emergency, the crew was supposed to accomplish such instant duties anyhow. In fact, salt water already was trickling through the air vent system.

While Washburn and the pharmacist's mate started forward toward the mess room, a stocky, 23-year-old electrician's mate third, from Greensboro, North Carolina, Lloyd B. Maness was propelling himself with major effort in the same direction toward his battle, or emergency station, the vital watertight door separating the after battery compartment from the control room. He had been aft routinely taking readings of the big lead/zinc sulphuric acid batteries.

To move against the submarine's slant, he had to pull his weight ahead by clutching the sides and springs of one bunk in this crew's sleeping area, and then grabbing the next one ahead, and so on. As he did so, he looked over his shoulder to see a buddy, John Batick, from Portsmouth, New Hampshire, an electrician's mate first, disappear aft into the crew's mess, slamming the hatch behind him.

Others also were reacting to the crisis in their own individual ways, not necessarily waiting for orders. Robert P. Thompson, a ship's cook, third class, from Nashville, closed himself in the after battery compartment, undogged the hatch to the deck, opened it, and left for the Atlantic Ocean and eternity.

Squalus was heading inexorably for the seabed as though this were her natural habitat. According to Judson Bland, an electrician's mate first from Norfolk, she "took a terrific angle, about 45° up by the bow." With no power (because of the flooded motor room) either to drive the propellers or blow out water ballast, the submarine began to sink like an elevator without brakes.

Maness, arrived at his station, was struggling with a door that weighed some 300 pounds even when it wasn't against an angle. Since the water was at least over his ankles, he realized "time was short if I was to close the bulkhead door . . . I had to exert all my strength to swing it into place.

"I had partially closed the door when several men shouted to me from the rapidly filling after battery. They yelled:

"'Keep it opened! Keep it opened!'"

Lloyd Maness permitted it to slip back on its hinges, allowing five dripping men to struggle through, breathless and scared. The last two were Washburn and O'Hara, who had barely made it. Then, Maness continued, "I immediately swung the door shut and turned down the watertight screws." When he looked through the small glass eyeport he could tell that water had already reached that level. Then, as he would recall, with "the first impulsive action over . . . I began to realize the awfulness of the men's situation in the after section."

To Naquin, the very act of closing was itself "a miracle," even though 26 human beings had been locked in that compartment, as surely as behind the cemented door of a mausoleum. Among the 26 was Sherman Shirley, torpedoman first, who was to be married Saturday in Portsmouth. His best man was to have been Lloyd Maness.

Francis Murphy, still helpless at his new, shiny controls with the neatly printed but suddenly meaningless words, such as "Up," "Down," "Open," "Shut," "Forward," and "Reverse," noted, "The ship fell into a sharp angle . . . we bumped the bottom with a jar . . . we knew we were going to be there a long, long time." He concluded that nothing—levers, wheels, buttons, switches, spring-loaded pull chains—would any longer respond on the control boards.

At 240 feet, a 10° angle by the bow, *Squalus* settled into bluish mud in the murk of the ocean depths at a temperature of no more than 40° F. Yet the immediate emergency was not quite ended. There remained. the crisis of salt water shorting out the batteries, which would inevitably cause fire, explosions, and chlorine gas.

Not waiting for orders, Chief Electrician's Mate Lawrence J. Gainer dived into a manhole-type opening leading into the lower battery deck, not wholly flooded. He groped his way to the first main switch, jerked it open, to be blinded by a huge, bluish arc of flame, recovered to find the second switch, and threw it open. He crawled back to safety through a now totally darkened submarine. Only emergency battle lights glowed yellow, feebly.

Naquin ordered red smoke rockets released. They would burn on the surface for a time. Also floated up in a great chain of bubbles was the telephone-container buoy. A yellowish orange four-foot cylinder with a hatch, it bore the grim message: "Submarine Sunk Here. U.S.S. *Squalus.*"

A phone watch was established to await the hoped-for "call-up" by someone on the surface—a lobsterman, cabin cruiser, anyone.

At the same time, Naquin split the 33 known survivors into two equal parties, one group in the forward torpedo room, the other in the control room. Commanding the former was Lieutenant (J.G.) John C. Nichols, Annapolis '34, torpedo officer, who was a native of Chicago.

"My main challenge," Oliver Naquin would recall (to this author), "was just to keep the people quiet, to conserve air, to conserve body warmth, to keep them calm."

When someone inquired about the 26 men behind the watertight door, the commanding officer ordered, "That'll be that!" The subject must not be mentioned, lest dwelling on the thought might conceivably grow into panic.

Besides, Nake Naquin entertained no doubt in his own mind that those remaining and accounted for would somehow be rescued. This would be no *S-4* or *S-51*.

Perhaps the last to appreciate the gravity of the moment were the two Filipino mess attendants, stationed in the officers' ward room, forward. Naquin overheard one inquire, "We soon finish drill?"

Then, after some apparent thought, his companion replied, "This no Goddamn drill, this real thing. . . . "

At 10:07 A.M., logged, "Fired red rocket." This was repeated at 10:24, with another notation, "Men in high spirits, joking and discussing various topics." A few whistled, then stopped when it was discovered it required too much wind.

An hour later, fuel oil was pumped through a toilet ("head") in hopes of attracting attention. More rockets were sent up. All, as Murphy would recall, were "taking it easy," bundled like Indians in winter, in their blankets. Some went into the officers' bunks, two together, for increased warmth. Even so, the outside temperature, within eight degrees of freezing, had almost fully penetrated, and the bulkheads were clammy and frigidly unpleasant to the touch.

And so the morning of this tragic "real thing" passed, somewhat in anticlimax.

At the Navy Yard, the typed radio message of the *Squalus's* dive lay on the desk of Rear Admiral Cyrus W. "Cy" Cole, the commandant. A veteran hard-bitten submariner himself, he was due to retire in a couple of years. When any vessel under his command was at sea, whatever her mission, he wanted periodic reports like a worried mother hen.

Especially nervous when he knew his submarines were on diving runs, he mentally logged submergence times as reported by radio and pegged his mental "stop watch" for the estimated surfacing. *Squalus,* he was well aware, should have surfaced just about 0940.

By not much more than 0950, allowing for transmission, typing, and messenger delays, his own "alarm bell" went off. At 10 A.M. he voiced his concern to Captain William F. Amsden, yard captain, responsible for general administrative duties. By 10:30, Cy Cole's apprehensions were mounting toward fever pitch, so much so that he rang up the lonely, windswept Coast Guard station on the Isles of Shoals.

No. There was not a submarine in sight through the spray and whitecaps, just a few wallowing lobstermen.

That did it. Cole, almost running, strode down to the dock where the sister submarine *Sculpin* was about to shove off for Panama, under Lieutenant Commander Warren D. Wilkin. Without advance warning, he crossed the narrow gangplank and went down into the first opened hatch. In the control room he confronted a startled skipper.

"Warren," snapped the admiral, "I want you to get under way at once. This is an order!"

He then explained that the *Squalus* was unreported about five miles southeast of the Isles of Shoals and that *Sculpin* must search for marker buoys and flares and immediately report by radio.

Cole had barely stepped off the deck of the *Sculpin* when her engines were throbbing and the first moorings cast off. The admiral then hurried over to the ancient yard tug *Penacook,* ordered steam up and to "get going!"

Back in his office, the commandant telephoned the submarine base in New London. He asked that the rescue vessel *Falcon,* of similar vintage as the *Penacook,* be alerted. She carried one of the precious McCann rescue chambers, with cranes and tackle to lower it.

Down on the *Squalus* Oliver Naquin had weathered a scare. Bundling a fresh set of blankets around him, he found tears streaming uncontrollably down his cheeks. His eyes stung.

"Good Lord!" he thought. "This is the end—black chlorine gas. The seawater's gotten to the batteries!"

Almost resigned to his choking fate, he started to sniff, sniffed some more. The smell was familiar—camphor. At once he understood. The attendants had forgotten to shake out the mothballs after they had drawn the blankets from the yard supply room.

Routinely, even in extremes, the ship's log was kept up:

1200 –1600. Lying on bottom, eleven degree angle.

1210. Cracked forward battery door, releasing pressure in control room and transferred hand emergency lights to control room.

1223. Entered dry storeroom and secured food, dinner, consisting of pineapples, beans, tomatoes, and peaches; men seemed to enjoy meal and in high spirit getting a great deal of amusement out of our breaking in dry storeroom and the ship's cook forward.

1240. Fired red rocket.

1250. Heard loud bang on hull, blew fuel out of crew's head.

Five minutes later they heard the unmistakable sounds of submarine propellers overhead, then reversed. Naquin knew it must be the *Sculpin*. So did Harold Preble, the naval architect, at his side, who had been present at the delivery and weaning of dozens of submarines. So might Charlie Woods and Don Smith, but the watertight door had been closed on them.

Wilkin on the *Sculpin's* conning tower had first sighted a red smoke rocket, then the bright telephone buoy. The latter was hauled on deck, the telephone removed. At 1321, by *Squalus's* log, contact was established.

While Naquin had remained optimistic that such help would arrive, he nonetheless had harbored a "premonition" that the phone line just might not be very permanent. The conditions were not quite as stable as, say, the telephone connecting the Navy Yard to Boston. He had, in fact, briefed Lieutenant Nichols during the morning on just what to say and how to say it should someone pick up the phone topsides.

"Nick," he said, "talk fast and tell 'em everything—depth, what happened, main induction valve opened, how many we know are alive."

And Nichols did just that, scarcely pausing for breath. Commander Wilkin himself was on the other end. Then, Nichols turned the phone over to Naquin. But he had time only to say "hello" when the line went dead. It had snapped.

Sculpin radioed the news to Admiral Cole. The effect was not only electrifying, it was comparable to cranking a movie projector suddenly into fast motion. Many officers rushed to telephones with urgent messages aimed in as many directions:

For New London: Get the U.S.S. *Falcon* under way immediately, with as many divers aboard as could be rounded up, also doctors.

For Boston: Summon another rescue tug, U.S.S. *Wandank,*

present at the *S-4* and *S-51* disasters; also alert Army engineers to open up Cape Cod Canal bridges for unobstructed passage of the *Falcon*, faithful old salvager that she was.

For Boston, Portland, Providence, and Newport: Start all available Coast Guard cutters to the Isles of Shoals.

For New York: Summon the 10,000-ton cruiser *Brooklyn*, carrying thousands of feet of high-pressure diving hose, and the tug *Sagamore*, to tow the ten pontoons used to salvage *S-4*. The *Brooklyn*, at 32 knots flank speed, could be in the disaster area before dawn.

For Washington: Report to the Chief of Naval Operations, Admiral William D. Leahy, and the Navy Department, nerve center for all sea defense concerns, great and lesser. From the Washington Navy Yard, get McCann and Momsen themselves and all available divers and metalsmiths from the diving school. Rush as many of them as possible up by plane. Give naval transport planes priority over all commercial airliners.

For Norfolk: Fly north all divers stationed or passing through that great naval base. (One fortuitous circumstance was that much diving equipment, from suits and helmets to boots and air lines, happened to be in Portsmouth, where it was undergoing tests.

By mid-afternoon that Tuesday in May, the world knew all about the drama being enacted 240 feet below the bone-chilling waters off the austere New England coast. Offers of assistance, if only as niceties of protocol, were pouring in to the State Department from London, Paris, Rome, even Berlin and Tokyo. By the same token, a large representation of the nation's press and radio had been mobilized and dispatched double time to Portsmouth. Hardboiled ship's news reporters were hauled out of waterfront bars and sat down before their typewriters.

There had not been such a hot breaking news story since the dirigible *Hindenburg* blew up at Lakehurst, New Jersey in May, 1937.

On the *Squalus* events did not accelerate with such swiftness. The minutes dragged, with ample time to play "ifs." Engineer's mate Gerald McLees had tossed a coin with John Batick to see who would take readings that morning in the forward and aft battery rooms. Batick, last seen by Maness closing an aft door, had "won" that area. Preble, in a few more minutes, could have wandered back to compare notes with fellow civilians Charlie Woods and Don Smith.

If William Isaacs, a ship's cook, second, from Washington, D.C., along with Washburn and O'Hara, had been seconds later getting through the door Maness was closing or, indeed, if they had stumbled en route . . . If Nick Nichols, the torpedo officer, had been checking the security of the aft torpedoes at that time, as he well might have . . . if, if . . . .

Virtually all on board, with the conceivable exception of Naquin, could speculate on the little things that might have kept them ashore on this nineteenth diving test.

Five and a half hours after she had lain on the bottom, at 2:12 P.M., carbon dioxide absorbent was spread to purify the air, and rain clothing was distributed as a further conserver of bodily warmth. Most of the drip-dripping through the air vents had been stanched, although a slight leak persisted in the pump room. The captain figured it would be several days before sufficient water accumulated to constitute a hazard. Certainly, he calculated, it wouldn't be too deep for four or five days, the estimated supply of pure oxygen.

At 4 P.M. the log reported "men in excellent spirits although extremely cold." Half an hour later, "men developing headaches; and breathing becomes difficult, and becoming nauseated." Supper at quarter of five, consisted of "beans, tomatoes, pineapples." No one had much appetite except for the pineapples, which seemed to compensate for the lack of drinking water.

Then, a few minutes before 5:30, the men heard a partly shrill staccato beating through the hull—morse code from an oscillator, a primitive but effective type of transmitter. The tug *Wandank* had arrived after a record dash from the Charlestown Navy Yard that had almost burst her old boilers and shaken loose every rivet.

"Can you hear us if you can make my call?" came the eerie message from 240 feet above.

Squalus replied, "Yes," then added, "you apply salvage air to compartments abaft control room. We have air for ballast tanks."

Wandank: "How many officers and crew in unflooded compartments? Are you taking any water in those compartments?"

Squalus: "Thirty-three; no."

Wandank: "We can hear your hammers but very weak. Send each word three times. What valve open and what degree list?"

Squalus: "Main induction. No list but 10 degree angle up by the bow."

Because of the cumbersome nature of the code (one hammer bang for a dot, two for a dash) and long pauses, the seemingly brief conversation actually required a full hour. Further, although those on the surface thought that communication was a means of keeping up morale, the effort to reply was Herculean. Without the advantage of an oscillator, or the power to activate one, two signalmen and two radiomen took turns smashing the bulkheads of the submarine with hammers and lug wrench, employing every bit of their failing energy. If they hit softly, they couldn't be heard on the surface.

Thus, a sentence of a very few words was all that one man could at first bang out at a time. By now, the four were so weakened that they smashed out each word individually, like four slightly maddened xylophone players each playing but one note successively.

During this time, Washburn, who had never received his cold medicine, was seized with a severe attack of chills. Worried that he might lose him, Naquin ordered extra blankets wrapped around his shivering form and told others to hug him to transfer their bodily warmth.   He responded little by little and finally ceased his convulsive shaking.

At 8 P.M., as the *Squalus* logged "men in good spirits," the *Sculpin* opened oscillator communication with her sister.   *Squalus,* after asking a seemingly obvious question—"Have you located us?"— then inquired, "What are plans to surface?"

Sculpin, instead of answering at once, posed another question: "What are conditions below?"

"Satisfactory but cold."

Now, *Wandank* joined the exchange: "*Falcon* arrives about three in the morning.   Expect to start operations evacuating personnel immediately, believe have grapnel attached your ship, report on personnel."

Squalus: "Fifteen in torpedo room, eighteen in control room."

Wandank: "Can you go from control room to forward torpedo room?"

"Yes."

Wandank: "Have you sufficient emergency rations, fresh water, and CO_2 absorbent?"

"Ample."

If necessary, Momsen lungs could be used to protect against chlorine.   However, they would not necessarily serve as an aid to escape, since crews were trained only in 100-foot tower tanks. Besides, in the interrupted ascents necessary for coming up from great depths how long could one live in waters hovering near the freezing mark?

With a pause in conversation, the quartermaster had time to catch up with his detailed log. That it was kept meticulously under such extreme conditions was a tribute to the determination of the submarine's navigation officer, Lieutenant (J.G.) Robert N. Robertson, Class of '34, from Quanah, Texas. Small, friendly "Robey" had been a member of Annapolis's 150-pound crew.

As the thirty-three settled down to await a dawn that they could not possibly see and, perhaps, salvation, the rescue fleet converged on Portsmouth and the Isles of Shoals. Some of the principal actors in this uncommon drama were already there: the divers.

They were tough, barrel-chested, leather-lunged, fearless men. A number of them could easily be tagged the world's most proficient—divers like Chief Machinist's Mate William Badders, holder of a 500-foot diving record, Chief Boatswain's Mate Orson Crandall, Chief Metalsmith James H. McDonald, Torpedoman John Mihalowski, Boatswain's Mate Martin C. Sibitsky, and Chief Torpedoman Walter H. Squire. There were more than 25 experienced divers in all, arriving at the scene, most of them veterans of previous undersea salvage.

Most, however, had to fight their way up the coast. Rain and fog had forced the Washington planes down at Newport, grounding McCann, Momsen and a dozen divers. They continued in automobiles as chiefs of police in Rhode Island, Massachusetts, and New Hampshire sent squadrons of patrol cars and motorcycles to clear the roads ahead to Portsmouth. Announcers broke into evening and all-night radio programs to warn motorists to be on the lookout for these unusual convoys and give them the right of way.

Once at the Naval Base, the growing rescue party, which included doctors, mechanics, and technicians of many skills as well as divers, was met by a fleet of fast Coast Guard cutters, commercial tugs, yard work craft, simple cabin cruisers, and even large speed boats classed as Coast Guard auxiliaries, waiting to ferry them out to the Isles of Shoals. There hadn't been such excitement at Portsmouth since the heady days of the World War when many believed that the Kaiser was preparing to invade America, or at least give her coast line a bad mauling.

Admiral Cole himself, his gold-visored cap pushed back on his head, was nervously pacing the wet, worn decks of the smelly old *Penacook*. He carried a conventional two-dry-cell battle lantern as if to augment the searchlights stabbing through the darkness and off the foamy wave crests from the *Wandank,* the Coast Guard's *Harriet Lane,* and other early arrivals. A light rain was falling to add to the salty clamminess of the moment, while whistler buoys off the shoals and bell buoys at the entrance to the Piscataqua Channel offered their own musical score to this strange, nocturnal setting.

As further punctuation of the scene there were the white, yellow, orange, red, and yet other colored marker buoys dropped with their light-weight anchors over an area of approximately 10,000 yards. The bizarrely festive appearance was reminiscent of the anchorage before a summer yacht club. The pivot buoy was that dropped by the *Sculpin* after the telephone cable had parted. Nonetheless, since the original communication line leading from the sunken submarine was gone, the second buoy necessarily could only hint approximately, not indicate an *exact* location.

All afternoon and into the evening, the *Penacook* had crisscrossed the relatively limited area with grapnels, trying to hook onto something. Eventually the grapnel did make firm contact, and the line was secured to a wooden grating and left floating with the assortment of buoys. None could know, either on the surface or below, that the grapnel had actually caught a part of the *Squalus's* decking close by the forward escape hatch.

At 2 A.M., in response to worried messages from *Wandank* asking about pressure in the submarine and general well-being of the survivors, *Squalus* replied, "Vents closed, comforts satisfactory. Men resting much as possible, spreading carbon dioxide absorbent."

The night passed. In a submarine, even under the most normal and efficient conditions there was no demarcation between night and day. Men became hungry, tired or sleepy merely in response to their own reflexive habits, degree of fatigue, their built-in time clocks. Navy routine, however, underlined by ships' bells and bosuns' whistles through loud speakers, supplied the lack of visual references. If anyone prayed the long, cold, lonesome night, he did so to himself and told no one about it.

A gray, damp dawn arrived. However, the rain had stopped and the wind abated, leaving only the characteristic swells of shoal water. Just as the sky was streaking with light along the horizon, the staunch old *Falcon* boiled in from the south. Shortly before 8 A.M. she was in oscillator contact with the *Squalus.*

The cruiser *Brooklyn,* however, with her reels of hose line, and the tug *Sagamore,* towing pontoons, would not answer dawn muster. Both had been delayed by fog off Cape Cod.

For two hours the *Falcon* maneuvered about the wooden grating buoy, then released four anchors, one by one, to maintain station as motionless as possible. At 10:15 A.M. Martin Sibitsky was ready to descend, using the grapnel line as a guide. He hoped against hope it led to something important, like the *Squalus.* At six feet, four inches, towering "Skee" Sibitsky was the Navy's biggest diver, possibly also the strongest.   It was less than simple to fit the 30-year-old boatswain's mate with a suit, which with its leaded boots and helmet added another 200 pounds to his own considerable weight.

By oscillator, the *Falcon* advised, "Diver descending now to attach down-haul wire for rescue chamber."

Sibitsky made his descent in seven minutes, finding the visibility through the icy cold murk of great depth surprisingly good—almost twenty feet.   His rather hard landing on the forward deck of the submarine was unmistakable to those inside—a clangor of salvation.

Next the down-haul cable was lowered to him. This he shackled to the pad-eye atop the escape trunk hatch. With his cumbersome gloves, the cold and the pressure, what would have been an almost instant operation on the surface required twenty minutes. His task completed, he asked to be hauled back up through the usual stages of decompression.

Waiting, Naquin worked on priorities for the trips to the surface. In the best traditions of the sea, "passengers" must be first into the "lifeboats." Preble, as apparently the sole surviving civilian, easily fit this category. As well, he appeared to be suffering more than others from the cold and the increasingly foul air. An officer must also be aboard to carry names of the known survivors and to answer questions from his special storehouse of technical and professional familiarity.   Nick Nichols, the torpedo officer, met Naquin's yardsticks.

Preble was the logical first out. The last would be Oliver Naquin, following the traditions of the sea.

On the *Falcon* frantic preparations were being made for lowering the rescue chamber. Its "parent," McCann himself, was in charge of "last minutes" assisted by Swede Momsen. Diver John Mihalowski would be in command, supported by Gunner's Mate Walter Harman. Some of his friends knew him as "Lucky" Harman. The sobriquet was well earned. He had been on leave from the *S-51* when it was rammed and sunk.

As the McCann Chamber hung, partly afloat in the water, from an "up-haul" cable running through a strong boom to a winch, the historic moment was thoroughly chronicled by reporters, radiomen, and press photographers in chartered boats, aboard the newly arrived cruiser *Brooklyn,* and aloft in small planes. Added to their numbers and to those actually involved in the rescue operation, the waters were jammed by another distinct group, the morbidly curious.

Small and not so small craft of every description, like so many misshapen lily pads, had transported the sort of crowds that would be attracted to the scene of a fire, a bad highway or train wreck, perhaps even a spirited dog fight. The Coast Guard was hard put to keep them at a respectable distance from the *Falcon* lest they snag the various lines and buoys.

As a matter of fact, the carnival aspect extended to or perhaps began at the dockside of Kittery and Portsmouth, where hucksters, newly set up, were selling hot dogs, hamburgers, lobster rolls, potato chips, coffee, and soda pop. They did a bumper business, especially to those putting out down the chill Piscataqua. One enterprising photographer had secured a navy glossy of a *Sargo* class submarine and converted it into a postcard with the label *"Squalus"* boldly across it. He found plenty of customers even at the outrageous price of $1 each.

This sort of sideshow had happened before, most recently in 1934, when the *Morro Castle,* still afire, drifted ashore beside—of all places—Convention Pier, Asbury Park, New Jersey. It was a promoter's dream, or nightmare. In February 1925, crowds had come from near and far to Cave City, Kentucky, to munch popcorn, stare, and wait while work parties dug vainly for two weeks to extricate Floyd Collins, trapped in a cave. It was a Roman holiday of the twentieth century, complete even with a court-martial and a "martyr."

At 11:40 the diving bell started down, pulled by the air-driven winch which reeled in the "down-haul" cable, pulling the chamber toward the deck of the submarine. Water ballast, in special tanks, controlled by the operators, reduced its buoyancy so it would sink without too much cable pressure. Thus, the winch was in many respects the heart of the invention.

Squalus inquired of *Falcon*, "How many men per trip?"

"Seven," the Morse reverberated through the 240-foot depth, as weary radio and signalmen clanged their hammers against the sides. Their arm muscles ached.

Naquin soon heard the unmistakable sounds of the circular skirt and gasket of the McCann bell thumping against the hatch. It had made a bull's-eye. The log continued:

"Opened lower hatch in airlock, secured it immediately due to receiving considerable water and opened drain line, approximately a barrel of water drained out."

However, the gasket between chamber and hatch was tight. There would be little more water. Mihalowski rapped on the hatch. It was opened again to reveal his stubbled, grinning face.

"Hello, fellows," he greeted the survivors. "Here we are."

Two hours after the bell started down and 29 hours after 192 had nosed down into her fatal dive—at 1:45 PM.—seven, including Nichols and Preble, were assisted on board the *Falcon.* From the surrounding vessels arose a symphony of deep horn blasts, such as that from the cruiser *Brooklyn,* and shriller whistles, such as that from the little *Penacook,* and there were cheers from thousands of spectators.

Below, no one was cheering. With rescue so near, patience wore thin with the tantalization of waiting one's turn. The log continued:

"Captain inquired of men in control room if anyone too weak to make to forward torpedo room. All men ready to make trip, Lt. (J.G.) Robertson to lead the way. Rigged lungs for breathing through chlorine gas, advised torpedo room to put on lungs and that we were abandoning control room [because of the diminishing oxygen there]. Captain last man in line. Put in mouthpieces and rigged nose clips. Cracked forward battery door, then latched it open.

"Men started through forward battery room. Captain secured door between forward battery room and control room. Cracked forward torpedo room door, then all men entered . . . closed door between forward torpedo room and forward battery room. Air. . . much better due to rescue chamber having vented compartment. Found men in torpedo room had conserved oxygen as much as possible for our use.

"Men in excellent spirits, followed same procedure of resting and waiting. Grouped as before in order to try and keep warm, extremely cold."

Soon, the log could note, "rescue chamber on way down for second trip. Heard bell making seal, after seeing flashlight through eyeport. Opened drain line to air lock and same amount of water entered compartment as before."

A special treat was delivered this time—hot soup.

Again, the chamber worked as it should, the down-haul cable and the water ballast regulating its rate of ascent. The up-haul cable was more of a guide, since it was not of sufficient strength actually to lift the great weight of the chamber and occupants.

A few minutes before 8 P.M., it started up on its fourth and final trip, carrying Naquin, seven other survivors, Mihalowski and his fellow master diver, Chief Metalsmith James McDonald.

It was none too soon. Chlorine gas was thickening, even though Naquin estimated that, paradoxically, about half of the oxygen and CO_2 absorbent remained.

Then, about 90 feet above the *Squalus,* the down-haul cable jammed, bringing the bell to a jerky halt. Try as they did, neither Milhalowski nor McDonald could persuade the little ·winch to move the underwater vehicle a fraction of an inch, up or down. The cable had obviously become worn, then frayed from so much usage. Since McCann's wonderful invention had never before been employed "for real," there was no graph on the subject of stress or fatigue. Now, when it was too late, the effective lifespan of existing down-haul cables had been determined.

McDonald and Mihalowski, trying not to allow their passengers to appreciate the seriousness of the situation, said they were going to call up the *Falcon* to order steak dinners, all around.

"You want yours rare or medium, Captain?" McDonald asked Naquin. Then, in lowered voice, he briefed McCann on what had happened.

The reply crackled back: Flood the ballast tanks and allow the bell to sink to the bottom. McDonald obeyed. The chamber soon came to rest in the mud, somewhere near the submarine. It could not, however, go back to the *Squalus*'s hatch, since the guide line was now a useless mass of frayed, gnarled steel wire.

The occupants could not return to the submarine, even on a temporary basis, if they wanted to.

Blinker lights 240 feet above the trapped men frantically recalled Admiral Cole from the *Brooklyn,* where he was catching a few needed winks. With his assent, Chief Torpedoman Walter Squire was hurried into his suit by many hands and sent down through the black night waters to unshackle the fractious cable. He followed the lighter up-haul, or "retriever," cable as his guide, seemingly down to "nowhere." Clipped to his big leather belt, just in case, was a pair of heavy wire cutters.

Squire, in a miracle of blind groping in the cold and pressure, found the submarine, the hatch and the shackle. But he could not unbolt it. The slime and the blackness had compounded the deadly tightness of Sibitsky's original fastening.

Already weakening, numb and groggy, Squire nonetheless was able to unhook his wire cutters and start hacking at the cable. They slipped. He obtained a grip again. They slipped off.

Squire kept at it, more and more out of breath. Finally, one strand, another . . . another . . . he was through. The cable parted. Squire was reeled back to the surface.

McCann, again with Cole and also Momsen concurring, ordered the up-haul cable to be winched in. This operation was discontinued after a few minutes since it was seen that this lighter cable was also fraying. If this broke, so would the telephone and air/oxygen lines and then ten men might die.

The rescue chamber once more settled in the cold mud off the Isles of Shoals. McDonald and Mihalowski, sick at heart, could no longer kid their passengers that all was well and that they'd be up and out in a few minutes.

Two more divers went down successively, their goal to shackle a new, heavy cable to the top of the chamber. Each man in turn became ensnarled in the air and phone lines and was brought up, blue and in a semiconscious state. It required prompt work by doctors and corpsmen to return them to normal heart action and bodily warmth.

Time was running out. The chamber had been stalled almost four hours. It was within seconds of midnight. Risking the lives of more divers in an operation which had shown no hints of success was deemed entirely inadvisable. There remained but one more alternative: blow the ballast and allow the bell to float to the surface like an air bubble.

The danger inherent in this expedient was that decreasing water pressure as the bell neared the surface could cause the chamber to emerge with the speed of a projectile, resulting in fractured legs, arms, and, certainly, skulls, inside. Too, shooting up out of control, it could smash in to the keel of one of the many rescue ships and shatter.

McCann looked at Cole. Cole looked at Momsen. There was no need to form into words the question, or the decision on the trio's minds. McCann took the initiative. He addressed McDonald, "Blow main ballast, 30 seconds."

McDonald twisted the valve releasing compressed air, which in turn forced water out of the ballast tanks. In exactly 30 seconds by his waterproof wrist watch, he shut the valve.

Ten men inside waited. Nothing happened.

On the *Falcon,* some ten husky seamen tugged at the up-haul cable. McCann did not dare trust so delicate an operation to a winch, lest too much and too sudden pressure snap the damaged line, the air, and the telephone lines.

Desperate, McCann ordered, "Blow 15 seconds more!"

This was done. The chamber clung to the mud as though it had settled in for eternity.

McCann, full of misgivings, perspiring, repeated, "Blow 15 seconds, *more!*"

McDonald obeyed, a third time. There was a slight vibration within the chamber. It began to move in response to the men pulling from the slippery decks of the *Falcon* . . . faster . . . faster. . . .

At exactly 12:38 A.M., Thursday, May 25, the McCann Chamber broke surface in spreading rings of foam and air bubbles under the sparkling glare of many ships' searchlights. The keel of the *Falcon* had been missed, but not by much.

In moments, tough old Admiral Cole, moist-eyed, still clutching his battle lantern, was staring face-to-face at Nake Naquin, struggling for words. Finally, half turning away, Cy Cole choked out, "Well done!"

8

The Little Ships of Dunkirk

". . . a strange noise like the cries of seagulls."

LATER THAT SAME THURSDAY, the indefatigable Mihalowski, accompanied by Chief Machinist's Mate Bill Badders, descended once more in the chamber, which had been fitted with strong new cables. Their destination this time: the after escape hatch.

As before, over the forward opening, the bell was tightly secured, then the hatch opened. Mihalowski shone his electric torch downward. The beam reflected back from a dark infinity of water. There was the silence of a tomb. The veteran torpedoman closed the hatch again and called to the *Falcon,* "Take us up."

Almost four months passed before entries resumed in the *Squalus's* log:

"September 13, 1939: *Squalus* was raised from 90 feet of water and towed to Portsmouth Navy Yard.

"September 14: Bodies removed from *Squalus.*"*

The recovery of No. 192 had consumed the entire summer. While furnishing incomparable new knowledge in underwater salvage, the operation had been punctuated with many frustrations, including the

---

* For the author's personal postscript to the *Squalus* incident see Acknowledgments.

wild porpoising of the submarine under pontoon and compressed air pressure, only to plunge back down again.

More awards, decorations, commendations, and promotions resulted from the massive *Squalus* salvage effort than in any previous naval peacetime operation—upwards of one hundred. Included were four of the land's highest decoration: the Congressional Medal of Honor. While Mihalowski, McDonald, and Badders were so recognized, Sibitsky, the first diver atop the submarine, was strangely overlooked.

A court of inquiry placed blame on "a mechanical failure in the operating gear of the engine induction valve." Whether improper lubrication, a small burr in the cylinder wall, or indeed the very design of the valve was most to blame had become academic—a quibble. A more efficient unit would replace the malfunctioning valve but so far as the nineteenth dive was concerned it did not matter a whit. Nothing, not even a valve of solid gold and diamonds worth millions would ever bring back the 26 lives sacrificed in the evolution of underwater expertise and engineering.

Naquin himself not only was held blameless but was commended for his bravery, devotion to duty, and "outstanding leadership" in saving the lives he did, as well as for his "great assistance" in the raising of the wreck.

Yet the inquiry left one question mark, a negative sort of postscript.

" . . . there is no adequate explanation of the failure to close the two hull stop valves in the after battery compartment. This together with the fact that a substantial doubt remains as to the habitual practice of closing the hull stop valve indicates that the training, supervision and indoctrination necessary to insure the timely closure of these important hull stop valves, while diving was lacking in emphasis."

And since no one in the after battery compartment survived to testify, the question mark would remain just that—forever.

As important to the navy as the raising of the *Squalus* and the findings of the court of inquiry were, the whole matter had become back page news by September 1, when Hitler's hordes, Attila-like, stormed across the Polish border to launch World War II. President Roosevelt had been awakened at 2:45 A.M. by an overseas call from Ambassador William C. Bullitt, in Paris, advising of the invasion. In a few hours, the chief executive pensively would be dictating a letter to Secretary of the Navy Charles Edison:

" ... I was almost startled by a strange feeling of familiarity—a feeling I had been through it all before. But after all it was not strange. During the long years of the World War [when he was Assistant Secretary of the Navy] the telephone at my bedside with a direct wire to the Navy Department, had time and again brought me other tragic messages in the night—the same rush messages were sent around—the same lights snapped on in the nerve centers of government. I had *in fact* been through it all before. It was *not* strange."

History appeared bent on a blueprint of the frenetic hours of 1914. Sunday evening, September 3, short hours after Great Britain had entered what had suddenly become World War II, the 13,500-ton Donaldson Liner *Athenia* was torpedoed off the Irish coast. Several Americans were among the 112 who lost their lives in this first "atrocity" of the new war. Memories of the *Lusitania* were rekindled.

This time, however, a disillusioned, isolationist-minded United States beat no drums, marched in no "preparedness parades." The mood in 1939 was, in fact, eloquently captured by cartoonist J. N. "Ding" Darling, of the *Des Moines Register,* as he depicted Uncle Sam sitting up in bed, with the observation, "But my dear, I wasn't even thinking of going out to play with *him.*" Outside the window was a helmeted figure beckoning "Yoo-hoo!" Uncle Sam's wife, labeled "American Determination," clutched a rolling pin as she retorted, " ... you're darn tootin' you're not!"

Still, there were thousands of American tourists to bring home. The State Department rushed steamships including the U.S. Lines' handsome *President Harding* to English and Irish ports, huge Stars and Stripes painted on their sides and floodlit at night. At the same time, German vessels, including the fleet *Bremen,* were playing cat-and-mouse in the North Atlantic with infuriated British cruisers, baying at their sterns.

Bremen made it in spite of long-delays in New York while Customs and Coast Guard inspectors, obviously inspired by a most un-neutral White House, thought of every conceivable ploy to give the Royal Navy more time to hurry her patrols down from Nova Scotia. Lesser ships flying the Swastika, even as in that long-ago

August of World War I, loped for the sanctuary of neutral ports. Danzig fell the first week of September to be at once annexed by Hitler. Britain again hurried off an ill-prepared, lightly armed expeditionary force to France, as the son of Tommy Atkins, pink-cheeked and unhardened to the ways of the war and the world alike sang a lilting doggerel, "We'll hang up our washing on the Siegfried Line!"

He alluded of course to the Reich's answer to the much-vaunted Maginot Line, France's multi-billion franc defense system from Switzerland to the North Sea. It was studded with bunkers, tunnels, and ominous gun turrets—"impregnable" by the estimation of the military minds of the day. Tens of thousands of poilus lived in relative comfort in its well-equipped and furnished casemates, boasting dry feet and hot meals—something Daddy only dreamt about in the muddy, rat-infested trenches of the old western front.

By the end of September, Poland capitulated, to be carved up by Russia and Germany alike. As the smoke of battle cleared and the rubble of ravaged Poland was somewhat "neatened up," the opposing lines in the west settled down to a curiously calm, watchful waiting. It was much like the lulls, the maddening boredom that had alternated with horror there in 1914 to 1918.

All in all, after the smashing Nazi victory in the east, this seemed to many Americans a most singular manner in which to wage war. The arch-enemy of the League of Nations, aging Senator William Borah, the "Lion of Idaho," very quickly coined a phrase, "the phony war."

This ill-founded label not only caught on but encouraged Hitler anew to avow his desire for "peace," and actually to suggest the impertinence that President Roosevelt act as mediator between Germany and Great Britain/France. The Fuehrer's navy, however, was less circumspect. On October 9 the powerful pocket battleship *Deutschland* captured the American flag freighter *City of Flint.*

Taken to Norway by a prize crew, she was freed by the plucky Norwegians, even though they might have reason to surmise that time for them, too, had almost run out.

Respecting relations with the United States, certainly this was the Wilhelmstrasse's first major diplomatic blunder. It provided Roosevelt with the very opportunity he had been waiting for: a special "Atlantic Squadron," to guard in theory a coastline that was vaguely demarked as extending 300 to 1,000 miles seaward, from New-foundland south to the Falklands. Four old battleships, four somewhat more modern cruisers, including the chief executive's favorite *Tuscaloosa,* and fourteen destroyers were the ships initially composing the new squadron.

Almost immediately, the president ordered these beefed up by 40 World War I four-stacker destroyers, to be demothballed, derusted, and rushed back into commission, leaky or not. As well, the Coast Guard was admonished to stop its customary rivalry and bickering with the navy and aggressively back up the Atlantic squadron.

The growing friendship between F.D.R. and the man he knew as "Former Naval Person," First Lord of the Admiralty Winston Churchill, was thereby cemented. Soon the "neutrality patrol" was baying at full knot about the North and South Atlantic sealanes, occasionally dropping depth charges, evincing such ever-mounting enthusiasm and pugnaciousness that its officers began to speak of "waging neutrality."

At the very least, the patrol would be of passive assistance to Britain and France. Suspicious craft of any nationality were to be tailed, and full information, including course and speed, was to be wirelessed in the hearing of all, in plain English. Such tailings and tattling contained special significance for the future of 66 German liners, tankers, and freighters in East Coast, South and Central American ports, grossing altogether 366,000 tons and waiting a chance to dash for home past the Royal Navy patrols. The largest of these was the 32,581-ton North German Lloyd *Columbus,* languishing in Vera Cruz.

At the same time, F.D.R. seconded his sea arm's thumpings for "a two-ocean navy" and continued his pressure on Congress for rearmament. He was successful the first of November in repealing the arms embargo, meaning that "cash and carry" of any military hardware, from rifles on up to airplanes and larger yet was now legal. The expansion of the war in Europe with Russia's invasion of Finland on November 30, doubtlessly had something to do with speeding a decision in the House and Senate.

U.S. cargo ships and tankers switched their registry to Panama in order to carry war cargoes and thus circumvent "neutrality" laws. Business, which never had fully rebounded from the gray depression years of the early '30s began to show an upturn. This, plus the positive help he was now able to offer Great Britain projected Roosevelt into the highest spirits friends and associates had observed in him for years.

Marquis Childs, of the *St. Louis Post-Dispatch,* perceived "fireman's blood" in the president, "and he responds to the three alarm bell like a veteran."

This "fireman" in the White House applauded at the scuttling of the pocket battleship *Graf Spee* off Montevideo, December 17, following her pummeling by units of His Majesty's Navy. Mortified beyond hope of consolation, her captain, Hans Langsdorff, locked himself in a hotel room, placed the muzzle of his service Luger against his temple, and pulled the trigger.

Neither Wagnerian sacrifice had been necessary. Langsdorff had fallen victim to British propaganda, which noised it about the Montevideo waterfront that powerful new units of the fleet, including an aircraft carrier, were waiting off the mouth of the Plate River to blow the *Graf Spee* out of the ocean. Only two British cruisers, badly damaged in the engagement, short of ammunition and serviceable naval rifles, were within hundreds if not thousands of miles of the pocket battleship.

That very same Sunday, December 17, a drama more directly related to the United States' "neutrality patrol" was unfolding. The *Columbus,* bathed in gray paint, under slender, quiet-spoken Captain William Daehne, had slipped out of Vera Cruz four days previously, to be "escorted" through the Gulf of Mexico, in a violent storm, first by the destroyer U.S.S. *Lang* and then the U.S.S. *Benham.* Whether they reported *Columbus's* positions or not mattered little. The British consul at Vera Cruz had already wirelessed Royal Naval Forces in the West Indies which in turn signalled Halifax. From that major Nova Scotian base the new 1,355-ton destroyer H.M.S. *Hyperion,* Commander Hugh St. L. Nicholson, went boiling southward at 35 knots.

Transiting the Florida Straits at eighteen knots, *Columbus* was picked up by two other U.S. destroyers relieving *Lang* and *Benham.* Then, Sunday, off Jupiter Inlet, Florida, she started to veer northeastward with the Gulf Stream away from land and warships and into the anonymity of the North Atlantic. That night, east of Cape Canaveral, she was spotted by a French tanker, the *Saintonge,* under charter from the Maersk Line.

Worried that this might be a German raider, Jurgen Knudsen, the tanker's master, sent out an uncoded wireless, "sighted large darkened ship steering a northeasterly course." He added the latitude and longitude. Curiously, British listeners in the West Indies did not receive the message directly. It *was* intercepted by the Atlantic squadron in Norfolk and immediately relayed to Royal Navy watch officers in Bermuda—as though, indeed, the two distinct naval forces, only one of which was at war, were already allies.

At the same time U.S.S. *Tuscaloosa* was diverted from patrol to "intercept the *Columbus.*" It was quite unnecessary. Two destroyers had been loping somewhere in the wake of the big North German Lloyd liner since she had put the Florida coast astern. Monday evening, *Tuscaloosa* picked her up, "towering like the Empire State Building," and relieved the destroyers.

Tuesday, the *Hyperion* arrived. The *Columbus,* 500 miles west of Cape Henry, had not made good her bid for home. Captain Daehne, anticipating a boarding party, ordered scuttling charges fired and seacocks opened. Within fifteen minutes 574 of her crew of 577 had abandoned. Only three members, soundly sleeping in cabin 246 of "A" deck, were somehow overlooked. The survivors were taken to New York by the *Tuscaloosa.*

(On December 11, 1941, in a long declaration-of-war tirade directed at the United States' "very grave crimes against international rights," Hitler singled out the *Columbus* as one of a number of alleged acts of provocation. The U.S. Navy, he alleged, was guilty of "tossing" the North German Lloyd liner into the "grasp" of the British.)

In February, 1940, with the Maginot and Siegfried lines alike locked in the icy dampness of a European winter, Roosevelt dispatched Myron C. Taylor, his personal envoy to the Vatican, and Under Secretary of State Sumner Welles on a mission aimed at assessing the possibilities of peace. The Nazi chancellor's reply was a new spate against "warmongers" and Jews, underscored by a cry of "Vorwarts," forward toward "decision!" in the coming year. The American President's two special ministers did not appear to take Hitler's pronouncements with much seriousness.

If Prime Minister Neville Chamberlain demonstrably went along with this apathetic view, others in England did not. Benjamin Cannell, for example, would recall (in conversations with the author) three years' tireless blueprinting, prior to the invasion of Poland, of airfields, port facilities, camouflage, all manner of defensive preparations. A surveyor, or industrial planner, Cannell was one of a farsighted group who knew that the next act of the World War of 1914–18 was nearing, inevitably.

Clearing for action in many ways, the Admiralty slapped gray paint over the hull of the unfinished *Queen Elizabeth* and sent her tearing across the Atlantic for New York at speeds well over 35 knots. There, on March 7, the world's largest liner—84,000 tons—emerged as a monstrous surprise from the morning mists. German bombers now would not find her in John Brown's Shipyard on the Clyde.

Six days later the Finnish war ended with a treaty of peace in which Finland ceded the Karelian Isthmus, Viipuri, and other territory to Russia. Thus, the heavy-handed Kremlin had driven her northern neighbor into the German camp.

On April 4, Winston Churchill was put in command of the entire British military and naval strength. Five days later, the blow was struck, with Hitler's invasion of Denmark and Norway. And yet, Western Europe still found it hard to believe that this seemingly invincible war machine of the Third Reich would seek further conquests, that the "Sitzkrieg" was no more. King Leopold III, of Belgium, so stubbornly sought refuge in the neutrality of his little Lowlands kingdom that he refused permission for the B.E.F. to cross his borders. This in spite of the cold-blooded rape of his country in 1914 by another war-oriented German leader, Kaiser Wilhelm II.

Light forces were sent by London to Namsos, Andalsnes, and Narvik. Too late, too little. Lacking strength, motorized equipment, naval support, air cover, skis, even warm clothing, they tried vainly to reach the key port of Trondheim. However, they were finding it hard enough to hang onto what they had. Within three weeks, by early May most of this pathetic but courageous expedition was being withdrawn back to England.

Then, on May 10, even the most myopic dull wits could perceive Germany's intentions as a brilliantly coordinated ground and air offensive smashed into the Netherlands, Luxembourg, and Belgium. This was known to the German High Command as *Fall Gelb,* or "Plan Yellow." The key fortress, Eben Emael, at the junction of the Albert Canal and Meuse River, fell to glider-borne troops within two days, sending the Belgian defenses toppling like tenpins. Sublieutenant J. K. Neale, a reservist aboard the minesweeper H.M.S. *Speedwell*, would pronounce an amen for many as he wrote, "The phony war had ended and Hitler was knocking hell out of Holland."

"Invited" too late to march into Belgium and Holland, British and French troops scarcely knew where they were, much less what they were supposed to do. Nearing the Belgian border but still in France, at Anzin St. Aubin, Major G. S. McKellar, commanding an antiaircraft brigade, was quartered in an old chateau. For want of something better to do he was engaged in a hunt for the neighbors' pigs when the air raid sirens began blaring in adjacent Arras.

The Maginot Line was breached for a distance of at least 50 miles in the Ardennes between Sedan and Namur. German armor blasted through toward the sea, with Boulogne perhaps the first objective. Other units were thundering over the plains toward Paris. The whole front was crumbling. Even as it did so, unreality persisted at all levels. Major McKellar once more bore witness as he was approached by a young Belgian lieutenant who offered him a drink of Scotch out of a water canteen *"a la victoire!"*

From then on, his unit was but one of many toasting this strange victory by steadily falling back to the French and Belgian sea coasts. They retreated side by side with road-choking streams of civilian refugees, who had been within short decades again forced from their homes by the rampaging Germans. Even a general staff officer, General Siegfried Westphal, would write, "The sights to be seen were sometimes so heartrending that for hours it was impossible to feel any real joy in our victories."

Many left so abruptly that dinner was on the table and the pets hadn't even been put out. Lieutenant Commander Thomas "Tommie" Kerr, with a Royal Navy beach/liaison party, would write as he came upon one house near Bray, Belgium, ". . . inside it was neat, a meal laid for, just an abandoned home, with the kitten being fed sardines by my men."

Unreality was manifested as well on the adjacent seas. As Lieutenant B.J.M. Wright, of the Royal Naval Volunteer Reserves, neared the French seacoast aboard the minesweeper H.M.S. *Gossamer*, he thought at first he was listening to a familiar seaside sound, as though it were sunset on the beach at Bournemouth or Brighton:

"... out of the darkness came a strange noise like the cries of seagulls—and in a few seconds we found ourselves surrounded by men calling for help."

If this were his impression it was but the juxtaposition of the mind's patterns of normalcy against the rasping and unfamiliar grid of war, the struggle to comprehend, then correlate. For that matter, his reaction was further acknowledgment that only microcosms of the vast and ugly canvas of conflict could be experienced or assimilated by any one participant at one given moment.

War is a dizzying firmament of millions of individual experiences and impressions. Thus, as the author looked out at the Indian Ocean from the beach at Galle Face, Ceylon, and wondered about enemy submarines, that became his immediate and uniquely tangible bit of the war. Later, when he abandoned a burning and exploding Liberty ship in the North Sea (in fact, across from Dunkirk) that, too, was a strangely personal experience.

The author's reality included such fleeting memories as coming ashore at Dover in stained khakis, without naval officer's cap or even shoes, and the challenge, later, of a U.S. Marine sentry in London, "Sir, aren't you out of uniform?"

Of such fabric is this presentation of Dunkirk, an operation involving a fleet upwards of 900 vessels, of which nearly one-third were "little craft." There is no attempt to paint a "big picture" or even analyze strategies, rather it is the account of a hurriedly conceived operation which saved an empire by rescuing its army from seemingly certain annihilation, as it looked, felt, and possibly smelled to a handful of its participants.

This, in a way, is the sensory narrative of Dunkirk, from the focus on a few lives caught up in it as indelibly and poignantly as though they had been witnesses to an apocalypse.

Part II

"PLAN YELLOW" surged westward with the imponderability of lava down a volcano's slopes. Like timekeeping for doomsday, the successive victories were scored in Berlin:

May 13.   Netherlands cut in two by the onrushing Nazi armies. Queen Wilhelmina fled to London.

May 14.   Rotterdam, an "open city," was bombed into rubble.

May 15.   The Dutch army surrendered.

May 16.   The old Somme battlefield once more shook to the thud of German boots.

May 17.   The Wehrmacht drove 30 miles into France. Louvain and Brussels occupied.

May 18.   Antwerp entered.

May 19.   Field Marshal Lord Gort, commanding B.E.F., started preparations for moving his army back to the channel, while trying to close breaches in the Franco-Belgian lines.

May 20.   German armor reached Abbeville, on the channel. Other tanks hammering at the approaches to Boulogne, Calais, and lesser ports.

A "splendid success," by the measure of General Heinz Guderian, commanding Hitler's XIX Corps.

To Winston Churchill, who had succeeded the timid Chamberlain as prime minister and was forming his war Cabinet, it was something else: a "hideous dilemma."

King George VI himself took to the BBC to exhort, "Let us go forward to our task with a smile on our lips and our heads held high!"

It wasn't easy. From the chalk cliffs of Dover, Britons, through powerful glasses, could watch the smoke puffs from the enemy's field pieces and Panzer tanks themselves. They knew, perhaps even more certainly than their own army commanders across the slim-waisted channel, that all must be lost. One of those watchers was a retread from both the Boer War and First World War, Vice Admiral Sir Bertram Ramsay, a small, quiet man who could go without sleep for an unconscionable length of time but then, at last, blow his temper so that none in hearing would ever forget. Ramsay, as Flag Officer Commanding Dover (hitherto concerned with logistics for the B.E.F.) was one of several high officers present on Sunday, May 19, at the War Office, London, to discuss what even at this late hour was considered unlikely—evacuation of the B.E.F.

Nonetheless, the code name "Dynamo" was agreed upon, and Ramsay went back to his lofty headquarters, old Dover Castle. In fact, the sobriquet "Dynamo" was inspired by the admiral's conference room in the castle, which had housed emergency generating equipment in the Great War. As a conservative military man, Ramsay had confided in the Lords Commissioners of the Admiralty that his "forlorn hope" was to rescue, should he be called upon to do so, as many as 45,000 of an expeditionary force which numbered one-third million. His major concern was the ships in which to transport so huge a military assemblage—what sort, where to find them, how to direct them? Time, now, was foe, not friend.

The great liners, such as the *Queen Mary, Mauretania* (a new namesake of *Lusitania*'s old sister), and *Aquitania,* could transport a division at a time, but they also presented a target too tempting to miss. Battleships were too cumbersome for inshore work, and, besides, they were needed elsewhere, in the Mediterranean, for example, or in continuing North Atlantic convoy. Cruisers were in much the same category and also in short supply for such a diversion.

This left the destroyers, minesweepers, minelayers, and hundreds of "little ships," from cross-Channel vessels and paddle steamers which plied principally the Thames and the Solent, to scores of private yachts and surf boats from lifeguard stations.

The minutes ticked away.

" . . . Continual telephone conversations," Admiral Ramsay was to report, "took place between Dover, the Admiralty, Ministry of Shipping and the Commander-in-Chief, Nore (another naval command, situated on the Thames), as to the provision of small craft for the final evacuation and provisions of Naval personnel for manning the small boats required for ferrying and skoots [Dutch coastal craft] and other small vessels taken up for transport purposes."

As a matter of fact, for the past week, there had been much word-of-mouth "telegraph" throughout the British Isles concerning the mobilization of pleasure craft. Even the BBC, on the day Rotterdam's heart was bombed and burned out, broadcast a guarded "order" to owners of such little boats to contact the Admiralty.

The effect on shipyards and yacht basins was electric. One of the former was Tough's century-old yard at Teddington on the upper Thames, half an hour's underground ride west of London. Here and at adjacent anchorages were some 150 yachts, cabin cruisers, and motor sailers which met the Admiralty's desiderata of more than 30 feet overall. In the shadow of one of the river's picturesque weirs were moored such objects of Sunday sailors' affection as *Our Lizzie, Kitcat, Blue Bird, Miss Modesty,* and *Mata Hari.* A 52-foot converted naval vessel, *Sundowner,* belonged to Charles Lightoller, who had been second officer on the *Titanic.*

Since they were pleasure craft, the heaviest armament any of them had known was a two-pound saluting cannon. But that didn't matter. Douglas Tough, then the owner, readied an initial batch of fourteen boats to be moved to Sheerness, on the lower Thames, even without formal orders. The man in charge was the senior warden of the yard, Ronald Lenthall, who recalled, "We removed masts, loaded them with petrol tins and generally made room in 'em . . . really wasn't much we could do, you know."

Soon, Lenthall was leading his proud little fleet, flags flying jauntily (including on some the Cross of St. George, the original flag of England) down the Thames, past Westminster and London's several landmark bridges. He pondered as he did so the availability of naval crews to man the boats since there were some "sticky problems" involved in civilians participating in military operations.

Actually, there were plenty of naval reservists called up or being called up or even hurriedly sworn-in recruits, bearing at least military I.D. cards. The lack was ships, not crews. One such reservist summoned to the colors on the fateful May 10 was Ted Harvey, a fisherman from Leigh-on-Sea, Essex. Within a few days, he too was at Sheerness, and assigned as coxswain to a 30-foot harbor launch, the *Moss Rose.*

A grizzled bosun, looking with some despair at the human sea of inexperience standing in front of him, asked, "Any of you chaps know the estuary of the Thames to Ramsgate?"

Ted Harvey raised his hand, and thus became an object of much awe and envy.

"So," he recalled, "all we had to do was load up with red cheese, chocolate, and two-gallon petrol cans—and wait."

Considerably more impressive was the gathering of the paddle steamers, of which the sixteen-year-old *Medway Queen* was not the least. Late of the Thames excursion run, she was 179 feet long, 316 tons. Converted into a minesweeper, she was already a veteran of the war, having swept the Thames Estuary all winter. Sub-lieutenant John Douglas Graves, a reservist who was a consulting surveyor in civilian life, recalled:

"This was the bitter winter of 1939, when even the Estuary partly froze over, and for weeks on end a tug was required to go before us morning and night so that our paddles would not be damaged by the ice floes, which were sometimes quite large. The seas that came aboard froze, and decks and rails became coated with ice which had at times to be chipped away to restore stability. Day after day, the little ship plunged out into the North Sea, streaming her sweeps and searching the depths, returning home each night with little to report except that the shipping channels were clear."

And so *Medway Queen* continued her scouring "while the nation slumbered and the German Army made ready to invade the Low Countries." Then, from Dover, in late May she received a signal indicating that she was about to return, in a fashion, to her old role of transporting people.

Early Sunday afternoon, May 26, Ramsay would record, "The military situation was thought to have deteriorated so rapidly that the Vice Admiral was informed by the Admiralty that it was imperative for 'Dynamo' to be implemented with the greatest vigour."

Providentially, partly because of heavy losses, partly through Hitler's impatience to drive on to Paris, tank forces which had crushed the Lowlands, halted at the Aa canal line, in some places in telescopic sight of the beaches. Even so, the B.E.F. and numbers of their French and Belgian allies were being compressed into an ever-shrinking beachhead, roughly 21 miles long, with Dunkirk more or less at the center, at least the epicenter, as of an earthquake.

At 5:40 P.M., the same Sunday, the War Office, by secret cipher telegram, announced, "Emergency evacuation from coast has been studied here in case required and is called Plan Dynamo. A fleet all sorts of craft is now under control Vice Admiral Dover. Shipping could take over 30,000 a day which could not be lifted from beaches alone but might be stretched even further if bulk of movement were from ports say Dunkirk and Ostend, Calais holding out though hard pressed. . . ."

An hour and a quarter later Dynamo officially commenced, even though troops had been pouring into the beaches for some hours. The cross-Channel steamers, chosen as the first to lift out the arms as "Personnel carriers," had yet to arrive. For shuttling from the shore there were only four Belgian passenger launches, a contraband control boat from Ramsgate, and a few assorted fishing craft. Nonetheless, the order had come none too soon. The picture was already that of a routed army staggering across a wasteland.

"As we moved through La Panne," wrote Sergeant W. B. Giblett, with the Second Battalion, Wiltshire Regiment, "the sight of devastation was everywhere. Bombed buildings had toppled into the streets and masses of debris were scattered around while flames flared and crackled as houses and vehicles burned after a recent bombing attack."

"The road running along to Dunkirk was choked with wrecked and burned out vehicles, among them a number of Red Cross ambulances. Many of the vehicles had belonged to the French troops, though some vehicles had been in the area from the beginning, including a few British vehicles."

Once on the beach, Giblett "looked around at an incredible sight, thousands of men stretched in a long line ten or twelve men deep from just ahead of where we came onto the beach right into the distance towards Dunkirk. Quite a number of vehicles had been run onto the beach and were scattered around, many of them burned out wrecks destroyed by bombing or shell fire.

"Along the water's edge were groups of men every few hundred yards, many of them had waded into the sea so that the foremost man had water almost at chest level as they waited patiently and hopefully. . . ."

"What a terrible night that was!" declared Lieutenant Commander Tommie Kerr. "For we had gotten hold of the odds and ends of an army, not the fighting soldiers. There weren't any officers, and those there were useless. . . . we worked without ceasing all the dark hours, restoring confidence . . . by speech and promise of safety and sight of our naval uniforms. Pathetic the faith in the Navy."

Confusion was compounded when Kerr was ordered to Bray Beach, "about seven miles away to embark 5,000 men . . . it took us some time to get there by bomb-cratered road and wrong turnings . . . then we gave a gasp, 5,000?

"Not a bit of it, there must have been 25,000 at the very least. . . ."

It was, as well, "a terrible night" for getting the Channel steamers safely across. "No less than five transports were shelled," reported Ramsay, "and returned to United Kingdom without making the trip."

However, Monday, May 27, dawned calm and clear. Little and big vessels started out from Dover, so crowded, according to Robert Lenthall, who watched from shore, it was "just like Piccadilly." Among the vast and wildly assorted fleet was Ted Harvey's harbor launch, *Moss Rose,* without a compass, just playing "follow the leader."

All the way from Dover, sailors aboard this curious armada, swelled at the last moment even by the lifeboats from great ocean liners, could see clouds of black, dirty smoke rolling toward the North Sea. The source was burning oil refineries, fired by the French to deny them to the Germans.

At nearby La Panne, on the Belgian border, Sergeant Giblett was being shelled by German artillery, "which quickly caused a dispersal as everyone sought what cover he could." He continued, "The shortening of the perimeter made La Panne no man's land and it was necessary for everyone to move up the beaches nearer to Dunkirk to avoid the heavy shelling . . . in the distance Dunkirk was burning fiercely after yet another bombing attack and the thick pall of smoke hung over the town as it had done for days past."

There were also groups of wounded, "some badly," attended for the most part by medical orderlies and a few nurses. Others pitched in, as Giblett added, "The men moving slowly along the beaches willingly took up stretchers and carried the wounded forward when asked to help owing to the shortage of medical staff, but many of the badly wounded needed the constant attention of trained medical staff who so few in number worked magnificently to give aid under the most dangerous conditions—due to the frequent shelling, bombing and machine gunning from which they and the wounded had little chance of taking cover."

Tommie Kerr continued to be impressed by the contrasts and contradictions such as "the sight of one little dinghy with 2,000 men waiting to get into it." And, "we couldn't persuade the troops it was no quicker to stand in the water than on the dry sand. They always felt that someone would get in front."

It was a desultory sort of day. First he started his little group marching toward Dunkirk, then "found a lorry and made it go and went back for orders and to fill up our water bottles."

There he boarded a "drifter," or medium-sized fishing boat, and was served "a drink of hot tea—wasn't it good!" But he did not have long to enjoy it . . ." presently shells started coming in, about twenty in all, then another terrific air raid of which only one lot of bombs were in any way frightening."

It was time, however, to resume his beach patrol, checking on the numbers waiting from La Panne down to Gravelines on the western extremity. Others of his unit had miraculously slept through the Germans' attack, one especially "snoring his head off," and he had to shake them awake.

". . . We pinched a car and lorry this time, and off we went, our party intact. One signalman ought not to have been in France at all. He was only just nineteen and he was a bit upset, poor boy, but he was jolly good. We bowled along the beach in fine style and finally took up our position. We had sent four men to pull from Dunkirk in a boat as a line of retreat for ourselves. It gave the men some confidence, though [we] had quite decided the odds were very much against our being anything else but prisoners of war in Germany.

"Having established our headquarters [we] decided we must try to contact Army headquarters, so we started off in the car, me driving. They told us the HQ was 7 or 8 miles along. Tide was high so we were up in the loose sand. As we went along we got into the French/Belgian troops and which slowed us down until the German machines started machine gunning the beach.

"We were able to bowl along then for it cleared things wonderfully. The car was hit by only one bullet, although I could see the machine out of the tail of my eye coming from the passenger side, it was so low, the machine guns blazing. But they go fast it is quickly over. The bullets scattered. Not so terrifying as you might think when you are doing something."

Soon, Ted Harvey was doing his own "something" in *Moss Rose*. He made four ferry trips from the beach to waiting destroyers and channel steamers, carrying between 40 and 50 British troops each time. Coming back, just east of the mole (the East Pier, or Jetée de l' Est, 1,400 yards long, five feet wide, with wooden planking), *Moss Rose* was rammed accidentally and barely made it to the beach without foundering.

Now Ted figured he was no better off than the rest of the men, awaiting evacuation. He sat down for a time, then noticed soldiers playing football, incongruous as the sight was, with smoke pouring overhead from the burning refineries and the ever-present rumble of shells and bombs in a background of varying proximity. Soon he joined the players, and the afternoon moved on.

Then the troops tired of that as they noticed an almost casual heap of dead soldiers, most in British uniform. They wandered over to the human mound, poked at some with sticks, turned one over, another, gingerly put a hand in a pocket. . . . soon, all were looting, mostly paper francs as the corpses stared back in bloated, unseeing reproach.

Harvey kept saying to himself, "I don't want to get like *them.*"

By this time, Ramsay's senior aide, Captain W. G. Tennant, had been landed by destroyer, following heavy and periodic attacks by dive bombers. He had two means of communication: ship's wireless and an intact telephone cable to Dover from the ancient plug switchboard at the Ambassador Hotel, LaPanne. This early Monday evening he advised his admiral, "Port consistently bombed all day, and on fire. Embarkation possible only from beaches east of harbor A.B.C.D. Send all ships and passenger ships there to anchor."

This was followed by a yet more urgent dispatch, "Please send every available craft to beaches East of Dunkirk immediately. Evacuation tomorrow night is problematical."

So far, the results were not encouraging: In the better part of two days' operation less than 10,000 soldiers had been transported to England from the beaches, lending weight to the original gloomy estimate of only 45,000 maximum. And there already had been losses. The big Dover-Calais ferry, *Queen of the Channel* this very night was bombed and sunk in a single dive-bomber attack. A "guardship," *Mona Isle,* and a hospital carrier, *Isle of Thanet,* were damaged by shore batteries at Calais in spite of the latter's prominent Red Crosses.

Two strings of small craft under tow were run down by larger ships in the dark, sunk or "scattered." It was believed that none was manned. Although he could not know about this loss at the time, Ramsay nonetheless sent urgent phone messages to all adjacent naval commands, commencing with the Nore, to round up every "shallow draught" boat that could be found, commandeered, or even stolen ("confiscated" was the nicer euphemism) then "stocked with fuel and provisions for two days."

The situation deteriorated with the acceleration of an avalanche. The armies of King Leopold III of Blegium had been "going to pieces like a wornout rope," the U.S. Ambassador to Belgium John Cudahy had confidentially advised President Roosevelt. At midnight, on his own initiative, the thoroughly shaken monarch surrendered his armies to Germany, thereby further exposing his British and French allies—a "pitiful episode," as Churchill would describe it.

Lord Gort, who had been trying to bolster his allies' sagging lines for a week, now sent what he could find of two divisions into the latest gap, along the Lys River.

Gort, in understatement, advised that the situation was "perilous," that "the enemy might succeed in cutting off this force from Dunkirk." Ramsay believed the report only confirmed "the results of air reconnaissance which indicated that German armored units were operating to the south of Dunkirk."

The vice admiral looked at his wall blackboard, then would make note, "there were assembling off the beaches 2 transports, 9 destroyers, 4 minesweepers, *Calcutta* [an antiaircraft cruiser], 17 drifters and a few skoots. . . . from signals received it appeared that the situation was desperate, that little could be lifted direct from the Port of Dunkirk and that the maximum effort must be made from the beaches.

"Commander-in-Chief Nore at this stage provided additional reinforcements of minesweepers and paddlers. . . ."

The "paddlers" assembled as the troubled hours of the night turned into morning, Tuesday, May 28. There were eight of them, some part of the Tenth Minesweeping Flotilla, *Medway Queen* flying the flag of Sub-Divisional Leader, followed by *Brighton Belle, Gracie Fields, Laguna Belle, Princess Elizabeth, Queen of Thanet, Sandown, Thames Queen*—a proud, squat squadron, somehow reminiscent of the ducks in Kensington Gardens, quiet Sunday afternoons, parasols, far pleasanter times.

Sub-lieutenant John Graves, *Medway Queen*'s second in command, would write, "In line ahead they steamed through the night to a point about half a mile from the shore where, in the first faint light of dawn, could be made out long lines of men standing still like human piers stretching out into the water—knee, waist, even neck high in it; standing so patiently there in full equipment, boots, rifles, packs, tin helmets and all, with sergeants passing or rather swirling their way up and down the lines with a word of encouragement here and a command there. Orders were to leave by daylight but in the face of what we found this was not possible, and as dawn broke, the ships put off their lifeboats to be rowed or towed to the heads of the human queues.

"The antiaircraft cruiser *Calcutta* stood by giving support against any German aircraft which ventured over, but apart from a few bombs which went wide, there were no untoward incidents, and at 7:00 A.M. *Medway Queen,* with the rest of the Flotilla, left the beaches and headed for Dover.

"On the way back and just outside the Harbour a heavy air raid developed, during which *Medway Queen* shot down a German fighter."

Graves estimated that there were "99 dive bombers" in the enemy formation, peeling off, taking each ship in turn, then, "In the confusion, *Brighton Belle* drifted over a submerged wreck, tore her bottom out and began to sink. We went alongside and took off her soldiers, together with her crew, before the old ship subsided to the bottom. We then continued on our way to Dover and disembarked the soldiers. They were mostly Base Personnel, Line of Communications Troops and A.A. Gunners. One wonders who gave the latter priority in the evacuation."

As Giblett witnessed this Tuesday:

"We could see the ships standing out to sea, often being harassed by bombing or shelling; from time to time a motor boat or other small boat came inshore to pick up a few men and carry them out to the ships, but it was only when ships could get into the harbour, or alongside the mole that any number of men could be embarked. During the hours of daylight the enemy's air attacks upon the ships prevented the ships doing much and only during darkness was it possible to get the ships alongside and carry out embarkation on a worthwhile scale . . .

"During the day the number of men on the beaches declined only slowly and the queue remained just as long and seemingly as big as ever. Every once or twice an hour there would be a bombing raid with the planes dropping bombs onto and machine gunning the beaches or as an alternative there would be shelling and mortaring of some part of the beach. These attacks meant instant dispersal to any possible cover where we remained for awhile before the queue reformed with everyone taking up his original place; there was no attempt at queue jumping.

"When not being attacked ourselves we watched the struggle between our ships at sea and the enemy planes attacking them. We could see quite clearly the bombs dropping towards their targets and the flash of tracer from machine guns; great plumes of water rose alongside the ships as bombs exploded in the water nearby and we hoped the ships might survive. The Navy's destroyers out at sea blazed away at the planes with their guns to give what protection they could. Although our ships were undoubtedly suffering damage it was gratifying to see the enemy did not get off Scot-free as some of his planes turned away with smoke trailing from them and one plunged into the sea with a mighty splash.

"A few of our own fighter planes arrived to challenge the enemy; they were a heartening sight though they only appeared rarely and in such small numbers. Although hopelessly outnumbered they sailed straight into the enemy formations and some fantastic dog-fights took place over the beaches or the sea.

"We watched the planes as they swooped, dived and turned and heard the rattle of their machine guns. With perhaps only two minutes of tense, dramatic action came the flash of flames as a plane caught fire, the scream of engines as it dived out of control, a pilot dropping to earth on a parachute, tracer lines in the sky and planes whirling around all over the place, then quite dramatically the sky cleared and the planes were gone."

None on the beach could appreciate the contribution of the R.A.F. While it was true that they were "outnumbered," although not "hopelessly," much of their effort was directed behind the beaches, out of sight of the troops, intercepting the Luftwaffe before it reached the sands, denying them the use of some recently captured Belgian and French airdromes.

Tommie Kerr, meanwhile, who had substituted a pair of "abandoned bedroom slippers" for his wet and irritatingly stiff boots slogged through the sand to brigade headquarters where the general offered him a drink of wine. Tommie refused. He reported his soldiers had told him of "one fifth arm bloke on the beach giving contradictory orders ... [but] it was too late before I could have him shot."

As he returned to the La Panne beach Kerr saw "a blazing ship full of soldiers." Since it was well offshore there was nothing Tommie could do about it.

While Ted Harvey and others who had lost their craft were crossing back to Dover or Ramsgate for fresh boats, reinforcements were already at sea in response to Ramsay's and Gort's earnest pleas. Among them was Lieutenant B.J.M. Wright, aboard the minesweeper *Gossamer*. Laconically, the captain had observed, "this is not the first time we've got the Army out of a hole."

Even then, the C.O. could not appreciate just how big and deep that hole was. *Gossamer* arrived at dusk, Tuesday, knifing into Dunkirk harbor, "which was brilliantly lit by the fires from blazing oil tanks at the back of the town." Wright continued:

"The chimneys and buildings were silhouetted against the flames and the place looked like an inferno. ... The wooden pier on the east side of the harbour was intact and as we went in we found it crowded with troops. We took off 450 with very little delay and got away while it was still dark, being troubled only by the number of ships all trying to get in through the tiny entrance to the harbor."

Heading for home port, *Gossamer* approached a large channel steamer which commenced signaling with dimmed blinker light. The vessel carried no Dunkirk chart and her navigator wondered if the minesweeper carried a spare. The naval officers debated; they were under standing orders not to stop if carrying troops. Yet, since there was "considerable danger" of grounding in the shoals, and with a large number aboard, it was decided to furnish a chart.

A whaler was lowered and the transfer effected. During this period a destroyer "tore past us," heading for England, which seemed normal enough considering the time, the place, and the circumstances, so "nobody paid much attention to her." About .ten minutes later there was a "dull thud" which sounded somewhat different from the gunfire that remained a background basso from the shore, "but again nobody took much notice."

Soon, *Gossamer* was under way in the early minutes of Wednesday, May 29. The captain felt all was well and turned in for some sleep.

"We had not been going more than about twenty minutes," Wright would recall, "when out of the darkness came a strange noise. . . ."

Was it the cry of seagulls? In seconds, the crew of the minesweeper knew it was not as the waters suddenly were dotted with men calling for help. Once more against orders, *Gossamer* hove to and started picking up the survivors, as it turned out, from the destroyer *Wakeful*, which had passed by earlier. She had been torpedoed, broke in half, and sank in less than 45 seconds.

"It was impossible to leave these men drowning," Wright continued, "although we knew there must be a submarine or M.T.B. [Motor Torpedo Boat, which was the case] lurking in the neighborhood. We lowered our boats and started picking up survivors, but when a drifter appeared our captain called in our boats so that we could leave further rescue work to smaller ships."

Confusion and tragedy was compounded after *Gossamer* continued on her way. The drifter *Comfort* was joined by another, *Nautilus*, the destroyer *Grafton*, and minesweeper *Lydd*. About 3 A.M. this Wednesday *Grafton* was torpedoed and machine-gunned, her captain dying on the bridge, while some 35 Army officers were sleeping in the wardroom, under which at least one of the torpedoes hit. *Comfort* was raised in the air by the explosion and when she leveled off again, the dying *Grafton* opened fire on her, thinking the drifter to be the enemy, while *Lydd,* the minesweeper, rammed and sank her.

Most of the *Wakeful*'s survivors succumbed with the *Comfort*. A "bright flash" subsequently observed from *Grafton*'s and *Lydd*'s wild firing was believed, at long last, to be from the destroyed German MTB. But had it been worth the cost?

On the beach, "somehow the night passed," according to Tommie Kerr. . . . "When daylight came I lay down and slept. Perishing cold the night had been (not really but one was weary) and shoulders ached from webbing equipment and unaccustomed weight ... I walked (staggered by this time) along the beach and found during the night a water tank had been floated ashore and was high and dry, so I got the party moved along and organized them to give out water which was badly needed."

Kerr then had a "brain wave to make a pier out of the lorries." To an extent, and for a limited distance the idea worked and soon men were walking along this improvised jetty "like a dose of salts."

As the morning wore on, the beach "filled with French troops and our usefulness there was obviously at an end. We had the lorry opposite the water tank and we made valiant efforts to get it afloat again and the engines running, and giving out water. We secured one whaler and bailed it out and moored it alongside the tank. . . . The shells started landing along our beach and they hit the hospital a number of times and killed and wounded many of the bunch. . . . "

The shellings and the bombings interrupted quite a variety of operations, and were mere punctuations in this wild and unreal world of beach clinging. For example, Philip G. Ackrell, a World War veteran now with an ammunition depot, had lathered up for a shave "when suddenly an enemy plane flew low, dropping bombs nearby, causing casualties. A period of quiet followed, enabling me to complete my shave."

Sub-lieutenant J. K. Neale, on the minesweeper *Speedwell,* arrived to find "the beach black with troops, and aircraft were flying up and down bombing and machine gunning them."

He noted a strange "pandemonium" added to the wild scene in the presence of "loose horses galloping about the beach." They had either run away or their attendants had already embarked.

Later in the afternoon, the dive bombers concentrated on the east pier, or mole, beside or near which a number of ships were loading. First hit was the paddle steamer *Fenella,* whose crew nonetheless succeeded in transferring most of the stretcher cases to another paddle steamer, *Crested Eagle,* freshly arrived from Dover. Aboard her was one of the youngest at Dunkirk, Peter Solari, a fifteen-year-old boy seaman who, as a matter of fact, had been on the merchant marine training ship *Exmouth,* Grays, Essex, since he was ten.

While the transfer was in progress, the destroyer *Grenade,* across the pier, was hit and started burning furiously. Through heroic efforts of a trawler she was towed away from the pier and out of the channel before she sank.

Crested Eagle completed the embarkation of 1,000 or more and cast off. She had paddled but a few yards when she was struck twice by a single dive bomber and, like *Grenade*, burst into flames. She was beached, but even so upwards of 600 perished. Young Pete Solari, hurt and dazed, was carried to one of the many impromptu dressing stations on the beach.

It was a bad afternoon for paddle steamers. At about the same time, off La Panne, *Gracie Fields* was hit. Her rudder jammed, sending her in circles, but she did not catch fire. Minesweepers managed to save most of the 750 troops on board before she slipped out of sight under the night waters.

Luckier, *Medway Queen* was now thumping back for another night's work. This time, a new danger became apparent: phosphorescent wakes from the twin, broad paddles. Twice German pilots followed this shiny trail and dropped bombs "uncomfortably close." What to do?

"We were nothing if not resourceful aboard *Medway Queen*," according to Sub-lieutenant John Graves, "and devised oil bags which were lowered over the bow on either side just as they are used at sea to break the force of heavy waves." The tattle-tale wakes disappeared, but even as they did so the funnel commenced to stream sparks, like millions of incandescent fireflies.

Still resourceful, the crew formed a bucket chain, ending with the tallest man on board, who dumped the pails of water into the funnel as they were passed to him. The expedient, while reasonably successful, nonetheless resulted in overflow down the necks of the engine gang and some very earnest profanity. Then, Dunkirk again:

" . . . the flotilla came under very heavy fire from shore batteries, and some of the ships hauled out of the line as the sea spouted columns of water around them. The scene was awe-inspiring. Rows of great oil tanks were blazing furiously, and the glare was reflected on the clouds. Heavy shells plunged into the harbor . . . docks and quay walls were rubble, and torn and broken ships lay everywhere."

Graves watched the soldiers as they "walked, stumbled or were carried" along the badly battered pier, in some places, down to its concrete piles, "the gaps . . . repaired by mess tables from ships, by ladders, wood planking, and other material taken from the debris around the harbor . . . silhouetted by the flames [as] the weary file of men stumbled along its length."

It appeared to Graves that "any man who presented himself abreast the ship was embarked. Only civilian families were excluded." Since *Medway Queen* rode low in the water, scaling ladders were placed against the mole down to her decks, with her crew assisting the soldiers above and below, as "work went on to an accompaniment of rough oaths and crude instructions, hurrying and harrying . . . in the exhausted state of most of the soldiers it proved to be the right approach.

"Finally, when the old ship was down nearly to her sponsons [paddle wheel encasings] in the water, the word would come to the captain, 'we are full up sir, time we went!' "

While in the past four days upwards of 80,000, or about twice the original "forlorn hope" had been lifted from the beaches, many more remained. As Ramsay wrote, in some self-contradiction, "The day closed with a formidable list of ships lost or damaged, a marked reduction in the number of destroyers available and with failure to achieve the high rate of evacuation hoped for."

Nonetheless, the Royal Navy could check off quite a fleet of destroyers, slightly in excess of 200, of vintages back to the Great War, but in conditions of seaworthiness and with degrees of modernity in armament and machinery. Ramsay hurried about seven of his newer ones off to Dunkirk, including H.M.S. *Esk.* Aboard her was another special deputy of the admiral, Rear Admiral William F. Wake Walker, unceremoniously hauled out of a fusty cubicle in the Admiralty, Whitehall, where with a dedicated staff he had been blueprinting an elaborate mine barrage north of Scotland.

One of those ordered to drop his pencils and calipers was Lieutenant Commander Cecil Wynne-Edwards, a lean, thoughtful, experienced navigator (and Yorkshireman, by the way), an indispensable member of the staff of any seagoing admiral. Even as Wynne-Edwards sailed through the dark, uncertain night, his pretty blonde wife, Bee Mary, a Cornwall native, was packing at their home in Portsmouth. Her activity was in response to the "private line" by which service ladies, especially those in His Majesty's Navy, knew at least simultaneously of a change in orders.

She gathered up extra uniforms, socks, warm underclothing, and some sweets and was soon at the station waiting for the morning's first train to Dover. She wasn't alone that predawn hour in Portsmouth, historically a Navy town. Other wives, too, had gotten the message.

As *Esk* nosed in toward Dunkirk in the first light of Thursday, May 30, Wynne-Edwards looked upon "one of the most astounding and pathetic sights I have ever seen.

"The whole ten miles of beach was black from sand dunes to waterline with tens of thousands of men. In places they stood up to their knees and waists in water waiting for their turn to get into the pitiably few boats. It seemed impossible that we should ever get more than a fraction of these men away."

Admiral Wake Walker, by plan, transferred his flag to the fleet minesweeper *Hebe*. When it was found that *Hebe* was needed to transport part of this "fraction" to England, he moved over to the destroyer *Windsor*, then to Wright's minesweeper *Gossamer*, yet another ship, then a torpedo boat, all in the space of a few hours. It became probably a record for continual transfer of command headquarters. Since Wake Walker had lost his flag somewhere in the confusion of this seaborne version of musical chairs, he soon was flying, according to the patient chronicler, Wynne-Edwards, "a converted bath towel, for we had no other."

It was a time of make-do. Struggling all week in the face of undeniably hopeless odds, E. H. Phillips was trying to salvage his ten Y.M.C.A. tea cars and their contents: cigarettes, chocolates, cakes, assorted "sweets," and, of course, tea. In between serving his refreshments to the cold, hungry, and thirsty troops, Phillips found himself ducking in a suddenly familiar routine inspired by the "incessantly" continuing air raids.

"Drop flat and stay still!" was a catechism he listened to hour in and hour out. That became easy enough to do, since the bombs drove into the soft sand and dissipated themselves without causing excessive casualties. However, by this Thursday he didn't have much of his stores to pass out. He had "parked" his tea cars beside a hotel as seemingly a safe shelter. Now, it had been struck by incendiary shells and fired.

As Phillips sought desperately to salvage what he could, he wondered if any of the soldiers were really sufficiently hungry to eat "scorched" cookies.

Farther up the beach, toward La Panne, Tommie Kerr was still attempting to get the engines of the water carrier to work. They resisted stubbornly. Then he was all but overwhelmed by "crowds of undisciplined French troops." Since he decided he couldn't "control that lot" he put his own men on the cumbersome water tank vessel and the whaler beside it and "lucky we did for the lorry was hit by shells."

Ted Harvey now was back on a new craft, the 50-foot Thames River boat *Silver Queen.* He had shuttled all morning to the *Esk,* carrying 100 soldiers at a time. Then, since the sea was not too rough and the *Esk* had steamed off, the young leftenant in command decided he'd take his latest batch direct to Dover.

"They were largely French colonials on board," Harvey recalled, "frightened, nervous."

However, as the smoke and the crump-crump of shells, together with the whomp of bombs, was left farther and farther astern, the men calmed and even began to sing "La Marsellaise." Although there was no compass, the young officer was following the shortest, simplest route, "Z," only 39 sea miles to Dover, close to shore, then heading across somewhere off Calais.

A haze drifted in, then gradually lifted slightly to reveal—white cliffs! The French poilus waved their hats and shouted for joy. Then, suddenly, "Bang!"

. Harvey himself saw shells, "big as pint milk bottles," slamming into the water, some ricocheting and zinging off toward the foggy horizon.

"*Le Boche! Le Boche!*" cried the soldiers, jostling each other in a frantic if hopeless effort to hide below the shallow gunwales. Without a compass, the *Silver Queen* had been steered straight for German-held Calais. In fact, she was right off the breakwater. Even then, under shore fire, Harvey mused detachedly to himself, "too bad for the leftenant."

Then he decided it was probably "too bad" for himself, too, as "a great battleship" loomed out of the mist directly at them. Surely it must be the *Scheer* or some much vaunted pocket battleship.

She boiled in so close that the wake knocked a lamp off the erstwhile river boat's stern and almost capsized her. Yet—salvation—it was H.M.S. *Calcutta,* the "ack-ack" cruiser. Not only did she return the shore fire, but she shepherded *Silver Queen* across the channel, almost into Ramsgate.

Harvey and his now shaken and gloomy leftenant discharged the troops, then cruised up to Sheerness. The near misses, it turned out, had opened up her old seams and off the pier, like a weary old elephant lying down to die, *Silver Queen* slowly disappeared beneath the opaque Thames waters.

Not far to the south, in Dover, Bee Mary Wynne-Edwards had sought, unsuccessfully, her husband. She asked for precise word as to his ship, if he were actually aboard a ship. She hurried, with others, onto the cliffs, where she saw the diverse rescue fleet moving back and forth through the mists, then went into the teeming city itself in quest of room and breakfast. She found none. People were sleeping in the hotel lobbies and restaurants.

She returned for her luggage, to the smoky, whistling railroad station, where even now trains were loading with the returned soldiers. She witnessed a stirring sight: " . . . people throwing flowers at them, cheering, passing out chocolates and cigarettes; hugging, kissing them . . . they were our newest and greatest heroes. The B.E.F. was coming home."

Part III

". . . the never ending stream of weary men . . ."

THE GERMANS knew the B.E.F. was escaping. And it was paradox. General Franz Halder, chief of staff of the Wehrmacht, would cry, "Thousands of the enemy are crossing the Channel under our very noses. We do not want to have to fight them again!"

Yet, Hitler would not order a resumption of the tank advance. Desperate British/French rear-guard action, employing the best of allied elite units—such as the Grenadier and Coldstream Guards —was maintaining the canal lines against the Nazi ground troops. The unsupported Luftwaffe, while inflicting painful damage, was proving it alone could not halt the exodus.

This crucial lack of coordination at the highest levels of German command was underscoring anew the continuing and frequently paralyzing rivalry among ground, air, and sea forces, especially between the navy and the Luftwaffe.

Ramsay, still sleepless, was fairly satisfied with Thursday's work. "Matters proceeded smoothly throughout the day," he wrote, "owing to the mist and there being a big smoke cloud over Dunkirk which prevented the enemy bombers attacking the ships in large numbers."

"In order to increase the rate of embarkation through the bottleneck of the East Pier gangway, the troops were urged to quicken their pace and eventually thousands . . . tired and without food and water for days, broke into the double and kept it up the whole length of the pier for more than two hours."

A ramp of lorries at Bray (probably in addition to Tommie Kerr's own brainchild) constructed by Army engineers was proving invaluable for embarking troops. At the same time, Ramsay had received a disquieting report that many of the small boats, casting off from this jerry-built pier and from the beaches, had been cast adrift once they reached the larger ships anchored or hove to in deeper water.

The vice admiral attributed this waste to "the lack of sufficient naval ratings as boat-keepers." Also, for the same reason "many of the smaller pulling boats were swamped and sunk due to overloading by uncontrolled 'rush' of soldiers."

There was one particular "rush" following the arrival at the mole of a storeship. Partially starved troops piled onto her, when she was only half unloaded. An emergency meeting was held between the ship's officers and their counterparts ashore. It was decided to cast off at once, and she did so . . . the ravenous soldiers still aboard, ripping open cartons, gulping down what they found, even cold salt fish.

Giblett himself watched the evening's debarkation, the "massive queue of men noticeably moving forward.

"I looked around me as we moved nearer and nearer to the mole and noticed once more the desolate scene, Dunkirk shattered and burning with the heavy pall of thick black smoke swirling over it. The mass of tired, hungry and thirsty men bunched together as they patiently moved forward nearer to where the ships were embarking as many as possible as quickly as circumstance permitted. The groans of wounded men on stretchers as stretcher bearers edged their way through towards the ships. Here some badly wounded men under the care of a nurse waiting for a chance to get onto a hospital ship which only could provide the medical care and attention they needed.

"Around the harbor and all along the beaches numerous wrecks of all kinds and on the shore several broken, battered, abandoned small boats no longer serviceable. A number of vehicles were scattered around, shattered and burnt out, and various debris littered the beaches.

"During the night the evacuation . . . continued despite occasional interruptions caused by enemy bombing attacks during which flares were dropped by the planes and both the ships and men on the beaches were bombed and machine gunned. As the planes droned overhead we would see a flicker of light and then a growing brightness as parachute flares dropped slowly towards the ground lighting up whole areas around the mole and the beaches. Then the planes swooped down to drop their bombs and machine gun the area, causing a rapid dispersal of everyone towards any possible cover the ground afforded.

"The night passed and with the coming of light I saw I was close enough to the mole to hope for evacuation . . . "

It was Friday, May 31, the sixth day of the operation. Wynne-Edwards, now with his admiral on the modern 1,400-ton destroyer

Keith (having a complement of nearly 200 and classed as a "flotilla leader"), logged "a fresh northerly breeze and enough sea to make inshore work difficult." Many boats broached at high water shortly after 8 A.M. and had to be left stranded up on the beach until the next tide came obligingly after them. Dividing his time between chart and staff work and the beach, the lieutenant commander added his voice to others who were exhorting the troops to "move westwards and close in on Dunkirk." It seemed "that the only hope of a complete evacuation lay in holding the harbour to the end and getting as many off from there as possible."

Direct lift from the beaches appeared to him to be hopelessly slow by comparison.

". . . the sky was clear, but despite this enemy aircraft gave little trouble during the earlier part of the day. Our fighter patrols were entirely adequate until the late afternoon and evening, when there were some gaps during which the enemy had things much his own way and many bombs were dropped. The bad weather and onshore wind, coupled with the stranding of so many small craft in the morning, slowed down the work on the beaches, sometimes almost to a standstill, and it became evident that there was no hope of bringing off the rearguard that night, as had originally been planned."

Up the beach, Tommie Kerr took advantage of the morning's same high tide to float his whaler.

"Just before it was too late to get anyone else on board," he noted, "we got some straggling British troops on board. It was blowing too hard for any more to get off from the beach and we told the lot we had to make themselves warm and comfortable and as soon as the wind eased down they would be rescued and as a lot of small pleasure craft and motor boats were coming and they would be able to get alongside at high water.

"In due course we manned our whaler and even with a trained crew we barely made it. Twice the seas broke over us. The destroyers had all moved off towards Dunkirk and we pulled with tired locks out to sea. Presently up came, of all things, the Margate lifeboat and we climbed on board. We towed the whaler to the best of our judgment where it would float ashore to the others, and then let go."

It was necessary to accelerate embarkation since the enemy was closing in hour by hour, and, as Ramsay reported, German "artillery were gradually finding the range of the loading berth." This was evident to Giblett, among the thousands of other soldiers nearing the mole, "the most hazardous time of all as everything the enemy could do was particularly directed against the ships lying alongside the mole embarking troops."

Then, moving across the narrow, patched up jetty with bomb craters all around it was to him "like running the gauntlet . . . we had to judge the right time to make our dash in between the salvoes of shells and falling bombs . . . there were wounded men on stretchers to be carried along to the ships and those carrying out this task could not dash along, so the quieter periods were needed for them to carry the wounded along, and with the jetty in a shaky condition it took care and time negotiating the tricky places. . . .

"The Germans were now putting on all the pressure they could . . . there was little time between the appearance of an enemy air formation and their departure after the inevitable bombing before the next formation was seen heading in our direction. We were obviously in for a hectic time; every now and then a number of planes would peel off and dive towards some target followed by sounds of gunfire as every available gun on the navy's ships blazed away at the planes."

Giblett then directed his attention towards a cross-channel steamer at the mole's very end, with destroyers beside her. As he did so a formation of enemy bombers dived and "all hell was let loose." Return fire from the ships kept the planes high and little damage was done.

Action was being stepped up all along the ever-shrinking evacuation perimeter. The destroyer *Hebe* was actually under shore artillery fire off La Panne, while Wake Walker, aboard the *Keith,* found himself ducking a similar barrage.

"At about the same time," Wynne-Edwards would recall, "a tremendous aerial battle was developing overhead. Our fighters were greatly outnumbered and while they engaged the enemy fighters many bombers broke through."

However, he found most of the attacks "ill-executed," and *Keith* curved at her 31-knot top and twisted, her mast tips almost on the water during tight turns, through the shell and bomb geysers around her . . . "at high speed it was possible to dodge the bombs."

Giblett himself, nearing one of the ships off the mole, continued to watch the aerial activity.

"... our own fighter planes though as usual in such small numbers, yet full of courage and determination ploughed into the enemy formation breaking them up and scattering them in all directions. The usual dogfights took place and planes darted about the sky twisting and weaving among the pattern of tracer bullets as machine guns rattled away. One plane disintegrated in a flash of flame and the pieces showered about as they fell to earth, while another dived down with its engine roaring and plunged into the sea with a mighty splash.

"... I was now at the beginning of the mole and started to make my way along it to where the cross channel steamer seemed about to cast off, having taken on all the troops she could manage. She was crowded with men and I doubted whether it would be possible for me to get aboard. Suddenly a couple of German fighters dived steeply out of the sky and streaked towards the ship with their machine guns blazing away as they swept over the ships and across the mole.

"Instinctively, I threw myself flat and waited a few moments before having a quick glance to make sure they were not on the way back, then getting up I hurried towards the ship which seemed about to sail.

" 'Come on, be quick!' called a naval officer standing near the ship and I and a few others ran the last thirty yards or so, and scrambled aboard just as the ship began very slowly to move away from the mole."

Not all soldiers were necessarily as determined as Giblett to leave the beach. Some had lapsed into a state of mingled shock and apathy, not only bone-weary and hungry, but shaken by the sight of so much death around them and by the constant spectacle of ship after ship being hit, usually set afire and sunk. Ackrell, for example, had seen one man lingering near the ruins of a house fronting the esplanade.

"Why don't you go home?" Ackrell asked.

"No, I'm staying here," he grunted. Then he adjusted the back pack he'd been using as a pillow and rolled over. So far as Ackrell knew, he did stay.

This day, the reluctant soldier could have availed himself of the largest offering of transportation yet. Ramsay had scraped the bottom of his sea locker and shaken into smoky, steamy life even the largely semiretired, creaky old coalburning channel steamers. Their very sight evoked memories in the middle-aged of the stirring days of 1914–18. As the vice admiral put it, their "short endurance necessitated coaling between trips," something not possible either in Dover or Dunkirk.

More remarkable yet was the appearance of the *Massey Shaw*, a fire boat, or "float," of the London Fire Brigade. With her shallow draft, she was designed for sloshing over the Thames mud between piers, not for going to sea. She carried a crew of only twelve.

Pumps, hoses, shining brass nozzles, she arrived this Friday afternoon in all her garish, red splendor, to be logged laconically in H.M.S. catch-all class, "other vessels." With her she brought much-needed water.

Plucked from the beach for her first return trip was, among many others, fifteen-year-old Peter Solari, from the lost *Crested Eagle*, suffering with a head wound. His memories of the three days at Dunkirk were necessarily a blur. *Massey Shaw* pulled out of the harbor in the day's lengthening shadows to join the unusually large flotilla of homeward-bound craft. As Giblett wrote, "every minute was taking us away from Dunkirk and as the coastline faded into the distance we began to feel hopeful we had finally got rid of our tormenters."

She had been bombed and machine gunned almost all the way into the open sea. Short rations continued as a plaguing problem. However, "water was passed around from the ship's supplies and loaves of bread were sliced among groups of men to help relieve our hunger and thirst."

Wright, on the *Gossamer*, also attested to this persistent over-riding hunger: "On every trip we found that the troops cleaned us out of food and the cooks were kept busy preparing stuff for them as we felt their need was greater than ours—we kept going on cups of tea, bits of chocolate and ship's biscuit (which I always think taste of castor oil)."

The soldiers appeared more famished yet to Thomas R. Russell, cook on the *Medway Queen:* " . . . starving animals, most of them too desperately hungry and thirsty to be polite—pushing, shoving and shouting. Someone opened the starboard half-door and they started to flood for service right into the galley, then tried to exit from the other door . . . it was pandemonium."

Along with "little people" like Giblett, Major McKellar, Solari, or Ackrell, the "big people" were also being taken out—Lord Gort and his large staff aboard *Hebe,* at 5 P.M., from La Panne. This Belgian beach was now under increasing artillery fire and all but untenable. However, since destroyers continued to be such a prime target for the Luftwaffe, Gort was soon transferred to a motor torpedo boat to continue his short voyage. Yet even the latter was not without its own tribulations, as Wynne-Edwards would observe:

"This vessel had earlier been in collision, and was holed just above her waterline on the starboard bow. She was all right when the bow lifted at high speed, but could ill afford to slow down without a sailor sitting in the hole."

At that the B.E.F.'s commander-in-chief had smoother sailing than Able Seaman Sam Palmer, whose 30-foot motor yacht *Naiad Errant* had been swamped. While he refloated the little craft, he could not coax its weary engines back to life. With eight soldiers on board who had no desire to return to the beach and larger vessels apparently not aware of his plight, Palmer determined to make England anyhow.

"Break up the hatches!" he ordered, in a flash of inspiration.

This the willing passengers did. "Now paddle!"

They paddled, and they made headway until, after several hours, one engine sputtered. Soon the yacht was creeping along at five knots. The men were on their way home.

Giblett almost *was* there: "At last we could clearly see the coastline of England and, as we drew nearer, the cliffs of Dover prominently stood out and grew larger. The ship approached the entrance to Dover harbour and down towards its berth at the quayside. What a feeling of reflief it was to be back once more in our homeland, the nightmare of Dunkirk seemed a long way away and I for one gave heartfelt thanks to those who had so unselfishly given of their best efforts to bring us safely home."

Now there remained only the trains and the "ladies awaiting us with hot tea, sandwiches and cakes."

Altogether it had been quite a day, this Friday, May 31. The evacuation peaked at 64,141, for a total of more than 196,000, or about two-thirds of the B.E.F. So heartening was the success of the operation that the British press was at last allowed to advise readers of what was going on. The news was inescapably exhilarating even at this stage of incompletion—so much so that Churchill already felt compelled to warn his cabinet and certain members of Parliament that "wars are not won by evacuations."

Ramsay, less constrained, was praising the "unremitting determination" of the navy, whose "surviving vessels had been operating ceaselessly for at least five days, and officers and men were approaching a condition of complete exhaustion."

Wright, on the *Gossamer,* could total up only "seven hours sleep in five days," as he shuttled with charmed existence in and out of the "inferno of Dunkirk," thoroughly convinced by now that there was "no more unpleasant noise than when you know you are the target of a screaming dive bomber and very conspicuous."

Then, as Wynne-Edwards would recall, "Black Saturday," June 1 dawned:

"During the night La Panne was under very heavy shell fire, which died down as daylight came. It was apparent that ships would have to withdraw to the westward at daybreak as the Germans had advanced to the Belgian frontier between La Panne and Bray."

With full dawn the gray, ravaged coast at La Panne seemed to be deserted. Only the litter of wrecked, abandoned military vehicles and sunken or half sunken ships and small boats was visible. The soldiers were farther down the beach, pushing into Dunkirk ahead of the Germans, who were closing in once more. At 7:30 A.M. large formations of swastika-marked bombers droned up from the south, escorted by fighters in apparent great strength. With no R.A.F. opposition, they dived at will on the Allied ships, by this time very short of ammunition and thus barely able to defend themselves.

" . . . we in *Keith* had not a round remaining. Attacks were made on most of the ships . . . and harbour. In one attack on *Keith* about a dozen or more Junkers-87 dived vertically from about 10,000 feet and released their bombs at 2,000–3,000 feet. All missed, but one salvo dropped so close astern that it jammed the rudder."

Paradoxically, there was lively betting among the officers on the bridge as to whether or not the successive salvoes would find their mark. *Keith* steamed at her full 31 knots in tight circles "impotently," unable to fight back. The destroyer *Havant* and minesweeper *Skipjack* nearby were sunk, and the minesweeper *Salaman-*

der damaged seriously.   H.M.S. *Skipjack,* with nearly 300 soldiers below deck, sank so quickly that almost none was saved.

This disaster was comparable to another shortly thereafter: the bombing and capsizing of the railway steamer *Scotia,* a coal burner. She lost about the same number of troops, all French, of which a total of 2,000 had been embarked, and 30 of her crew.

Keith's phenomenal luck finally ran out.   First she was hit amidships by one salvo; then a single bomb plunged down the aft funnel and exploded with a doomsday roar in No. 2 boiler room. Wynne-Edwards wrote, "The ship lost steam and had to anchor . . . in the fairway.   After summoning two tugs to stand by *Keith* the admiral [Wake Walker] disembarked into a motor torpedo boat, and we proceeded towards Dunkirk to find out the situation inside the harbour.   Attacks were still going on, and a squadron of dive bombers attacked the M.T.B. as we steamed westwards."

The admiral and his staff were then machine gunned most of the way to Dunkirk.   Still, they fared better than most of the complement of *Keith,* sunk by a final attack after most of remaining crew had been picked up by the attending tugs.   One of the two tugs, struck by a bomb, blew to bits.   There were no survivors.

Wake Walker, noting that "things are getting very hot for ships," decided it was time to report to Ramsay in Dover, since the evacuation was assuming a disastrous character.   At 9:30 A.M. he started off in a torpedo boat, once again being sped on his way by continual bombing and gunning.

At Dover, Bee Mary was waiting for Cecil Wynne-Edwards. Persistence had won out.   Not only had she haunted the debarkation docks, but, the Navy wives' "private line" had worked.

"Oh, he was grimy, tired, unshaven," she recalls, "and wrapped in a blanket was a present—a little alcohol primus stove, the only thing he had salvaged from his ship.   He thought he'd need it when he went up to Scotland and the mine barrage."

Halfway across and almost in sight of the chalk cliffs was the durable Ted Harvey, now on the 30-foot cabin cruiser *Thark,* one of several small craft under tow.   There were nearly 200 persons aboard, including several French women.

Then, with little warning, the cable snarled, tipping the overloaded cabin cruiser over and projecting everyone into the cold waters.   Most, possibly all, were picked up by the tug.   One of the drenched women, through an interpreter, explained that this was indeed *"assez!"*(enough!). She had lost her whole family, and who did she have to blame?

"Le Boche, Le Boche!"

Ramsay had every reason to wonder how many more troops could be rescued as he wrote, "The toll of casualties of ships during the day was mounting, particularly amongst the destroyers and shortly after midday the Commander-in-Chief, Nore, called the attention of the Admiralty to this, suggesting the discontinuation of the use of destroyers by day off the French coast."

In London, officers at the Admiralty studied their charts and worked out projections. The casualties to the rescue fleet including auxiliaries had passed 25 percent and were still climbing. The destroyers had been hurt the worst: six sunk, 23 damaged, for a casualty rate of an unbelievable 75 percent. Such attrition was clearly intolerable. In conventional warfare it would have been epitaph for a battle already lost. Even in Jutland's clash of mighty juggernauts in 1916, the Grand Fleet sustained only ten percent losses, the German High Seas Fleet roughly the same.

Preeminent, however, among those who continued to steam jauntily through fire and torment, the *Medway Queen* continued on her cross-channel commuting. On the aft deck a sandbagged enclosure had been set up. As Graves wrote, "On *Medway Queen* we believed in concentrated fire power. I took a party ashore at Dunkirk and succeeded in 'borrowing' a number of abandoned bren guns, these were lashed to stays and shrouds with a single turn of rope which formed an ideal swivel. Provided with a pile of ammunition beside each, they were handy for whoever was nearest to use in an attack. Beyond this, all troops and sailors who had a rifle were encouraged to blaze away at approaching aircraft on the sound principle that a storm of rifle fire could be as effective as a number of machine-guns. The total result was impressive in discouraging any close approach by hostile aircraft and certainly contributed to . . . our good score of three low flying aircraft shot down."

Now they had taken aboard among their mixed passenger list a group of Spanish sailors, refugees from the recent Spanish Civil War who had been overtaken by the German advance. Leaving Dunkirk, the paddle steamer was hailed by a lone naval-uniformed officer in a small motor boat urging the vessel to proceed down the coast to a position where some troops were supposedly cut off and awaiting evacuation.

"We set off," Graves reported, "but speaking by chance to the Spaniards, they were horrified and gave us to understand the place had been in German hands for two days. They had escaped from there!"

Ramsay, this "very dark night," was made aware of such false information being passed to ships. He was led to believe that it originated from "a non-identified skoot," the Dutch coastal class of vessel which had proven so useful.

"The plan of the night," the admiral continued, "provided for all minesweepers including paddlers, skoots, and all small craft, except special flotillas especially organized, to go to the beach stretching eastward one and a half miles from Dunkirk. Dunkirk Harbour was to be served by up to seven personnel ships, eight destroyers, and the inner harbour nine drifters and special power boats organized from Ramsgate.

"The French vessels were to serve the Quay in the new outer harbour and private small boats, the Quay Felix Faure and in addition about one hundred French small beach fishing craft and drifters for the beach immediately east of Dunkirk. It was estimated that the British vessels could lift about 17,000 between 2100/1 and 0300/2, probably in the proportion 50 percent British and 50 percent French.

"The plan was set in motion without incident until 2200 when it was reported that a number of towing craft and small boats were returning empty from the coast. All ships were warned to look out for these and to send them back to their duty on the coast."

As Saturday night drew to a close, *Gossamer* was feeling her way through the wreck-strewn channel on her fifth trip.

"The decks were cluttered," Wright wrote, "with empty shell cases and, inside, the ship was like a shambles. The stench of stale wounds and sweat was enough to make the toughest stomach vomit."

On the last crossing two of the badly wounded succumbed "and we had no alternative but to tip them overboard."

In the first minutes of Sunday morning, June 2, as Wright, "listening," peered through the night, now the blacker from haze and smoke, he had the feeling that "the troops had probably been captured and that the beach might be in the hands of the Germans. We knew that this was the very last lot of troops who had to be holding this village to protect Dunkirk.

"We could clearly see the fires of Dunkirk five miles away and hear the occasional boom of guns inland. About 0130 we heard a faint splashing noise in the water. Someone was swimming out to us.

"Presently there was a yell of 'help! I'm finished! I've got an important message for your captain!'

"A young rating who was a very good swimmer—the assistant cook as a matter of fact—dived overboard and brought in a half-drowned man, who turned out to be a Lieutenant Commander McClellan. He was from one of the ships which had been sunk the previous day. Since then he had been ashore with the troops. He had a bad shrapnel wound in the ankle and when we first got him on board he was so exhausted he was unable to speak."

Then the captain of the minesweeper knelt beside him on the quarterdeck and listened while he gasped out a message that all ships eastward of us should be signalled to proceed to Dunkirk to which 6,000 British troops were marching.

"The scene as I saw it in the dim light with a circle of men standing silently round the two central figures, made me feel for the moment as though I was taking part in a Hollywood film."

McClellan recovered in a surprisingly short time, aided by cups of hot chocolate, swigs of rum, warm clothing, and blankets. He added that the troops "should soon be on the beach."

About the same time Ramsay received the intelligence, "considerable number British troops still on mole. Military are expecting further arrivals there."

There was indeed a "considerable number." As *Gossamer* pushed in closer, Wright would report, "soon the troops began to emerge and were standing in hundreds on the beach and in the water. They were yelling and shouting to us to fetch them off quickly and saying that there were many wounded there. We could only yell back that we had no boats and that they must find some."

The tired men's patience was tested this Sunday as the larger ships hove to offshore and the little craft were assembled to chug in when darkness returned. Among the latter was Ted Harvey, now on his fourth boat, the *Hilfranoor.* Waiting for orders, Harvey was struck by the wasteland appearance, wreckage everywhere, including the beautiful steamer, *Queen of the Channel.*

Hardly able to keep awake, he wondered if this would be his last trip.

While normal evacuation by the little ships like the *Hilfranoor* and the larger ships like the *Gossamer* was suspended, it was decided, nonetheless, that hospital ships could be operated, in spite of blatant past attacks on them. Ramsay received a radio message from the beaches:

"Wounded situation acute and Hospital ships should enter during day. Geneva Convention will be honourably observed, it is felt, and that the enemy will refrain from attacking."

The *Worthing* sailed out of Dover only to be bombed about two-thirds of the way across. She turned back for repairs, refueling, and new orders. At the same time, another Red Cross-marked vessel, the *Paris*, got up steam for one more try.

That Sunday evening, as the rescue fleet once more prepared to receive the troops, Wynne-Edwards, back at Dunkirk, was impressed by a number of sights, sounds, emotions, and some finer nuances somewhere in between. The rear guards, most predominantly, were now arriving at the beaches, among them the historic Grenadier Guards, as Wynne-Edwards would write.

". . . after three weeks of continuous fighting marching in file down the pier, yes and some even singing as they marched, very different in bearing and discipline from the earlier thousands who had come off from the beaches. These were the real fighters, the heroes who defended Dunkirk to the last, who had borne the brunt of the fighting, and made all this outstanding evacuation possible."

Something in addition had been stamped indelibly on the lieutenant commander's mind and senses, the "dramatic" spectacle "by night of the eastern arm of the harbor lit up in silhouette by the huge flames behind it with the never-ending stream of weary men moving down it, sometimes hurrying into a tired run, sometimes plodding blindly on towards safety, sometimes packed up stationary on the narrow parapet waiting for the next ship to berth."

Wynne-Edwards was sure this was "a sight which will live for always in my memory."

Others might have said the same concerning the repeated attacks on the hospital ships, which, as Churchill would observe, were "a special target of Nazi bombs." *Paris*, flood lights playing on the huge Red Crosses on her sides, decks, and superstructure, started off in the early evening. She had progressed to about the same position where *Worthing* was attacked when she herself was heavily dive bombed.

An S.O.S. brought several tugs, which towed her to a buoy ten miles off the French coast. There she sank after her crew had been removed. Less bitter than Churchill, Ramsay reported, "the last attempt to evacuate the wounded by Hospital Carrier from Dunkirk was brought to naught."

Accumulating on the beach and pier were 230 stretcher cases, with more still arriving. Those who could walk or hobble were making Herculean efforts to leave the litters, some pitifully insisting they were "all right." Since prospects of removing them appeared increasingly dark, the medical staff drew lots to see who would remain with the wounded. It fell to three doctors and 30 orderlies.

With the first haze of evening, the "armada," as Ramsay described it, led by thirteen surviving Channel steamers, including several of the coal burners, moved in. The wounded would not be left behind.

In the early hours of Monday, June 3, copy desk writers at the *London Times* manifested unfamiliar enthusiasm as they set in type the two-column headline: BULK OF THE B.E.F. SAVED.

It was just about true, since nearly 300,000 had been ferried from the French and Belgian sands. Yet more, still, waited.

A few minutes after 3 A.M., Ramsay received a message that all ships were hauling away from the beaches and harbor, while "the flow of French troops had dwindled away." In fact, it was reported that one ship idled two and a half hours to embark her load, so thin was the trickle to come aboard.

"No assurance could be obtained," the vice admiral added, "that this coming night would terminate the operation and considerable anxiety was felt regarding the effect of the gradual exhaustion of officers and men of the ships taking part in the 'Dynamo.' This exhaustion was particularly marked in the Destroyer force, remnants of which had been executing a series of round trips without intermission for several days under navigation conditions of extreme difficulty and in the face of unparalleled air attacks."

He then advised the Admiralty, in the predawn hours of Monday, that continued operations would surely prove "beyond the limit of human endurance." He asked that fresh forces, *if* they could be found, be used should the evacuation continue.

Ramsay waited. The morning mists cleared, revealing the now familiar dots of ships sailing towards Dover, ships of all sizes and shapes, with battle scars of varying degrees of severity. Paddling the other way was *Medway Queen*, on her seventh trip, possibly a record. None, not even Ramsay himself, could keep tally of any more records, since superlatives and the "impossible" had become the rule, rather than exception. As the little steamer berthed against the mole, Graves distinctly heard approaching machine gun fire.

"The sands were running out very fast," he wrote. "We took on board about 400 French troops—all the B.E.F. had by this time left. Shelling in the harbor was very heavy. A destroyer astern of *Medway Queen* was hit and flung forward against our starboard paddle box, extensively damaging the sponson."

In early afternoon, Ramsay passed the order that all ships were to leave Dunkirk by 2:30 the next morning. It was none too soon. Monday night, advance German army troops appeared on the streets of Dunkirk, along the battered, wreck-strewn esplanade, and finally onto the beaches.

Medway Queen, with one of her officers "strumming a mandolin on the after deck to cheer up the tired Frenchman," finally pulled clear of the shell-pocked pier. It was 1 A.M. Tuesday, June 4. Now, the dark silhouettes of enemy soldiers, like precursors of doom from the lower regions, could be seen running along the mole. Bullets began to rattle off the paddle steamer's sides.

Near her, the destroyers *Express* and World War I *Shikari* (totally undamaged after the long evacuation) also glided out into the harbor waters, "still lit by blazing oil tanks falling astern," as Graves saw the scene.

A fog rolled in, somehow symbolic of a curtain falling upon the final act of a great and bizarre drama. *Medway Queen* and the two destroyers pushed into the dampness of the North Sea. Slowly, the machine gunning faded, the light from the fires dimmed into a glow. Once more, the throb of the vessels' engines and the swish of foaming, occasionally phosphorescent, salt water under the bows predominated.

To Graves, to Wynne-Edwards, to all en route to England or already there, the whole, unreal experience was becoming but the fitful memory of a nightmare.

Epilogue:

Home from the Sea

THAT VERY TUESDAY AFTERNOON, about 3 o'clock, half an hour after the Admiralty had formally declared Dynamo "terminated," Winston Churchill stood before the House of Commons to review a momentous nine days. After warning that "we must be very careful not to assign to this deliverance the attributes of a victory," he continued:

"Even though large tracts of Europe and many old and famous States have fallen or may fall into the grip of the Gestapo and all the odious apparatus of Nazi rule, we shall not flag or fail. We shall go on to the end, we shall fight in France, we shall fight in the seas and oceans, we shall fight with growing confidence and growing strength in the air, we shall defend our island, whatever the cost may be, we shall fight on the beaches, we shall fight on the landing-grounds, we shall fight in the fields and in the streets, we shall fight in the hills; we shall never surrender, and even if, which I do not for a moment believe, this island or a large part of it were subjugated and starving, then our Empire beyond the seas, armed and guarded by the British Fleet would carry on the struggle, until, in God's good time, the New World, with all its power and might, steps forth to the rescue and the liberation of the Old."

As the radio commentator Edward R. Murrow put it, Churchill was underscoring anew his ability "to mobilize the English language and send it into battle."

Just under 339,000 troops, about two-thirds British, had been rescued. Some 2,000 had died during the operation. Of the civilian ship crews, 126 had been killed or drowned.

The Royal Navy would never furnish overall figures on its human toll, although of the "principal" ships (destroyers, minesweepers, sloops, gunboats, trawlers, "personnel" carriers, and others) 35 were sunk and 41 damaged. Not all losses were as catastrophic as that of the destroyer *Wakeful*, most of whose complement of 150 went down with her. On the other hand, her destruction provided at least a hint of the magnitude of the naval losses, including the French, whose navy lost three destroyers among other vessels.

Ramsay himself did not know the exact size of the evacuation fleet. Estimations, including the "little ships," range from 693 to 845, with those destroyed stated to be between 25 and 35 percent. Yet, staggering as these casualties were, the B.E.F. *had* been brought home, and a negotiated peace, which would have altered world history, thereby obviated.

But, *how* had this "miracle of deliverance," as the Prime Minister termed it, actually been achieved? Churchill asserted:

". . . by valour, by perseverance, by perfect discipline, by dauntless service, by resource, by skill, by unconquerable fidelity . . ."

Those who participated could hardly disagree. But they carried away additional thoughts as well.

It was "the naval organization, once it got underway," David Divine, correspondent at Dunkirk, has told this author. As part of that "organization" he pointed to the navy's ability not only to sweep channels for mines but to constantly divert traffic to different channels, and just another example of the genius of Ramsay. Even the enemy aided in the operation by halting its tanks and by falling victim to the Nazis' often paralyzing rivalry among their own forces, land, sea, and air.

Officers such as Wynne-Edwards "felt most of the time we wouldn't complete it," adding, "it must be accounted little less than a miracle that the five-foot wide wooden pathway along which so many tens of thousands walked to safety should have remained intact to the end."

Peter Solari firmly believes that Divine Providence sent in protective screens of fog many nights and early mornings, augmenting the smoke by day from the burning refineries to at least harass Luftwaffe bombardiers. He also considers that nine days without storms as something more than coincidence.

John Graves, while paying credit to "the wonderful work of the army rear guard," finds that "incredible cheek" in daring to attempt something "obviously impossible" had much to do with the "miracle of deliverance."

Ted Harvey, convinced that "Dunkirk may be equalled but never exceeded," adds, "never assess one's ability until the occasion arises." In part, his comment was inspired by his belief that the Germans suffered from an underestimation of their foe as typified by the remark attributed to one of their generals: "What are the stupid British up to?"

Ramsay, while expressing disappointment at the "extremely disheartening" R.A.F. cover, paid tribute to "a continued flow in ever increasing numbers of small power boats and beach craft" which insured a "continued evacuation from the beaches."

Without "the little ships" to "feed" and generally support the larger, the operation would have been impossible. The mole alone was not sufficient.

There is hardly one, all-encompassing answer for the "deliverance," although raw courage must necessarily place high upon any list. It was, for example, the same courage manifest on November 5, 1940, in mid-Atlantic when Captain E. S. Fogarty Fegen fought the pocket battleship *Scheer* with his hopelessly outgunned, aging, 14,000-ton armed merchantman *Jervis Bay*.

In sacrificing his vessel and himself Fegen saved the bulk of his convoy of 37 ships and hammered out another chapter in the history of valor at sea, even as his "Island Kingdom" was hanging on until "in God's good time, the New World" stepped forth "to the rescue."

". . . Fogarty Fegen? Yes, I knew Fogarty Fegen. Served with him when I put *Jervis Bay* in commission. Big man, with an Irish temper. Used to throw his cap on the deck and stamp on it . . . awful temper he had. I knew Fegen."

Speaking was James A. P. Blackburn, whose own command, the *Voltaire*, also an armed one-time passenger liner, "dressed up as a fighting ship," met her fate in April, 1941, en route to Sierra Leone under the merciless guns of the German auxiliary cruiser *Thor.* Blackburn "stepped" into the water as the burning *Voltaire* went down, carrying with her one-third of her crew of nearly 300. The rest of the war was spent by her captain in a German "Marine Lager."

Now nearing 90, a bright-eyed, sharp little man, Blackburn had come back from the sea which has been virtually synonymous with his life since he was a boy climbing the rigging of sailing ships and fighting the Germans in two World Wars, winning a D.S.C. But neither he nor his wife, Hilda, ever moved far from the water, residing today in Eastbourne where the Channel fogs come in and bell buoys toll their long, nostalgic lullabies.

Blackburn, who doesn't regret a moment of his career, not even the months in P.O.W. camp, is peculiarly symbolic of all the sailors who have come home, who have fought wind and sea and sometimes a human or perhaps inhuman enemy. He is at once distinctly his own person, yet joined in that common bond evoked only by the sea and its own restless, unrestrained omnipotence.

Like Semmes, George Washington De Long, Bill Turner, Oliver Naquin, Sir Bertram Ramsay, Cecil Wynne-Edwards, or Ted Harvey, the multitudes who preceded and followed him to become one with the sea's continuing epics, this old sailor in Eastbourne has come home.

Bibliography

1: The Ordeal of William Bligh

This narrative does not focus on personalities and motivations. It deals solely with the epic struggle of men in a small boat to save their lives. The character of Captain Bligh has been so fuzzied over the years by fiction and half-truths that there is considerable doubt as to what the man really was like. Certain only is the fact that where Bligh walked or sailed, trouble and turmoil dogged his steps, or his wake. That, too, he was product of rough, turbulent times and dreadful conditions of existence at sea is undeniable.

Further, the rights or wrongs of the mutiny, whether Fletcher Christian was hero or villain or in a gray milieu somewhere in between is beyond the scope of this chapter.

To this author the only hope of presenting a factual canvas of castaways attempting to reach civilization over thousands of miles of unfriendly sea appeared to lie in an original source. Such are William Bligh's own journals. Recently they were printed, just as written by him, in Australia, under the U.S. Library of Congress entry:

A Voyage to the South Sea—Undertaken by Command of His Majesty for the Purpose of Conveying the Breadfruit Tree to the West

Indies, in His Majesty's Ship Bounty, *Commanded by Lieutenant William Bligh.* London: George Nicol, 1972. Australia Facsimile Editions No. 121. Reproduced by the Libraries Board of South Australia. Adelaide. 1969.

A number of books on Bligh and the *Bounty* have been produced in recent decades, drawing on primary records, especially those of the court-martial. While this chapter is based wholly on William Bligh's own, unadorned account (certainly the most logical person to recall that long ago adventure), the titles listed below are recommended as possible additional reading.

Anthony, Irvin, ed. *The Saga of the Bounty: Its Strange History as Related by the Participants Themselves.* New York: G.P. Putnam's Sons, 1935.

Hough, Richard A. *Captain Bligh and Mr. Christian, the Men and the Mutiny.* New York: E.P. Dutton, 1973.

Mackaness, George. *The Life of Vice Admiral William Bligh.* Australia: Angus and Robertson, 1931.

Rutter, Owen. *The True Story of The* Bounty. London: Newnes, 1936.

2: The Blue Riband

Slowly fading from living memory is the once all-important Blue Riband. That there actually was no such physical entity seems to have remained boldly beside the point. For more than a century the peculiar lure of this salty will o' the wisp sparked the contest for fastest across the Atlantic and, in so doing, the competition for bigger and better steamships to attain that goal.

Speed, which sailing ships measured in weeks, was translated into days when steam vapors and coal smoke demarked new lanes across the North Atlantic. Then came the long-distance airplane, and days became hours. Now, with the supersonic transport—minutes?

Source material for this chapter extends back to Charles Dickens and yet earlier. A great number of newspapers on both sides of the "Big Pond" supplied much of the grist, at least the mood. Unfortunately, for the purposes of this somewhat condensed section, they are just too many to list. While the same (to a lesser extent) is true of books, the titles listed below were among those consulted.

Beaver, Patrick. *The Big Ship.* London: Hugh Evelyn, 1969.

Benstead, C.R. *Atlantic Ferry.* London: Methuen & Co., 1936.

Braynard, Frank O. *S.S. Savannah.* Athens: University of Georgia Press, 1963.

Brinnin, John Malcolm. *The Sway of the Grand Saloon, A Social History of the North Atlantic.* New York: Delacorte Press, 1971.

Brown, Alexander C. *Women and Children Last.* New York: G.P. Putnam's Sons, 1962.

Buchanan, Lamont. *Ships of Steam.* New York: McGraw-Hill Book Co., 1956.

Clark, A.H. *The Clipper Ship Era.* New York: G.P. Putnam's Sons, 1910.

Dickens, Charles. *American Notes.* Paris: Baudry's European Library, 1842.

Dodman, Frank E. *Ships of the Cunard Line.* London: Adlard Coles Ltd., 1955.

Dugan, James. *The Great Iron Ship.* New York: Harper Bros., 1953.

Farr, Grahame. *The Steamship Great Western, the First Atlantic Liner.* Bristol, England: F. Barber & Son, 1963.

Forwood, Sir William B. *Recollections of a Busy Life.* Liverpool: Henry Young & Sons, 1911.

Hoehling, A.A. *Great Ship Disasters.* New York: Cowles Book Co., 1971.

Hoehling, A.A. *They Sailed Into Oblivion.* New York: Yoseloff, 1959.

Hyde, Frances E. *Cunard Liners of the North Atlantic 1840–1973.* London: MacMillan Press, 1975.

Lane, Wheaton J. *Commodore Vanderbilt; an Epic of the Steam Age.* New York: Knopf, 1942.

Lee, Charles E. *The Blue Riband.* London: Sampson Low Marston & Co., 1930.

Low, Garrett W., and Haney, Kenneth, ed. *Gold Rush by Sea.* Philadelphia: University of Pennsylvania Press, 1941.

Lytle, William M. *Merchant Steam Vessels of the United States, 1790–1868.* Steamship Historical Society of America / University of Baltimore Press, 1975.

Marvin, Winthrop L. *The American Merchant Marine.* New York: Charles Scribners & Sons, 1910.

O'Brien, Frank M. *The Story of the Sun.* New York: D. Appleton & Co., 1928.

Pond, E. Long. *Junius Smith, a Biography of the Father of the Atlantic Liner.* Freeport, New York: Books for Libraries, 1927/1971.

Rydell, Raymond A. *Cape Horn to the Pacific.* Los Angeles: University of California Press, 1952.

Wells, Evelyn, and Peterson, Harry C. *The '49-ers.* Garden City, New York: Doubleday & Co., 1949.

Yeomans, Frances Y. *A Voyage to the United States of America.* Manchester, England: Privately Printed, 1851.

3: Cruise of the Alabama

The principal source for this chapter is *Cruise of the Alabama and Sumter,* the journal kept by Raphael Semmes and published by Saunders Otley & Co., London, in 1864. Successive editions, somewhat altered in text, appeared over the next 40 years. That no American editions arrived until a century later, in time for the centennial, may be testament to a lingering antipathy toward this mass destroyer of the U.S. merchant fleet, and the lack of Southern publishing houses.

There are, of course, corroborating sources detailing the depradations of this colorful, if austere, raider, especially the *Official Records of the Confederate and Union Navies,* Series I, vols. 2 & 3 (Washington: U.S. Government Printing Office, 1894–95), although references to the *Alabama, Kearsarge,* and other Confederate cruisers as well as the Union vessels pursuing them are to be found in other volumes.

Another source is the bible of the Civil War enthusiast, *Battles and Leaders of the Civil War,* edited by Robert Underwood and Clarence Clough Buel (New York: The Century Co., 1887–88). This basic reference source contains articles originally published in the *Century* magazine. Volume 4 contains accounts by John McIntosh Kell, Surgeon John M. Browne, and by Professor James Russell Soley, naval historian.

Other pertinent sources are listed below.

Civil War Naval Chronology, 1861–65. Washington, D.C.: Naval History Division, Navy Department, 1971.

Clark, William H. *Ships and Sailors.* Boston: L. C. Page and Co., 1938.

Elliott, John M. *The Life of John Ancrum Winslow.* New York: G. P. Putnam's Sons, 1902.

Jones, Virgil C. *The Civil War at Sea.* vol. 2, 1961. vol. 3, 1962. New York: Holt Rinehart & Winston.

Krafft, Herman F., and Norris, Walter B. *Sea Power in American History.* New York: Century Co., 1920.

Sinclair, Arthur. *Two Years on the* Alabama. Boston: Lee and Sheppard, 1895.

Slinkman, John, and Editors of the *Navy Times. Duel to the Death.* New York: Harcourt, Brace & World, 1969.

4: The Jeannette Expedition

This chapter is based on the author's work, *The Jeannette Expedition, an Ill-fated Journey to the Arctic*, published in 1967 by Abelard-Schuman, New York. That book was inspired by De Long's own *Ice Journals*, which were recovered, edited by his widow, and published in 1884, two volumes thick. Also useful were Emma De Long's own memoirs, those of Danenhower, Melville, and Newcomb, plus the voluminous hearings conducted in 1884 by the House of Representatives Naval Affairs Committee, and the Navy's Court of Inquiry.

Two descendants of expedition members, Miss Emma De Long Mills, of New York City ("Little Sylvie's" daughter) and James C. Ambler, of Richmond, Virginia, also assisted.

Source material for other sections of the chapter include Philip B. McDonald's *A Saga of the Seas, the Story of Cyrus W. Field* (New York: Wilson-Erickson Co., 1937) and Wilton J. Oldburn's *The Ismay Line* (London: Journal of Commerce, 1961).

Special mention should be made of Edward Ellsberg, whose historical novel of the *Jeannette, Hell on Ice; The Saga of the Jeannette* (New York: Dodd, Mead, 1938), awakened interest in an almost forgotten quest. Prolific author and distinguished naval officer, Ellsberg graduated from Annapolis in 1914 to serve in two World Wars, especially as a salvage officer.

5: The Return of the Mammoths

Some of the 'feel' for this chapter was gained through osmosis when the author, as a small boy, listened to his father and his father's friends reminisce about voyages circa the turn of the century and during the ensuing two decades. As a child, he also accompanied his parents to Europe on the great old *Majestic.* In 1937, as a copy boy on the *Washington Post,* he agonized out his first story on the *Leviathan,* which he'd happened on at her Hoboken pier prior to her final voyage to the shipbreakers. "Queen of the Seas" was his somewhat less than original heading.

At the outbreak of World War II and before he was called to active duty in the Naval Reserve, the author wrote an article for *The Evening Star,* of Washington, on the 'ghost fleet' of World War I transports, in a Patuxent River anchorage. Most were seized German liners.

Part of the bibliography of Chapter 2 applies, as do the titles in the following list.

Anderson, Roy. *White Star.* Prescot, Lancashire, England: T. Stephenson & Sons, 1964.

Braynard, Frank O. *World's Greatest Ship, the Story of the* Leviathan. New York: South Street Seaport Museum, 1972.

Corbett, Sir Julian. *Naval Operations.* London: Longmans Green, 1920–24.

Diggle, Captain E.G. *The Romance of a Modern Liner.* London: Sampson Low, Marston & Co., 1930.

Hoehling, A.A. *The Great War at Sea.* New York: Thomas Y. Crowell, 1965.

Ocean Liners of the Past, the Cunard Triple-Screw Atlantic Liner Aquitania, a reprint of Souvenir Number of 1914, The Shipbuilder. London: Patrick Stephens, 1971.

Rostron, Sir Arthur H. *Home From The Sea.* New York: MacMillan, 1931.

Also useful were *Era Magazine,* January 1903, and *Literary Digest,* November 29, 1913.

6: Why Did They Sink the *Lusitania?*

This chapter finds its wellsprings in *The Last Voyage of the Lusitania,* by A. A. Hoehling and Mary Hoehling. It was first published in 1956 by Henry Holt (New York). Since that time the documentary has been translated into several languages, printed in several editions, hard cover and paperback, excerpted, condensed, serialized, and so on. A softcover edition (Dell) remains in print. The book was prepared after interviews with some 50 survivors of the sinking. Only a very few of these same individuals are alive today. Voluminous printed sources consulted included newspaper and magazine accounts on both sides of the Atlantic, memoirs, diaries, and letters.

The official British inquiry, conducted for the Board of Trade by Lord Mersey, who had earlier presided over the *Titanic* investigation, magnanimously absolved Captain Turner and Cunard, placing guilt "solely with those who plotted and with those who committed the crime."

Overlooked were Turner's several flagrant violations of instructions. From the author's own experience in World War II as a gunnery officer aboard merchant vessels, he can appreciate, however, that there was nothing willful in William Turner's judgmental errors. Rather, he was reacting as most merchant masters do to the regimentation and demand for unquestioning obedience of wartime. Long used to independent command, they were unable to understand or comply with the peculiar and mortal challenges of war. In a word, many of this number of otherwise able and distinguished navigators tend to become confused in danger zones, whether running alone or in convoy.

If the *Lusitania* sank in the ephemera of minutes, her ghost is long lived. It refuses, to this day, to be put to rest. Almost a decade after her torpedoing, a Mixed Claims Commission finally awarded damages to next of kin through the U.S. Government, the amounts being based in great measure on need. The Frohman heirs, for example, received nothing, while the Elbert Hubbard clan won $60,000.

In the 1930s, *Lusitania* was remembered for the gold bullion still rumored to be in her encrusted hull (this in spite of testimony to this author by the then-surviving officer that the one so-called "strong room" was empty the voyage long).

In 1935, a British diver, Jim Jarrat, believed he actually walked across her plates, identifying her by the diameter of the rivets. While underwater photography was in its infancy, sound tracings did produce an interesting silhouette of the portentous wreck. Then World War II relegated to a distant background the flotsam of a predecessor conflict.

Yet, two World Wars failed to dampen one persistent charge—that Britain had knowingly sacrificed the Cunarder to hasten American sympathies to her side. It was fueled by a diary entry of Anglophile Colonel Ed House, special adviser to Wilson. He recalled a noontime appointment with King George at Buckingham Palace on May 7, not much more than two hours before the great Cunarder had been torpedoed.

"We fell to talking, strangely enough," he wrote, "of the probability of Germany sinking a transatlantic liner. He said, 'suppose they should sink the *Lusitania* with American passengers on board.'"

To interpret a chance remark as more than coincidence required a broad stretching of the imagination. But it was stretched even into the 1970s when at least one writer set his typewriter keys smoking with the accusation that England had done her diabolical best to turn *"Lusy"* into a sacrificial lamb. The poor quality of the Irish Coast Patrol and its excessive amount of dock time was offered as a case in point.

However, Jutland was more than a year in the future at the time of the *Lusitania* sinking. First line warships could not be spared. They were desperately needed as a standoff for the German High Seas Fleet and at the Dardanelles.

In early 1915 the United States served as a sort of officially neutral quartermaster for the Allies. As just one example of war orders, Westinghouse, the very day *Lusitania* had sailed, had confirmed a $28 million contract for their war supplies. The economic effects of the submarine blockade remained to be felt. England was not short of funds, manpower, or food.

In dramatic contrast to the sobering losses already tallied by France, Russia, and Germany, Great Britain's announced total casualties remained below 140,000 at the time of the liner's torpedoing. London, *then*, did not want or need U.S. troops "over there."

As another facet of the enduring *Lusitania* mystique, divers in recent years have sought to prove that the liner was armed. Frustratingly for them, they have been unable to produce the necessary evidence. Yet it would not have mattered if they had salvaged so much as one small machine gun, since there never was any question that the ship was a Royal Navy auxiliary.

Equally abortive have been efforts to prove she was, in a manner of speaking, down to her Plimsoll in munitions of war. As noted in Chapter 6, the Cunard liner was no freighter. Her cargo space was extremely limited. It was reserved in peacetime for such premium items as mail (which was why she was RMS, or Royal Mail Ship, *Lusitania*), perishables, high quality machinery, glass or cutlery, paintings, antiques, and the like.

Perhaps the most reasonable mystery, unclouded by prejudice, pro-Allied, or Central Powers, is why the liner sank so swiftly—in 15 to 18 minutes. The *Titanic*, in dramatic contrast, with a 300-foot gash below the waterline, had remained afloat for nearly three hours. In fact, Kapitanleutnant Walther Schwieger was registering shock at the rapid deterioration of the impressive Cunarder when he logged, "I could not have fired a second torpedo into this throng of humanity attempting to save themselves."

In the absence of any significant quantity of ammunition aboard, it would appear that exploding coal dust and bursting boilers must have augmented the force of the single torpedo to blow out so large a portion of the vessel's bottom. Otherwise, she would have remained afloat somewhat longer, the list would not have been so acute, and many more lives would have been saved.

The wreck has been found to be so imbedded in the sea bottom that divers have been unable to shed reliable new information on this puzzle. By the same token, the *Lusitania*'s condition defies the possibility of raising her even though new methods have been proposed (including filling the hull with tens of thousands of nitrogen-core Ping-Pong balls). Aside from the will-o'-the-wisp lure of gold bullion, the amount of copper used in her construction makes the old liner a tempting prize.

Mysteries, doubts, and sinister question marks may persist surrounding the sunken superliner, but one fact is clear beyond refutation—in addition to writing finis to any last vestiges of chivalry at sea, the loss of the *Lusitania* set world history on a new course.

A recent comprehensive book that focused on the political history of the Cunarder is *The* Lusitania *Disaster,* by Thomas A. Bailey and Paul B. Ryan (New York: Free Press, 1975).

7: U.S.S. *Squalus*—The Nineteenth Dive

On a warm September evening, 1939, this writer was one of a

hushed group standing at dockside in the Portsmouth Navy Yard. U.S.S. *Squalus* was finally in, battered, torn, rusted, crisscrossed with cables, wires, and hoses of every diameter and description. Yet, stubbornly "192" still answered muster in big black numerals from her conning tower.

Although I was a cub reporter on the *Washington* (D.C.) *Herald,* at the time I was vacationing and content to allow the veteran wire service men to cover this mute requiem to a story which had clattered through city rooms with incredible drama back in May. What I recall, in addition to the silence interrupted only by necessary commands as the submarine was finally tethered in her drydock, was the smell: the disinfectant that had been slopped around everywhere.

It was as though by fumigating the area the heavy, brooding presence of so much death, entombed in front of us in that elongated steel casket, would somehow be cleansed away. Then there wouldn't be any more death. It didn't work that way, though.

The reality and the horror only increased as the white-clothed hospital corpsmen with their face masks moved silently over the narrow gangplanks and into the opened hatch of the fatal rear compartments. Then they reappeared, two by two, carrying stretchers with the still, sheeted shapes that after all these months of immersion remained unmistakably those of men.

This closed the books on *Squalus* if not on No. 192. Thoroughly refurbished, her homicidal induction valve replaced with one less disposed toward malfunction, she was rechristened *Sailfish.* Slipping out onto her first patrol from Manila the day after Pearl Harbor, she fought through the war, sinking at least seven Japanese naval and merchant vessels and winning nine battle stars.

There was, tragically, an example of the cruel irony of war in her torpedoing of the escort carrier *Chuyo.* On board were 21 American prisoners from the recently depth-charged *Sculpin.* But one survived in this bitter postscript to a drama which had commenced four and one half years earlier near the Isles of Shoals, on the other side of the world.

Too, the guardian angel of some off the New England coast would prove fickle in distant, strange Pacific waters. "Robey" Robertson, the navigation officer who kept so meticulous a log of the ordeal on the bottom was lost in an early foray on the submarine *Argonaut.*

Lloyd Maness, who closed the watertight door, himself met death on *Growler.*

A previous captain of *Growler,* Howard W. Gilmore, in another action, had won a posthumous Medal of Honor through his last dying command from the conning tower, swept by enemy fire, "Take her down!"

It would take position beside such other naval catechisms as "Don't give up the ship!" and "Damn the torpedoes!"

Oliver Naquin's good fortune, on the other hand, did not forsake him. Not wishing to waste his considerable engineering talents on the relatively minor machinery of submersibles, the Navy ordered him to vessels of far broader challenge. Thus, he was chief engineer of the battleship U.S.S. *California* on December 7, 1941. As luck would have it he was painting the walls of his new home on Black Point when the bombs started to fall.

He was aboard the *New Orleans* in the sixth battle of Savo Island when that handsome cruiser had her entire bow blown off. Later, he served in Noumea on the staff of the famous Admiral William F. Halsey. "Bull" Halsey variously was commander of forces in the Southwest Pacific and of the Third Fleet.

Naquin, like Halsey, came through the war unscathed. He retired a few years afterwards to enter private business. An active, healthy man, Rear Admiral Naquin divides his time between a handsome colonial mansion in Alexandria, Virginia, and a large cattle farm in the southern part of the same state.

The author is much indebted to this fine gentlemen for his help in recapturing the mood of that long ago May on the bottom, off the Isles of Shoals. Several years previously he had aided the author, who was then editing a book for the Army Times Co., *They Fought Under the Sea, the Saga of the Submarine.* Two editions were published by the Army Times Publishing Co., in 1962 and 1966. It was compiled by the editors of *Navy Times.*

Included in this book, which is a history of submarines, is the complete log of the *Squalus.*

Another primary source for this chapter, in addition to Admiral Naquin, is the Navy Court of Inquiry. This encompasses several hundred pages, including correspondence and various attachments and endorsements. Among the signatures is that of Admiral Chester

W. Nimitz, then Chief of the Bureau of Navigation, later to be the United States' top naval commander in the Pacific. These valuable records were made available by the Judge Advocate General's Office, Department of the Navy, and through, in particular, Lieutenant Commander Conrad A. Buhler, U.S.N., of that legal office.

The full history of the *Squalus/Sailfish,* as prepared immediately after the war by the Office of Naval Records and Naval History, was produced by Rear Admiral David M. Cooney, Chief of Naval Information, and Anna C. Urband, of that office.

A considerable number of newspapers, and a lesser number of periodicals of that period were consulted, including the *Boston Globe, Boston Herald, Greensboro* (North Carolina) *News, New York Daily News, New York Times,* and the *Washington* (D.C.) *Evening Star.* Among the magazines referred to were *Life, Newsweek, Popular Science, Scientific American* and *Time.*

The first book on the *Squalus* disaster was written by a *Boston Globe* reporter, Nat A. Barrows, who was on the scene that summer long. *Blow All Ballast* was published by Dodd, Mead & Co., New York, in 1943. Unfortunately this hard working and careful reporter did not long live to enjoy the fruits of his success. He and fellow correspondents were killed in a plane crash at the time of the Yalta Conference, 1945.

A classic on submarine salvage was written by Edward Ellsberg in 1929, detailing the recovery of *S-51: On The Bottom* (New York, Dodd, Mead).

The following three books are also valuable.

Lockwood, Charles A., and Adamson, Hans Christian, *Hell at 50 Fathoms.* Philadelphia: Chilton Co., 1962. (The commentary on the "ganomes" is contained in the foreword by the late Admiral Momsen.)

Maas, Peter. *The Rescuer.* London: Collins, 1968.

Navy Department. Bureau of Construction and Repair. *Submarine safety—Respiration and Rescue Devices.* Washington: U.S. Government Printing Office, 1938.

A further note: while the Momsen Lung has long since been replaced by a simpler underwater "hood," the McCann Chamber remains on standby duty. Nine are at East and West Coast bases and at Pearl Harbor, although not one has been used "in earnest" since the *Squalus* rescue. In fact, the distances and great depth at which nuclear-powered submarines operate rather preclude the McCann's utilization. The loss of the only two such modern submarines, *Thresher* and *Scorpion,* involved another factor as well: crushing of the hulls by exceeding pressure depth.

(Early in this chapter, the account of the *Leviathan*'s final voyage is from a letter by Captain Binks published in *The Atlantic Monthly,* November 1938.)

8: The Little Ships of Dunkirk

". . . it is such a contrast writing this in my bedroom at the Charing Cross Hotel. French windows wide open . . . the buses passing, the pealing of the bells of St. Martin's, people passing on this Sunday of rest. . . I walked in the evening to Westminster Abbey and attended evensong, a lovely service. . . it soothed my spirit."

So wrote Tommie Kerr, back in London from the numbing experience of Dunkirk. And at a "reception" camp in his familiar Wiltshire, Sergeant Giblett would write, ". . . we were fed, had baths and then glorious sleep free from the strain and tension of the past three weeks. What an experience those three weeks had been. Three weeks, incredible! and unforgettable!"

It is likely they did not truly appreciate the depth of their shock. When this author jumped from his Liberty ship to the deck of the Dutch trawler *Tromp,* which had courageously come alongside the furiously burning freighter, and was asked if he were "all right?" he glibly replied "yes!" As he started down a ladder leading to the warmth of a hatch some ten feet below, his knees unaccountably buckled and he fell the rest of the way.

"All right?" The British Army, shocked, would recover, but was scarcely "all right," any more than the author was for an appreciable time. It required another year before effective raiding parties could be organized against targets pinpointed on the Norwegian and French coasts (Dieppe in particular), against Spitzbergen and the Lofoten Islands. It was two years before the Germans were put on the defensive in North Africa, three years before they were driven out, and four long years of incalculable effort and sacrifice before the Allies, on June 6, 1940, returned to France to stay.

"Unforgettable!" it was, as Giblett observed. So were certain other violent and acute punctuations of the war, especially the V-1 or "buzz bombs." John B. Cannell, of London, commodore of the Association of Dunkirk Little Ships, for example, was hurt by one himself while hurrying to the hospital where his wife was being treated for injuries caused by another V-1.

Lying on a stretcher in front of a pub, near which the V-1 had struck, Cannell placed his finger on the pressure point of the arm, or stump of an arm, of a woman beside him, pumping blood. Years later, he encountered the same woman, with one arm, walking past the same pub.

And there were the rocket bombs, the V-2s which arrived without warning to detonate with double explosions and rumble over the great city with the rolling anger of some unending summer thunderstorm. The author, in his oil-stained khakis, jumped visibly as he experienced his first V-2 while being registered at the Golden Square Red Cross Club, off Piccadilly.

"I believe," said the hostess, with a faint and perhaps superior smile, "that women are braver than men."

Perhaps. But if not being frightened, sometimes, were a condition for serving in an army, a navy, or an air force, there exists extreme doubt that any nation would be able to maintain a defense force composed of other than congenital liars. It is certain that those brought home from Dunkirk spent the remainder of the war being afraid, or at least apprehensive, once in a while. All that mattered was that they kept on doing what they were supposed to be doing, while being frightened.

Some, exposed to the German fury, have not learned to forgive. In the lovely village of Hythe, with its Roman ruins, near Folkestone, dwells Peter Solari, with his wife, Emma, following a distinguished career in the merchant marine. He has not forgotten.

"When I encounter a German tourist," he confided, "and he asks me how to get somewhere, you know what I do? I send him in exactly the opposite direction."

Also near the Channel, but on Hayling Island, near Portsmouth, a retired R.N. captain, Cecil Wynne-Edwards, is of opposite mind. As a naval officer in postwar Western Europe he learned to work with his erstwhile enemies.

Wynne-Edwards and Solari are but two of a number of persons

who gave generously of their time and hospitality to help make this very long chapter possible. Solari, for example, drove to Canterbury on a Sunday morning to meet the author and his wife, Mary Hoehling, and take them back to his home for a long afternoon of sociability and browsing through Solari's private "museum" of statistical notebooks and memorabilia. His brief experience on the shell and bomb torn beach and his scanty memories had nonetheless become a powerful factor in his life. One of the most devoted members of the Dunkirk Veterans Association, he attends its regular reunions in France or Belgium. In fact, there is photographic evidence that he has at least once been Grand Marshal of the parade through La Panne—against a background of a rebuilt waterfront which affords no hint at all of what happened there during several late May and early June days and nights in 1940.

On Woodgaston Lane, Hayling Island, Cecil Wynne-Edwards enjoys the life of a gentleman farmer. With three fertile acres abutting inlets of the Channel, he raises all the vegetables he and Bee Mary need, and then some. In the kitchen, and occasionally used, is the primus stove the then lieutenant commander brought back from the sinking *Keith*. An ample, tasteful living room is made the warmer by an attractive raised stone fireplace. On the far wall hangs an oil portrait of a beautiful woman, Bee Mary.

"I love the military," she confides. "I'll follow a band marching, anytime . . . "

The captain, as a matter of fact, is a friend of Oliver Naquin, of the *Squalus,* which happens to be how the author was so fortunate as to meet this charming couple.

Ever since World War I, if not somewhat before, there has existed a close liaison between the United States and Royal navies. For example, Captain Alan D. H. Jay, retired in Nottinghamshire, first made acquaintance of his American counterparts in the mid-1930s while on Yangtze River patrol. Later he was a staff officer, Minesweeping Command, Normandy Allied Naval Expedition.

Jay, although not at Dunkirk, is compiling a personal recollections history of Royal Navy minesweeping operations in World War II. Through his kindness, the experiences of Wright, of the *Gossamer,* and Neale, of *Speedwell,* are excerpted in this book. B. J. M. Wright is since deceased.

Jay, whom the author first met in the pleasantly nautical environment of the Navy Club, Mayfair, was both friend and admirer of Admiral Ramsay.

"He was the sort of officer," recalls Jay, "who if not satisfied with one plan, or if his staff was not satisfied with one plan would say, 'tear it up, try another!' He was flexible, and imaginative. His was surely the genius behind Dunkirk."

Ramsay, however, did not survive to witness the Nazi surrender. Allied Naval Commander at Normandy, he was killed in an airplane accident in September of that year, 1944, en route to the ill-starred "Market Garden" plan to capture bridges at Arnhem, Holland and nearby, and thus turn the Siegfried Line.

Nonetheless, this meticulous senior naval commander left behind a very lengthy and detailed report, "The Evacuation of the Allied Armies from Dunkirk and Neighboring Beaches," dated 18 June 1940, which was made available to the author by the Naval Historical Branch, Ministry of Defence. Not only does it provide the basic, factual framework for those nine days but the writing at times is most expressive, if only through understatement.

The perspective is quite different from someone like Ted Harvey, who lives in Leigh-on-Sea, Essex, at the mouth of the Thames, and still earns his living on the waterways. The author made the acquaintance of this friendly and highly articulate gentleman through John Cannell and The Association of Dunkirk Little Ships. Cannell remains a well-known and active surveyor, or industrial engineer (although there is no exact counterpart in the United States), and has been concerned recently with the major North Sea oil and natural gas procurement.

In a similar profession is John Douglas Graves, of *Medway Queen* association, of the Liverpool firm, Peel and Graves, "marine and cargo surveyors." The author is much indebted to him, both through conversations and his reminiscences as published in 1975 in a small brochure, "The Story of *Medway Queen*," by the Paddle Steamer Preservation Society. John B. Millar, of the unique society, put the author in touch with Graves.

Medway Queen returned to minesweeping, then to her alter ego as excursion steamer, and now has come home from the war, the rivers, and estuaries as a permanent exhibit at Cowes, the Isle of Wight.

Near London Bridge sits a sister paddler, the *Princess Elizabeth,* also Dunkirk-scarred, now a sometimes restaurant and pub. Longevity and durability, however, is inherent in these friendly, duck-bottomed craft. The *Duke of Devonshire,* for example, wheezed and waddled through two World Wars to be retired only in 1968 at the age of 72 years! Queen Victoria had conveyed felicitations at her launching in 1896.

No stranger to paddle steamers, although his 100-year old firm does not build them, is Robert O. Tough, director of Tough Bros. Ltd., up the Thames, at Teddington, Middlesex. He was a boy when his father, Douglas, his yard manager, Ronald Lenthall, and others with the familiar shipwrights on Teddington Wharf helped prepare the pleasure boats for their great adventure. Robert Tough generously made available his files of that period, while Lenthall searched his memory for the flavor and the immediacy of those heady, almost improbable days.

The yard also built "Fairmile" antisubmarine boats during the war, and also motor launches. On its ways, at the beginning of 1977, were several handsome—and very expensive—private yachts.

All the way across London from Tough Bros., in Lambeth (also near William Bligh's house and tomb) is the Imperial War Museum. There Rose Coombs, special collections officer and authority on World War I, once more assisted the author in research. Made available specifically were the letters/memoirs of P. G. Ackrell, W. B. Giblett, Tommie Kerr, and G. S. McKellar.

He is indebted, too, to Leslie Reade, of London, an author who first aided him in researching *The Last Voyage of the* Lusitania. In addition to initial probing for, first, the existence and then the locations of the Dunkirk societies, Leslie shivered through one wet, cold November afternoon en route to fish and chips aboard the *Princess Elizabeth,* herself a sort of low-key symbol of the durable qualities of Britannia.

The author is appreciative, too, of the time accorded him by David Divine, retired military editor of the *Times* and easily the most knowledgeable authority on Dunkirk. He resides in a handsome old home in Hampstead, within easy commute of the museums, the ministries, and Fleet Street when the urge dictates. His principal works on Dunkirk (from which he, too, carries scars) are

Dunkirk (New York: E. P. Dutton, 1948) and *The Nine Days of Dunkirk* (New York: Norton, 1959).

While much has been written about Dunkirk, the historic evacuation has nonetheless been accorded nothing like the great volume of recapitulation and analysis of other massive and fateful military operations: Austerlitz, Jena, Waterloo, Gettysburg, Cold Harbor, Tannenberg, Verdun, the Meuse-Argonne, El Alamein, Iwo Jima, Normandy, any number of others.

Perhaps the answer in part lies in the fact that the professional military strategist contemplates an evacuation with profound frustration, irrespective of his own sympathies. In the case of Dunkirk, the dedicated analyst no doubt would find enough errors on both sides to cause much dismay. Napoleon's classic retreat from Russia, however, remains an exception so far as literary interest, especially of the novelist, is concerned.

Following is a sampling of books treating Dunkirk in various degrees to which the author has referred, in addition to Divine's documentaries.

Beaux, Jean. *Dunkerque 1940*. Paris: Presse de la Cite, 1967.

Bloxland, Gregory. *Destination Dunkirk, The Story of Gort's Army*. London: William Kimber, 1973.

Chatterton, E. Keble. *The Epic of Dunkirk*. London: Hurst & Blackett, 1940.

Churchill, Winston S. *The Second World War: Their Finest Hour*. vol. 2. Boston: Houghton Mifflin Co., 1949.

Collier, Richard. *The Sands of Dunkirk*. London: Collins, 1961.

Hoehling, A. A. *America's Road to War 1939-41*. New York: Abelard-Schuman, 1970.

Masefield, John. *The Nine Days Wonder*. London: William Heinemann, 1941.

Williams, Douglas. *Retreat from Dunkirk*. New York: Brentano's, 1941.

Young, Peter. *World War 1939-45*. New York: Thomas Y. Crowell Co., 1966.

Magazine articles on Dunkirk are scarce. However, the recollections of E. H. Phillips and his mobile "Y" canteen were found in the *Fortnight* magazine, of Great Britain, July 1940.

Epilogue: Home from the Sea

It was tea time at the apartment/nursing home in Eastbourne when the author called on James A. P. Blackburn and his pert wife, Hilda. The elderly captain is very deaf and Hilda has recently lost her eyesight, but it doesn't matter. Both communicate a great deal more satisfactorily than many who possess perfect auditory and visual senses.

"I think I know him pretty well after these years," she confesses, with a smile.

"These years" are 57 in number. They have counted four children, ten grandchildren and eleven great-grandchildren. Both sons, as adults, were lost in tragic marine accidents.

"I wanted to be a sailor before I saw salt water," says Captain Blackburn, adding of his long and notable career at sea, "I am very proud I have done it."

Captain Jim Blackburn, modest even though he is a part of history, soft-spoken, very friendly, home from the sea . . .

There is one recent book on *Jervis Bay* by George Pollock, titled simply, *The Jervis Bay*. (London: William Kimber, 1958). In 1941 Gene Fowler published "The *Jervis Bay* Goes Down," a poem (New York: Random House). Its recitation by Ronald Colman on nationwide radio some ten months before Pearl Harbor added further fuel to the emotional fires already burning for Britain and the Allied cause.

*   *   *

Finally, risking as always the danger of overlooking those who in some way might have aided in the research for this book, the author wishes to thank several stalwarts in the Department of the Navy who must, by now, wonder if they are doomed to keep answering this author's requests. Among those not previously mentioned are Dean Allard, head, operational archives branch, and Charles Haberlein, photo section, both in the Office of Naval History, as well as Robert Carlisle, head photo journalism and public inquiries branch, office Chief of (Navy) Information.

He is indebted, surely, to John Fink, executive editor, for his patience and encouragement alike; also to Mary Hoehling who accompanied her husband on his research trip to England. Earlier in the book's genesis she had mused over the challenge of making William Bligh appear at least credible, the possibility of "likeable" not even being entertained.

In sum, rarely has the author owed so much to so many.